JANINA FIALKOWSKA

A Note In Time

novum premium

This book is also
available as
e-book.

www.novum-publishing.co.uk

© 2021 novum publishing

ISBN 978-3-903861-97-8
Editing: Ashleigh Brassfield, DipEdit
Cover photo: Ulrich Wagner
Cover design, layout & typesetting:
novum publishing
Internal illustrations: Janina Fialkowska;
p. 352: Sgt Joanne Stoeckl, Rideau Hall
© OSGG, 2002

The images provided by the author
have been printed in the highest
possible quality.

www.novum-publishing.co.uk

For Harry

CONTENTS

ACKNOWLEDGEMENTS

There have been a few friends who, with their memories, their enthusiasm, their patience and their expertise, have been of invaluable help in the writing of this book and I'd like to thank them all. I think the greatest debt of gratitude goes to Nicola Schaefer who read the book right after it was first written and convinced me it was of some value. Since then, she has never stopped pushing, prodding and providing motivation until it was finally finished and sent off to the publishers.

Others who played a vital role are Judith Rice Lesage who helped me with all the foreign translations, Lady Annabelle Weidenfeld, my brother Peter, my cousin Alison Hackney, John Pearce, Linn Rothstein, Flora Liebich, Elaine Plummer and Jeffrey Swann.

And many thanks to my friends Richard Sauer and Josefine Theiner who got tired of hearing about the book as it gathered dust on my studio shelf, and found a publisher for me: Novum Publishing and the excellent and thoughtful Bianca Bendra who has expertly guided me through the entire publishing process.

Finally I would like to thank my husband Harry; quite frankly, without him, there would be no book.

CHAPTER 1

Whirlwinds of Snow ("Chasse Neige")
by Franz Liszt

My eyelids flickered as I slowly drifted back into consciousness. A pale, sickly blue light filtered through my damp lashes and, bit by bit, I became aware of my surroundings. There was an unnatural stillness. Sounds were muffled, distant. I knew that I was in a hospital recovery room, and the realization that I was still alive caused a smile to cross my face before more complex thoughts were generated in my brain, dulled by anesthesia. There was a numbness in my left arm and the peaceful insouciance of a drug-induced state was soon dispelled when, in a sudden panic, I attempted to wriggle my fingers under the bedclothes. But all was well; they moved as before: pianist's fingers. My heart continued to thud at an alarming rate and cold sweat spread across my forehead.

The world eventually shifted into focus; lights brightened, sounds amplified, and I remembered: this was a cancer hospital and I had just lost a chunk of my left arm. I could see that I was not alone in my predicament, which was somehow reassuring. That day there were many of us, lying in our cots in three tidy rows, waiting for the surgeons to deliver their verdicts. Some patients were still unconscious while others were surrounded by family members speaking in low, encouraging tones. There were those who, like myself, lay silently with a knot of anxiety growing within, and those who seemed to find delight in calling out loudly and repeatedly for the nurses, unable to cope for even a few seconds on their own. The cries of the few who were in extreme distress were heart-wrenching; I felt empathy, pity, but mostly fear in the presence of such suffering. In the bed next to me someone was moaning softly, but although I tried

11

to turn my body around to see, I found I was more or less tied down and couldn't budge. My left arm felt heavy and lifeless but, mercifully, I felt very little physical pain.

Nurses flitted efficiently from patient to patient, brightly cheerful, dealing briskly with the stress of a room vibrating with palpable anguish. The sounds of disembodied voices, machines beeping, curtains being pulled to and fro, wheels turning and oxygen pumping soon became exhausting. I was freezing cold and shivering so badly the bed was rattling. My body felt sticky and saturated with hospital stench, dried blood and disinfectant, and I had been pumped full of liquids during the procedure, so my bladder was constantly and painfully full and oh, how I loathed even the thought of bedpans! Also, like the sword of Damocles, the pending results of my biopsy hung perilously over me.

Presently a nurse, noting that I was awake, stopped by to ask how I felt. In a display of totally inappropriate fortitude, I reassured her that I felt fine when actually I felt quite dreadful, having suddenly been engulfed in waves of nausea. Minutes later I disgraced myself by being sick, mostly – although not completely – into the little basin conveniently stationed within reach.

From the clock on the wall opposite I calculated that I had already been in the hospital for nearly twelve hours. It was 6:00 pm on January 31st, which just happened to be Harry's birthday. Sitting miserably in a hospital was not the way I had envisaged my newly acquired husband celebrating his birthday, but it seemed as though greater forces had seized control of our common destiny, altering the course of our lives and steering us into dangerous whirlpools and eddies.

Up until that day my life had been a seesaw of the glorious highs and desperate lows typical of a performing artist with a demanding schedule. Nevertheless, over the years both body and mind had received quite a battering, which I had ignored. I had managed to bounce along unchecked, riding on my innate stubbornness, basic good health, and a large dose of childish naivety.

This time, however, the events leading up to the biopsy had been simply too much even for a tough campaigner. The camel's back was succumbing not to the proverbial straw, but to a giant bale of hay. As I waited for medical science to reveal the next phase of my life, my mind, in a futile attempt to disassociate itself from the present, harkened back not to a happier distant past but to the past year, starting with another birthday and another life and death drama that had occurred eight months previously.

We should have been celebrating my fiftieth birthday, but the day was spent in transit from Knoxville, Tennessee, where I had been playing on tour, to Montreal, where my mother had been rushed to the hospital. I spent the next two weeks at her bedside watching her die. She had a virulent form of leukemia and had developed bronchitis, a fatal combination. I learned a lot during those two weeks about courage and dignity, about unconditional love and about the incalculable power of a sense of humour. My mother showed no fear, was invariably courteous and accommodating to the overworked nurses, and made witty comments to try to lessen my concern and grief, right up until the moment she slipped into a final coma. She had taught me how to play the piano with honesty; she now taught me how to die with integrity.

Shortly after, at the beginning of June, Harry and I were married in a private ceremony held in the Bavarian village where he had grown up. It had required the written permission of the Highest Court of Bavaria and an onerous, transatlantic quest to assemble all the correct and pedantic documentation (not helped by the fact that, fifty years prior, the wine at my christening must have been flowing quite freely, as the officiating priest had misspelled both my father's and my names on the baptismal certificate). Considering the death of my mother only weeks before and given that neither Harry nor I had ever wished for a huge wedding, only Harry's mother and brother and a few of our closest friends were present. Everyone except me seemed to be shedding copious tears during the service. As for myself, I was intent on understanding what the nice lady registrar, who was marrying us, was saying. My comprehension of German was somewhat feeble at the time, and I was desperately trying not to say the wrong thing at the wrong time. However, in the end I managed a resounding *"Ja."* at the appropriate moment, which was a colossal relief.

In the back of the room, Sena Jurinac, legendary star of the Vienna State Opera and one of Harry's closest friends, commented in a clear stage-whisper that the registrar's speech was unintelligible: no one seemed to know how to project their voices nowadays. The sobs now became punctuated by an occasional giggle.

Our wedding lunch was held, romantically, in the little country restaurant where Harry and I had had our first meal together alone.

There was no suggestion of a honeymoon due to time restraints. Instead, we had a weekend in the mountains at a delightful bed and breakfast, accompanied by three of our closest friends who had come from Northern Germany and California. It rained the entire time, but our party was merry, and I regretted having to go back to work on Monday.

Over the next three months I flew back and forth to Germany as often as possible between concerts in North America, trying to maintain some semblance of a normal married life. For years I had firmly maintained, both publicly and privately, that marriages and concert careers for women were incompatible. I was now determined to disprove my own theory. Being the spouse of a performing artist can be a thankless task; always tiptoeing around the neurotic spouse on concert days, making sure there are no disturbances, always playing the secondary role, the person in the background, the support, the nanny, as well as the lover, suffering right along with all the pre-concert anxieties but never having the opportunity to dispel the personal stress. The performer has the cathartic concert, the applause, the compliments, while the spouse continues to suffer long after the concert reception is over. Then there are the long separations – I didn't know how we would manage, but I was determined our marriage would work.

Harry, who was running a "period instrument" festival in the Allgäu region of Germany, had a hard time getting away, so I did most of the travelling back across the Atlantic. He did, however, manage to escape for a weekend in July, when I performed the Paderewski concerto in the pouring rain during an outdoor concert in Quebec City for a sold-out crowd of umbrellas, followed by a wonderful memorial party for my mother in the old family home near Montreal. My brother and I celebrated her life with family and best friends showing old family movies dating back to the 1920s and consuming vast amounts of delicious food and champagne. It was a marvelous party; my mother would have loved it.

The next day I drove back to the States and Harry returned to Germany. I had a string of concerts to perform and a CD to record, which translated into over six hours a day practising hard at the keyboard. I never minded this kind of intensive work. In fact, I loved seeing the pieces slowly taking shape and reaching performance level. It's a little rough on the body, but I had always been one of the lucky ones, never having suffered from the normal pianistic ailments of tendonitis, carpal-tunnel syndrome, or just plain old muscle strain.

By the end of August the concerts were over, the CD of Liszt Etudes was complete, and I slipped eagerly into my unaccustomed role of "Frau Intendant" or "Mrs. Director" throughout Harry's festival. The "Klang&Raum" (Sound and Space) festival was Germany's premier period instrument festival and had been administered and nurtured by Harry since its inception nine years previously. It was a unique blend of excellent concerts and recitals, all performed on historically accurate period instruments of the baroque and early classical eras. It was held in the church and in the adjoining seventeenth-century Benedictine monastery (now transmuted into a hotel/conference centre) of the picturesque village of Irsee in the foothills of the Bavarian Alps. Coincidentally, the festival's orchestra in residence was the Canadian-based Tafelmusik, so at least half the orchestra members were people I already knew.

There were also marvelous meals, excursions through the lovely Allgäu countryside in horse-drawn carriages, and picnics in Alpine meadows. Harry, who had built the festival up from scratch, was on friendly terms with just about everyone who bought a ticket, and there was a family atmosphere that encompassed not only the public but the administration, the kitchen staff, the stage crews, the musicians, and the sponsors. People returned year after year from as far away as California and Japan.

But smooth-running, happy festivals don't happen by themselves, and a price must be paid by someone. It was an intensive two weeks – rehearsals, then six days of performances with up to three concerts a day, intertwined with gourmet feasts, official dinners, sponsor events, lectures, and endless speeches. I loved it all – except for the speeches, which tended to drag on for hours, and the cocktail parties, where I attempted to converse wittily and intelligently in German. I took my role of "Frau Intendant" very seriously, but most likely failed miserably, since the art of small talk, even in my own English and French, eludes me totally.

The music, played on unfamiliar instruments and tuned in a way to which I was unaccustomed, sounded alien to me at first. But the performers were, for the most part, outstanding, and good music played at a high level will always stir the soul, whether the instrument is a Stradivarius or a tin whistle.

For a week we hardly slept, so that by the time the last goodbyes were said and the final post-mortems were over, we were beat. I had two days before I had to fly back to the US for a cruel two-month separation. To have had the good fortune of finding the love of my life well into my middle years, only to be faced with the constant prospect of future separations, was hard to bear. In an attempt to alleviate the pain as best we could, we planned a brief trip to Paris, a city we both loved but had never visited together, for two nights before I continued on to New York. We were both so exhausted that jokingly we told all our friends that we were flying to Paris to take a nap. Which is exactly what happened – unintentionally. When we foolishly lay down on the bed after our arrival on a golden Parisian autumn day, we promptly fell asleep, losing the entire first afternoon.

Luckily the next day was also glorious and we decided to do all the touristy things that for years, as seasoned, snooty Francophiles, we had scorned. So, we climbed to the top of the Eiffel tower, drank tea and ate pastries in Montmartre, and rode the Bateau Mouche at sunset. It was a heavenly day; my first day of true relaxation since well before the death of my mother.

A few days later, on September 10th, I was in New York City for a meeting with my accountant and my financial advisor. The meeting wasn't very taxing, and I didn't have to fake looking interested or nodding in deep understanding when, in truth, I hadn't a clue what they were talking about, which was normally the case; the hour passed very pleasantly.

The next morning was so beautiful and the sky so crystal clear and piercingly blue that Bill, my financial advisor, made the spontaneous decision to walk to work even though it would mean he arrived a bit later than usual. As he approached his office at the World Trade Centre, he saw a huge passenger jet crash into one of the twin towers. The Solomon Smith Barney building, where Bill's office was located, was the third and last building to completely disintegrate as a result of the brutal attack on 9/11. In seconds, America the complacent was plunged into chaos.

The psychological impact of that day's events was horrific and far-reaching. The fact that human beings could be driven, by whatever motives, to plan, execute, and rejoice over the murder of thousands using planes filled with live individuals as grotesque battering rams – and all this in the name of God – defies comprehension. But then, evil has always existed, and human nature has clearly not progressed since our days in caves. It is just that our methods of harming each other have been modernized, and 9/11 was a particularly shocking new twist on man's moral depravity.

All day we were glued transfixed to our television screens, Harry in Germany, myself in our house in Connecticut. The pictures of devastation and destruction were replayed over and over again, forever branded in our memories.

Somehow, life had to continue, and it limped painfully along over the next few weeks. In spite of the turmoil, I had contracts to fulfill and concerts to play – with the considerable impediment caused by the temporary closure of all American airports. To get anywhere I either had to drive myself or find circuitous routes via Canada and Canadian airports. I managed to reach all the venues in time for the performances, but missed a few of the vital orchestral rehearsals – once with dire consequences, since putting together the massive Brahms D minor piano concerto in a small town with a good but secondary orchestra requires more than just a quick run-through before the concert. I was quite mortified by the flawed result, every bar a nightmare of insecurity, though there was a form of redemption when the concert was repeated the next day and Brahms was treated more honorably. The whole experience wore me out completely.

Even when US airports reopened, there was an atmosphere of hysterical paranoia everywhere, as new, oftentimes defective, security machines were being installed, and security personnel floundered. Passengers sweated and waited in the long, hot lines, unused to the removal of shoes and jackets for the airport scanners and to the unpacking and scrutinizing of computers and telephones. Delays became routine and, although no one complained, tension was omnipresent.

It was ironic that this was one of my busiest fall seasons ever. The repertoire I had to prepare – seventeen concertos for piano and orchestra, two full recital programs and a Lieder recital program – was enough to tire out even a seasoned veteran. I barely noticed when my upper left arm felt sore after a weekend in Kingston, Ontario, where I had just performed all five Beethoven concertos. It had been a thrilling experience, but by the end my arm felt like lead and throbbed with pain. I ignored it and moved on to Chopin in Calgary and Bartok in Stavanger, Norway, where the December sun made only a vague appearance at midday and Harry and I shopped for Christmas tree ornaments. Harry had joined me there and the orchestra had put us up in a rustic little cottage near the hall. We enjoyed ourselves thoroughly; the concerts went well, and we were finally together again.

After Norway there were no more concerts until January, so we booked ourselves into a "Wellness Hotel" in the Bavarian Alps for three days. I had generously given Harry my lingering cold, which I had caught in Iowa months previously, so he spent two of the three days in bed reading books and surrounded by mounds of Kleenex. The mercury dropped to –20 and a winter storm raged outside. Gone were all thoughts of picturesque hikes in the snow-covered mountains. We were more or less prisoners in the hotel, but I had discovered they had a beautiful swimming pool and was using it frequently. I remember quite clearly walking past a mirror clad in only my bathing suit and noticing that my left arm appeared to be quite swollen. I remarked on this to Harry, who took a look at it, but neither of us was particularly perturbed. I had read somewhere that tennis players often develop big muscles in their right arms from overuse and decided that in my case the over-development just happened to be in the left arm.

Christmas, our first as a married couple, was pleasant and greatly enhanced by our newly acquired Norwegian ornaments. There was plenty of snow in Bavaria, and the Christmas markets were enchanting. I slipped back into "Frau Oesterle" mode and found myself caught up in the intense social whirlwind of a German Christmas. For a shy person like myself, this was sometimes intimidating, but people were very tolerant and I was eager to fit in amongst Harry's vast circle of friends. I was becoming more and more enamored of Bavaria and its Baroque churches, awe-inspiring abbeys, fairy-tale cities and divine countryside.

On New Year's Eve, Harry and I walked up to the top of a nearby hill, the snow crisp under foot and glistening under a brilliant moonlit sky. At the stroke of midnight, the fireworks began and church bells from all the surrounding villages rang out in celebration of the New Year. It was a precious moment of happiness and of hope.

The next morning, I was back at the piano working furiously on my upcoming recital program. In an attempt to kickstart my somewhat neglected European career, which would enable me to cut back on North American concerts so that I could spend more time with Harry, I had offered to presenters a blockbuster recital program which included the ferociously difficult, complete Transcendental Studies of Franz Liszt for the spring of 2002. Much as I passionately love the music, I admit this was a bit of a gimmicky "tour de force" for, up to that point, few men and perhaps no women, other than myself, had ever attempted this feat in a live concert. Various presenters on both sides of the Atlantic were seduced by the idea and invited me to their cities, with the end result that, although I had my usual recital tour in North America, there was also a magnificent tour of Europe lined up, beginning in March of 2002 and including London, Paris and Rome, as well as appearances in Sweden, the Netherlands, Germany and Great Britain.

On January 13th, 2002, I tried out this ferociously demanding Liszt program in front of a large group of friends in the concert hall at Irsee. The following day I traveled back to Connecticut alone to prepare for a month of concerts in North America. Harry was to join me the following week.

At this point my upper arm looked gigantic and was extremely stiff and sore. I decided to visit a chiropractor who had once helped me. He took one look at the swelling and made an appointment for me to visit a local orthopedic surgeon. I also decided to try acupuncture. For a few sessions long needles were stuck into my hands causing extreme pain and frightening the daylights out me. The acupuncturist assured me that the growth was diminishing inside. It was not; quite the contrary. The surgeon decided that I should have an MRI taken of my shoulder and upper arm. Out in Connecticut, they had the latest machine, not the old ersatz coffin version, so mercifully it wasn't too claustrophobic since I could see out the sides; rather like having a very large hockey puck hanging over oneself.

Although the pain was a bit worrying, what with the upcoming, grueling schedule, I wasn't at all concerned that whatever was wrong couldn't be treated and rectified quickly. The absurd notion of cancer barely crossed my mind. My brain was too busy with the Liszt etudes and refused to be distracted by anything else.

The first inkling that things might not be quite so simple came with the results of the MRI and the doctor asking me in which hospital I would prefer to have my biopsy: the Memorial Sloan Kettering Cancer Center in New York City or the hospital at Yale University in New Haven. In my innocence I answered this serious question lightheartedly and without much thought, plumping for New York over New Haven because I thought it would be more amusing for Harry. The results had indicated that there was a large growth wrapped around my upper arm muscles and the doctor felt there was a certain amount of urgency involved. An appointment was made to meet Dr. Carol Morris the following Tuesday in New York. As one is wont to do, I immediately built up a picture of Dr. Morris: someone short, bespectacled, with black hair streaked with grey severely tied back in a bun, wrinkled forehead, bad teeth, in late middle age and, of course, brilliant. Except for the brilliant part, my imagination had gone badly awry. For it was not a gnome but a goddess who walked into the examining room where I sat joking and waiting with Harry that Tuesday. Young, tall, slender, fine-featured with the most beautiful, delicately formed hands, she entered the room surrounded by her acolytes, an aura of stillness and authority about her, like a high priestess. She was extremely serious, carefully explaining my options and strongly suggesting an immediate biopsy, warning me that even if I didn't have cancer, the tumour (it was now officially called a tumour) should nevertheless be removed, and I would risk some damage to my arm muscles.

"How much damage?" I asked, "Would it affect my piano playing?" The answers were ambivalent.

I chose to believe that all would be well and was upset only because the biopsy was forcing me to cancel several concerts. Very early on it had been drummed into me that one never cancels concerts, that it was somehow unethical, so many of my concerts had been played with a raging fever or worse. And to lose a concert due to illness sometimes meant never being invited back to certain cities. The battle for my career had been hard fought and there hadn't been a cancellation in over twenty years. It hadn't been easy to reach the plateau of relative stability I now enjoyed, and I hated to risk jeopardizing it even by the loss of only a few engagements.

Dr. Morris was very serious and offered no optimistic platitudes. But I remained basically cheerful and almost without doubts. I blotted out the negatives. The concept that a cancerous tumour could exist in my arm with the power to damage my pianistic skills and consequently destroy my life seemed preposterous.

On the morning of January 31st, 2002, just over two weeks after I had played my Liszt recital in Germany, Harry drove me to the hospital. We had left our house in Connecticut at 5.30 a.m. and without any traffic to impede our progress we sped along the deserted Parkway in the steely grey light of pre-dawn, arriving in New York just as a winter storm began to blow in earnest. Neither of us had slept much the night before, mainly because we had to get up very early and, typically, had no faith in our alarm clocks. I still wasn't particularly frightened by the pending surgical procedure: rather, I was fascinated by the whole experience.

At first, after I had checked in, signed various forms, submitted to the various tests and answered various questions, I sat quite happily with Harry in the waiting room observing the other patients. A very large family of Romanian descent sat huddled together at one end of the room. There were at least four generations present and they had brought along masses of delicious looking food, all carefully wrapped in aluminum foil and stuffed in large containers. They created a rather festive atmosphere in their corner, chatting and eating with enthusiasm, although I felt a little sorry for the grandmother in her hospital gown who was, of course, not allowed to partake of the feast. She was soon called to the operating room and the family left, probably to have breakfast nearby as their appetites seemed boundless.

In another corner a couple quietly intoned mantras. He was desperately ill, emaciated and with skin the color of parchment; I could hardly bear to look at him but, filled with guilt at being so healthy, I forced myself every so often to meet his eyes and proffer an encouraging smile.

Before long, though, everyone was gone, and Harry and I were alone. We were eventually told that Dr. Morris was performing emergency surgery and that my procedure would be delayed.

Harry and I sat silently holding hands in the deserted room. Clad in only a thin hospital gown and the regulation, hideous, puce-colored cotton dressing gown, and not having eaten since the previous evening, I became chilled to the bone and developed a throbbing headache. Harry hadn't eaten either but refused to leave my side. The magazines provided were eventually all read, and I was left alone with my thoughts while Harry read the books he had foresightfully brought along to help pass the time. Luckily, a nurse stopped by during the afternoon with blankets for me, as I was, by then, blue with cold.

Gone was the devil-may-care-attitude of the morning. We no longer giggled and told each other jokes or made bad puns to amuse ourselves and other patients. The uncertainty of when I would be called and my physical discomforts began to affect my nerves, although I tried to maintain a brave countenance.

Since this was supposedly an out-patient procedure, and as the minutes continued to tick by, it looked more and more as though we would have to drive back to Connecticut in a raging winter storm right in the middle of the New York rush hour with me in, presumably, less than stellar form. Some birthday for poor Harry!

As I stared at the walls, my thoughts inevitably strayed into dark regions. The Memorial Sloan-Kettering Cancer Center was not new to me. I had been there years earlier to visit my dying friend Dana. She had suffered from various forms of cancer since the age of thirteen, but had managed to bear two beautiful girls and survive until her 40th year when she was ultimately defeated by the disease in this very hospital. We had grown up together in three different countries, gone to school together, shared apartments, had been best friends. Why should she have died and why should I have been spared? What, in fact, was this thing, this alien creature growing rapidly and repulsively in my arm? How did it get there? Why was it there?

I decided these thoughts were counter-productive and tried to concentrate on anything else. When my mother lay dying I would "give" her happy memories to think about. I tried out this tactic on myself and thought of our recent trip to Paris, of our walks in the mountains, of pieces by Chopin, the composer to whom I feel closest, whose music speaks directly to my heart, affecting my emotions with an almost preternatural power.

Finally, around 5:00p.m. I was ushered into the freezing cold, rather shabby operating room. It was such a relief to actually have the endless waiting over that my good mood instantly returned and I chatted happily with the kind nurses and with the anesthesiologist, who had me laughing just before he put me under.

"Ms. Fialkowska!" A voice woke me out of the troubled sleep into which I had slipped. Most of the other patients had either gone home or had been transferred to other wards. Harry was standing by my bed smiling at me with anxious eyes and Dr. Morris was speaking to me. She looked exhausted and was still wearing the blue "shower cap" that surgeons wear, and which looks ridiculous on most but not on her. I wasn't taking in all she was saying but the message was clear and blunt. I had cancer; the tumour had to be removed.

She spoke of radiation therapy, of chemotherapy, and I tried to comprehend and to be brave. Above all, I kept telling myself not to make a fuss – not to make it difficult for her – for

Harry. She said that we would have to discuss how to proceed but that she would first confer with her colleagues about how best to save my arm. I had only one question: would I be able to play the piano after the operation? She couldn't give me a definite answer and left soon afterwards.

It was close to 7:00 p.m. and I was to be discharged soon. I felt in complete turmoil and very ill. The tubes in my nose and in my wrist and the large cuffs wrapped around my lower legs to enhance circulation started to prey on the more neurotic segments of my brain. I felt as though I was being buried alive. The combination of lack of food and the anesthesia made me feel dizzy and nauseated. My heart started to race. Suddenly there was a loud, fast and scary beeping coming from the monitor by my bed. A cardiologist was hurriedly summoned, and something was adjusted in the intravenous medication.

There was now no question of my returning home that night, and I lingered for hours in the recovery room, drifting in and out of an uneasy sleep. Harry was finally told that I was out of immediate danger and that he should leave and come back for me in the morning. Upset and distracted by the events of the day, he drove home alone in the storm. He had only been to New York a few times in his life, and had never negotiated the trip in and out of the city. My concern for him was so great that I temporarily forgot my own predicament – an effective counterirritant, I thought to myself, and smiled wanly for a few seconds before slipping back into self-absorption.

Would I ever play the piano again?

CHAPTER 2

Scenes from Childhood ("Kinderszenen")
by Robert Schumann

My first public performance was not what one could term an unmitigated success. History relates neither the obstetrician's nor the nurse's reaction to my initial appearance on the world stage in 1951 but, according to family legend, the first words which fell from my mother's lips following my birth were: "Oh God! Take it away! That's not a baby – it's a dried prune!"

Presumably such a remark, inflicted at such a tender age, could damage a person's psychological makeup for the rest of their life. But this kind of wickedly humorous honesty was a family hallmark and therefore part of my genetic code. At home remarks that would send others scurrying to psychoanalysts were nonchalantly absorbed on a daily basis; to survive one needed to develop either a very thick skin or the capacity for lengthy periods of selective deafness.

That said, there really is a strong streak of eccentricity in my mother's family that, coupled with a tendency to obsession, makes for an interesting agglomeration of personalities. To mention but two, I had a cousin who, at age seventy, streaked down one of the main streets of Victoria, British Columbia, stark naked, hand in hand with one of the most notorious town prostitutes, because he felt it was an amusing thing to do. And another cousin, a dear, loveable person who, for the Queen Mother's 100th birthday, sought out and bought the very outfit Her Majesty wore on the day of her celebration, put it on, had his photograph taken proudly wearing it, and then sent copies of the photo to all of the members of his family as well as to Clarence House. But then, my own mother, having received a hand-knitted tea cozy as a wedding present from an elderly friend, decided it was far more suitable as headgear than as a pot cover, and for years wore it during the winter months without a trace of embarrassment. The scary part is that the family found nothing remotely odd in this behaviour.

In addition, the women of my mother's family have tended to be strong-willed and bossy. And when, by some quirk of fate, there is a member of the family with a slightly more normal (boring?) outlook on life, chances are this poor person, feeling somehow inadequate and at a disadvantage, will seek out a glorious eccentric in marriage just to keep up the family's reputation and pass the interesting genes on to the next generation. As for myself, the obsessiveness and strong will are definitely there; and eschewing a life of leisure for never-ending hours of struggle in front of a black box with white keys, could be interpreted as mildly eccentric.

We are definitely proud of our "oddness" – no question about it. But when the human cocktail of eccentricity and obsession is mixed with despotic tendencies, the result is sometimes a rather entertaining, perhaps rather overwhelming personality; my mother instantly springs to my mind.

The genealogy of my maternal grandmother is a typical Canadian mixture of Scottish and English adventurers who rose in the ranks of the Hudson's Bay Company and made their fortunes. One of them, Robert Miles, my great-great-great-grandfather, actually became chief factor of the company and married a remarkable lady from the Cree nation. It has always been a source of great pride to know that I have some First Nations blood running through my veins.

The marriage of Robert and his wife, Betsy, was happy and successful, and their grandson, my maternal great-grandfather, rose to prominence as a great financier, becoming president of the Bank of Montreal and founding the Royal Trust Company of Canada. For his efforts, he was knighted and thereafter was known as Sir Edward Clouston. He was obviously a bit of a rogue, but he enjoyed life and was a kind and philanthropic man, particularly towards his less fortunate relatives, who regarded him always with great affection.

Sir Edward had three daughters; two died very young, and the third, Marjory, was my grandmother. An extraordinary beauty, she also appears to have been extremely strong-willed, especially in her choice of husband. Having been brought up in the lap of luxury and as part of the cream of Canadian Society (such as it was at the end of the 19th century), she was expected to make a high-profile marriage, preferably to a titled Englishman or, at the very least, to someone from a family of equal wealth and power. She chose, instead, a persistent suitor from Victoria who was a "mere" Doctor of Medicine. Although her parents overcame their initial prejudice, some of her other relatives and friends were aghast. The fact that my grandfather was one of the most renowned and decorated research scientists in his field didn't sway them one bit. In just three generations the family had gone from carrying canoes in the wild and trading fur pelts, to considering an alliance with a professional man as a social faux-pas and a definite "step down." My grandfather, a parasitologist, had already distinguished himself as a young man with his work in Gambia and the Belgium Congo, isolating the tsetse fly as the carrier of the dreaded "sleeping sickness." Shortly after the First World War, he was sent to Poland, where a terrible epidemic of typhus was raging. For his magnificent work there, he was given Poland's highest civilian decoration. Decades later, in 1976, when I was engaged to perform three concerts with the Royal Liverpool Philharmonic, I spent a day as an honoured guest at the renowned Liverpool School of Tropical Medicine. The fact that I was a concert pianist was considered all very worthy, but the delightful attentions and kindnesses that I received from the Dean and the professors were mostly due to the fact that I was the legendary Dr. John Todd's granddaughter.

My mother, Bridget or "Biddy," was the youngest of three sisters. Incredibly strong-willed, like my grandmother, she seems to have been totally unsuited to the life she was expected to lead. Many of her early years were taken up in the pursuit of fun, since there were continuous house parties with masses of young people in their home, riding, playing tennis and hockey, acting in amateur theatricals, travelling luxuriously, and leading a life of utter ease. But my mother, early on, apparently developed a strong streak of rebellion, hating her governess–ruled education and desperately wishing she could go to a "regular" school and university to earn a degree and follow a profession. She refused to be a "debutante" and at the age of nineteen, while the family was spending a year in Paris, she suddenly decided she wanted to be a pianist. She enrolled herself into the École Normale de Musique which, at that time, boasted such luminaries as Alfred Cortot and Nadia Boulanger amongst its faculty, and she worked frenetically and fanatically for four years, until 1939 when the family, for obvious reasons, could no longer allow her to remain in Paris. Reluctantly my mother returned home, and her musical career was put on hold indefinitely ... or at least until I appeared on the scene. Her only non-musical interest during those Paris years was ice hockey; she played Centre Forward in the European Woman's Hockey League representing Great Britain, but then defected to the French team.

When her fiancé was killed in the early months of the war, my mother enlisted and earned a degree as a mechanic. She was sent overseas with the armed forces and, once in England, was assigned as a driver/mechanic to the Polish forces in exile stationed up in Scotland, which is where she met my father.

During the early stages of World War II, the Poles were hugely popular in Britain, especially after the heroic performance of the Polish pilots during the Battle of Britain. However, once Hitler had attacked the Soviet Union and Stalin became Britain's ally, the Poles became somewhat of an embarrassment to the English and American governments who desperately wanted to keep Stalin appeased and the Russians fighting hard on the Eastern front. With Poland occupied by Russian troops who had no intention of leaving, what followed was a tragic betrayal on the part of the allies. It wasn't that anti-Polish sentiment became government policy, but it certainly wasn't discouraged in any way, and it flourished amongst left-wing groups in England and Scotland.

And so it happened that one day my mother, sitting in her truck with the window open, waiting to drive a Polish officer to a staff meeting, was spat upon and insulted by a young Scot. My mother returned to the officer's mess that evening and recounted her story. The Polish officers, who doted on her, made a huge fuss, exclaiming that they would never forget how she had suffered for Poland etc. etc. – all the officers but one, who had just arrived and who was unknown to my mother. His only comment was that perhaps the next time she went out she should take an umbrella! Thus, my parents met, and two years later they were married in London, where they both had been transferred. My mother had become so proficient in the Polish language that she was assigned to the Polish headquarters in the Rubens Hotel, where she served as a translator for the Polish Underground Army.

As I've mentioned, my mother was obsessive, quite unreasonable and, on occasion, a bit of a tyrant. But she had a wonderful sense of humour and a wicked sense of fun. A lifelong rebel, she enjoyed flaunting orders, driving through red lights, backing up on major highways when she missed an exit, jumping to the head of queues with panache, and filling out serious forms with witty and thoroughly disrespectful comments. Even in her late seventies, when she was under strict instructions to stay indoors because of a bout of pneumonia, she sneaked out and went skating on the lake in front of our house because, as she put it with her own infallible logic: "The ice was so perfect." And just to annoy all of us, she recovered from her pneumonia the next morning! She was exasperating, but I loved her.

Of my father's family I know far less, my father not being interested in such things. All I know is that my grandfather was a Pole who came from the Austrian section of Poland (Poland before World War I was divided into three occupied sections: the Russian sector, the Austrian sector, and the German sector) and that he was fortunate enough to come from this more tolerant section, where he had a successful career in the military, becoming the Commandant of the Austro–Hungarian officers' school in Wiener Neustadt and eventually rising to the rank of General. He married his best friend's daughter, Ludmilla von Regwald, whose family owned great tracts of land in Bukowina as well as in Poland. An alleged *bon vivant*, full of charm, he died suddenly in 1919, leaving my grandmother destitute with three small boys, the war having devastated the family finances.

My father Jerzy, or George, was the youngest son and only eight years old when his father died. They were living in Lwów (formerly Lemberg), where times were terribly hard following not only the horrors of the first World War, but also the failed attempt to re-occupy Poland by the Bolsheviks in 1920–1921, when my uncle Konrad, still only a young boy, acted as a courier for the resisting Polish forces. At one time the family survived only with the help of the American Red Cross and their soup kitchens. But the Fialkowski boys were all over-achievers, and by 1939 my uncles Konrad and Gabriel were already successful doctors of medicine and heads of hospital departments. My father was an electrical engineer with a bright future, working for the German firm of Siemens in Warsaw. Called up to active duty after Poland was attacked by the Nazis, he took part as a young reserve officer in the defence of Warsaw, where the sadly under-equipped Polish army heroically staged the last cavalry attack of modern history against the German tanks. He then was ordered to evacuate and re-join the Polish army in exile. Through many hair-raising adventures, including dodging bullets, avoiding bombs and a daring escape from a prison camp in Romania, he made it to Greece, where he apparently had a marvelous few days sightseeing before embarking on a transport ship to France. My father had a passion for travel, and nothing made him happier than visiting exotic places, preferably in warm climates (even in the middle of a war!). After France he finally ended up in London via Scotland. During the war, he worked in the Polish underground as a communications expert.

Miraculously, my strong-willed grandmother and two uncles survived both the German and Soviet invasions, my uncle Konrad having been interned by the Gestapo and later persecuted mercilessly by the post-war communist regime. My uncle Gabriel, although a less intense, more happy-go-lucky fellow, also suffered mightily from deprivations and persecution; among other things, his home in Lodz was first commandeered by retreating German troops and then by Russian troops, who he found had chopped up all of his furniture to use for firewood! The rest of the family – cousins, uncles and aunts – were either killed or deported to camps, Nazi or Soviet. Some survived and one, a resistance fighter, escaped to South America after the war, but was hunted down by the communists and assassinated. My father spent over seven years without knowing if his mother was dead or alive, and only ventured back to Poland to see his family in 1958, after Stalin had died. Had he returned earlier he would most likely have been shot.

In Canada, my father worked for General Electric and then, when my maternal grandfather died, he retired from engineering and took over my mother's third of the family estate, located on the western tip of Montreal Island, transforming it into a beautiful apple farm. He loved the property and was very happy living there, so long as he could travel each year to Europe or somewhere unusual. My father's idea of heaven was to walk for hours in Paris, where he had studied as a young engineer, revisiting the "quartiers" of his youth. Since this coincided very much with my mother's feelings about her early experiences in Paris, I always felt that their best times together were during our frequent trips to France as a family. My father was passionate about politics and read constantly, but although extraordinarily charming, in Canada he was very much a recluse, and could go weeks on end seeing no one but the family. Once he was in Europe, this changed dramatically and he became gregarious; I believe he just felt more at ease with the European style of life, of thought, of rapid conversation and discussion, as opposed to the natural reticence of English Canada.

But what my father cared for above all was his children. He was devoted to us and was always there whenever we came to him with any problem, wise and ready to support and reassure with reason and calm. My brother Peter had a particularly close relationship to him, and they often travelled all over Europe together while I stayed home with my mother and practised the piano.

Thanks to my parents, I grew up at ease with both cultures and inherited a profound love of Europe, a strong interest in politics and a passion for gardens and apple trees.

My ambitious mother suffered mildly from the notion that, because as a girl she had never received a university degree or even a regular high-school diploma, her intellectual upbringing was somehow disadvantaged. *Au contraire*, her massive general knowledge of history, politics, art, music, literature, and poetry (of which she could recite hours and hours in three or four different languages) would have put many a university professor to shame. What she possessed was a remarkable mind that positively thirsted for knowledge and remained sharp and ever curious right until the end.

She was also an inveterate organiser and a perfectionist and, perhaps due to her upbringing and early social status, was extremely self-confident in social situations. So, it was partially out of her own frustrations at not having had the chance to continue her musical studies or, indeed, pursue any other kind of profession, that she focused on her children's development with passion and commitment.

My brother Peter, three years older than myself, is one of the family's most delightful and gifted eccentrics. But he was definitely not the appropriate recipient of this barrage of ambition and discipline from my mother. Instead, he escaped into a fantasy world, which he generously shared with me. He created an entire universe with kingdoms and time machines, armies and palaces, knights, cowboys and gangsters (all inspired by books he read or countries we had visited) and magical, imaginary places like "Ishkabible" and "Iccadiccadaccidak." Peter would be the narrator and would play the part of all of the characters but mine. I was entranced and enthralled by his imagination and his absurd sense of humour. I can still see us walking up and down the driveway for hours and hours after I had finished my work, in any kind of weather (even snowstorms and days of 30 below Fahrenheit), totally oblivious to the elements, completely caught up in our fantasy world.

I sometimes wonder what would have happened to me if I hadn't had a brother who had utterly no interest in kicking balls and playing with other little boys but preferred my company and the world we created between us. He was always popular at school because he was so witty and such a good mimic, but his thoughts were never concentrated on anything scholastic or group oriented. For a little girl who was already sitting for five hours a day at the keyboard as well as attending regular school, those few hours with my brother each week were a true lifeline.

It was a crushing blow when he was sent away to boarding school in his early teens. My mother had had to give up forcing him to practise the piano because at one point Peter just dug in his heels and refused to co-operate, although he has loads of talent and had really become quite proficient. My father would patiently help him with his schoolwork and at university, seemingly without ever cracking open a book, he breezed through the courses and obtained his degree. Because of his

good looks and talent, he was much in demand and always landed the lead parts in university theatricals, but the rigours of
the acting profession were not for him, and in the end, he preferred a quiet life working for years as a television news-anchor
and meteorologist in Peterborough, Ontario. His obsessions
still include ocean liners, operas, railroads, sailing and trips
to France. He was my closest ally as a child, as I was his, and
he remains the best brother imaginable. My gorgeous Italian
sister-in-law, Luisa, keeps him reasonably grounded, although
many would affectionately consider him to be mad as a hat-
ter. They have five children between them, and it is a relief to
report that Peter's two, Caroline and John, whom I love dearly, carry on the family tradition of eccentricity. Luisa's three,
Valerie, Andrea and John-Paul, are genuinely delightful and
are an excellent counterbalance.

My mother found more fertile ground for her ambitions in
her daughter. Peter was already playing the piano quite well
when, at the age of four, I was clamouring to learn how to play
myself; the sounds my brother was producing by pressing down
the keys intrigued me. And so it was that my career began. My
first piece was a Polish Christmas Carol, "Jezus Malusieńki,"
that I played for my father as a Christmas present. Shortly thereafter, I was enrolled in the Sacred Heart Convent in Montreal
as a day-pupil. My parents were unusual in Quebec society at
that time, as my mother was a non-practising Anglican and my
father a practising-on-his-own-terms Catholic. They decided
the children should be brought up Catholic, as my father did
actually attend church every Sunday and my mother never saw
the inside of a church except for a funeral, a wedding or, more
likely, as a tourist in Europe. I'm pretty sure they wanted us
to be exposed to some sort of religion so we could develop our
own theological philosophies later on. My father attended the
village church regularly, but when we grew up and no longer
went with him, he discontinued the practice because he found
the local priests to be at best uninteresting and, at worst, as he
would put it rather bluntly, "idiots." He had strong beliefs, in-

cluding some significant spiritual feelings for the pilgrimage town of Lourdes, where he had gone to pray at difficult periods in his life, including his time in France during the early days of the war. But he often found Church doctrine meddlesome and intrusive, mixing into areas he felt were none of its business. In many ways my politically ultra-conservative father was, in fact, an extremely forward thinker.

Actually, my mother was a far more religious person than my father; I think she had a very strong sense of faith, even though she was a child of agnostics with no real religious background at all. She had a wonderful sense of irreverence towards organised religions and never failed to chuckle over some of the passages from the reams of Catechism I was forced to learn by heart every day at the convent.

I loved going to school and I enjoyed all the rituals of the Catholic upbringing: the lily parades, the first communion, the incense, retreats, candles, ribbons, and medals. Confession every week did strike me as a little ludicrous and, already a performer, I worried that the priest would get bored with the tiny scope of my sins and found myself spending a great deal of energy and imagination dreaming up more exotic ones to keep him entertained; I believe he was quite amused. Unlike most of the other little girls, I never felt any desire to become a nun, probably because already, at the age of five or six, the concepts of freedom of thought and individualism had taken hold in my young mind. Also, I was already ambitious, and the thought of wearing black robes every day seemed rather dreary; the life of the Cloister and of obedience didn't strike me as much fun or worthy of aspiration.

The education at the Convent in the 1950s was based heavily on learning pages and pages of grammar, Catechism and history by heart. Luckily for the nuns, early Canadian history is full of the exploits of Jesuit and other Catholic missionaries (not to mention nuns), so they had a field day, and it was all very exciting for a young mind – to ghoulishly revel in the horrific stories of Fathers' Brébeuf, Jogues and Co.'s martyrdoms at the hands of my aboriginal ancestors. I also believe that this early memorising provided excellent training for when I later started to develop my repertoire at the piano. To this day I memorise new pieces extremely quickly, and I attribute this small but useful talent to the style of education I received at the Sacred Heart Convent.

Many of the nuns were from poor Irish backgrounds or French-Canadian country families, and their characters ranged from boorish to mostly very pleasant and kind. But occasionally one struck gold, as I did in my third and fourth year, when I was taught by a remarkable woman, the younger daughter of a distinguished Montreal family – the Duchastels – who were friends of my grandparents. Quite elderly at that time, she was highly civilised, well educated, had a wicked sense of humour and was a totally delightful person. I loved her dearly and believe the feeling was reciprocated. I flourished under her guidance, loving school and eagerly absorbing any bit of knowledge she would impart. However, she never seemed to award me any of the ribbons or medals so beloved in Convent life and that she would lavish on the other little girls. In frustration, I once asked her why I was always overlooked, citing my good marks and general good behaviour; Mother Duchastel just nodded wisely and, smiling, pointed out that I didn't need any extra encouragement and that I was already far too pleased with myself!

In 1960, when I was nine, my world changed drastically and irrevocably. That summer we travelled to France, ostensibly for a family holiday. However, Biddy had ulterior motives, a vision of my possible musical career having taken hold in her mind. At the time I never questioned my mother's actions or motives. One didn't in those days. Besides, I was a self-satisfied little creature with plenty of ambition and a major desire to impress my parents. It was still all a big lark to me.

I had learned a short program to play for her pre-war piano teacher, Mademoiselle Anne-Marie Mangeot in Paris. The program (unimpressive by the standards of today's mini-monsters, who play Rachmaninov's 3rd piano concerto at the drop of a hat, shortly after leaving the cradle) consisted of a Bach two-part invention, a movement from a Mozart Sonata, Debussy's "Golliwog's Cake Walk," and a Cramer Etude. After hearing me play, Mlle. Mangeot suggested to Biddy that perhaps now was the time for me to start up serious music studies at a conservatory or music school. This gave Biddy the green light to intensify and lengthen my practice sessions with her and the search was on to find me a teacher.

It was my great good fortune to be living in Montreal at a time when arguably the greatest piano pedagogue in Canadian history was teaching at a local music school. The school itself was impressive enough. Newly finished, it was the brainchild of an extraordinary nun, Soeur Marie-Stéphane. She had been in Paris as a young nun and had met the rather obscure French composer, Vincent d'Indy, who was renowned in Paris for having created his own unique music school, the Schola Cantorum. Armed with ideas, inspiration and a divine mission to succeed, iron-willed little Soeur Marie-Stéphane came back to Canada, started lobbying and by the time I appeared on the scene, in the fall of 1960, the impressive École Vincent d'Indy was practically completed; an imposing structure built on the side of Mont Royal overlooking the predominantly French Canadian sector of Montreal known as Outremont; it had a state-of-the-art recital hall, facilities for boarders, many practise rooms and pianos, a cloistered area for the nuns' living quarters, a lovely chapel, library, kitchen, and studios and reception rooms. The quality of teaching was first-rate. My aunt Rosanna, who had never heard of Vincent d'Indy but was Quebecker enough to know that 90 per cent of the place names in Quebec are those of obscure saints, would innocently refer to the school as Saint Vincent des Indes, and so the name stuck in our family; it was affectionately and more commonly referred to, by irreverent students, as V.D.

When I arrived there with Biddy one early September day for my
first lesson, we were met at the entrance by a beautiful young
nun named Soeur Stella Plante. The daughter of a doctor in far
away Thetford Mines, Quebec, she had originally wanted to be
a nurse and had been promised by the Order that if she "joined
up" at the tender age of seventeen, they would train her so that
she could pursue her dream. She did take her vows, but the high-
er-echelon nuns had other plans for her. So obvious was her
unusual talent for music that it was no surprise she ended up
teaching piano at their best music school and the nursing was
put on hold. She became my teacher for the next seven years –
two lessons a week. She was enthusiastic, ambitious and had an
incredible spark for igniting students' interests and inspiring
them to strive for perfection. I loved my lessons and was also,
for a while, happy to practise for hours every day, as it was all
very exciting and new. Biddy was happy as well; the teaching
was sound and followed along the lines of the French school-
ing she herself had received in Paris: a great deal of Solfège and
Dictation, Theory and History, Counterpoint and Gregorian

Chant. The repertoire I learned consisted mainly of Bach, the classics and French music.

During the fall of 1960, there was another change. Biddy took me out of the French- speaking Sacred Heart convent and put me into the English Protestant school known as The Study, where they generously worked their entire schedule around mine so that I could have ample time to practise the piano every day.

By the age of ten, I had progressed enough to be playing the first movement of Mozart's Piano Concerto K. 466 with the Montreal Symphony, the venerable Wilfrid Pelletier conducting. To play with an orchestra for the first time was breathtaking. I was overwhelmed by the different sounds and orchestral textures all blending in so magically with what I was playing. I felt this amazing burst of warmth radiate through my body, and my inner eye was blinded by a kaleidoscope of fantastic colours.

By the age of eleven, although still going to The Study full-time, I was also practising at least five hours a day. I seemed to manage fine, juggling everything without fuss, although, other than seeing my classmates at school, there was never time for socialising during the off-school hours. If it hadn't been for Peter, I might have turned into a far greater social recluse than I actually became.

Before entering The Study, my I.Q. had been tested and the results emboldened Biddy to take a few radical measures. I started skipping classes to be able to participate in piano competitions. I also started to skip whole years and ended up graduating with girls three years my senior. How I ever passed all my exams is a mystery, as I had been forced to miss so many of the lectures. But, once again, I was fortunate: most of the teachers were indulgent and perhaps a little sympathetic as well, helping me along while trying to keep me as level-headed as possible. For me, going to school was a joy and an escape – almost a holiday – and a welcome respite from what was becoming, after the first euphoric months at V.D., the increasingly stressful hours at the piano. Indeed, signs of stress were definitely showing; before every performance I was becoming physically ill, throwing up uncontrollably, much to the consternation of those around me. I soon learned to keep this disgusting occurrence secret, never panicking since I knew I'd feel fine once on stage.

When I was eleven, it was time for me to start lessons with the master pedagogue, Yvonne Hubert, who came to V.D. on Fridays to teach the advanced students. Biddy, who sat with me and supervised my practising every day, and Soeur Stella, who taught me twice a week, had prepared me well so that my lessons with Mademoiselle Hubert were quite thrilling. A tiny little Piaf-like French woman whose breath always smelt of the gallons of coffee she drank, very highly strung and very serious, she had settled almost by accident in Montreal years before and became the most revered piano teacher in Canada. She had been a pupil of the legendary Alfred Cortot and, among her many gifts, she possessed the most extraordinarily agile left hand. Never demonstrating with both hands, she would sit on my right side and play everything miraculously with her left hand alone – a feat that never failed to amaze. A perfectionist, she instilled in me a desire for clarity, structure, and intelligent music-making. Her students produced mostly lovely sounds – they never banged – and she counted among them at that time André Laplante, my great friend William Tritt, whose brilliant career was tragically cut short by his premature death, then, a little later, Marc-André Hamelin and Louis Lortie, who are now pursuing major international careers.

Great rivalries grew up not only between the students but also between their black-robed teachers. As there were many national and international competitions taking place in Montreal, the rivalries thrived, but for the most part (at least among the students) they were amicable and beneficial. One little nun, though, was quite enterprising; she actually hid in the broom closet of the room where an international jury was deliberating so that she could get advance notice of which pieces her pupils would, potentially, be playing in the next round. She also gave her students little snorts of brandy before they went on stage. Sometimes, when she decided the pupil seemed lethargic, it became more than just a sip or two ... which made for some wild performances.

Biddy, however, had her own agenda, and remained unfazed over whether I won or lost competitions. Of course, she was pleased when I won, but what concerned her most was the quality of my playing and that it should deserve to win (my father George, on the other hand, just felt I deserved to win everything regardless). She was not your typical stage mother because she never pushed me to perform in public and, for two years, much to the good nuns' horror, she refused to allow me to enter competitions or to perform at all, insisting I use the time to learn repertoire and to develop my technique. Probably I was very overworked at the time and there was never really any break, since even holidays in Europe now consisted of daily searches for pianos on which to practise in hotel bars and restaurants, piano shops, even night clubs – a nightmare for me as I was convinced my playing was obtrusive and annoying to other guests or to the staff. But Biddy was adamant that I put in the hours every day.

Although holidays had lost any vestige of relaxation and the pressures of work were increasing at home, I still felt quite content most of the time. I was sure I could cope with everything and was proud to be able to do so, convinced I was enjoying my life. Nothing made me happier than having good music lessons, getting good marks and being no trouble to my parents. But there were dark shadows lurking: a few early indications of the discrimination I was to suffer in later years at the hands of the occasional xenophobic, separatist-inclined French-Canadian organisations made their appearance. Even as a child I was often overlooked for performance or prize opportunities because of the political incorrectness of my surname. Janina Fialkowska is a very Polish name and didn't fit into the French-Canadian philosophy of the 1960s. Neither was it particularly popular with the arch-Anglo society of Toronto at that time. I may well have not noticed the occasional unfairness, but my parents suffered mightily on my behalf, and it was their suffering that hurt me.

I was still a confident and cheerful soul back then, however, even with my terrible pre-performance nerves. I had discovered early on how to compartmentalize different emotions in different parts of my brain, locking away the more unpleasant aspects of life quite successfully during the greater part of the day. Playing the piano was just something I did better than most children of my age, and I enjoyed the distinction it gave me. I realised that to remain at the top was a struggle and the work had to be done, but my fundamental passion for music had yet to be ignited.

I was already studying with Yvonne Hubert when Arthur Rubinstein came to Montreal. The first time I heard him play, in the mid-sixties, he performed Mozart's concerto K. 466 and Beethoven's Emperor concerto with Zubin Mehta conducting the Montreal Symphony. The following year he returned and played the Schumann and the Chopin E minor concerto, again with an admirable accompaniment from Mehta. Each piece was sublime, but it was the Chopin that was a revelation for me. I had never heard playing like this – not only the sound from heaven, the burning emotion, lyricism, divine phrasing, and structural perfection, but the fact that Rubinstein communicated all this incredible beauty to me, so personally. I was transported. That night I wrote succinctly and accurately in my little diary: "Thank you Chopin and thank you Arthur Rubinstein – now I understand what it means to be a musician." From then on my whole attitude changed; music was now a noble profession in my eyes, not just a child's game or a mother's ambition, and I intended to strive as hard as I could to be worthy of its responsibilities and demands.

But then Peter was sent off to boarding school. I missed him desperately and practising piano began to overwhelm my life. I now went to school only to attend classes for the ten subjects I needed in order to pass my Matriculation. Recess, sports, school outings, Girl Guides, debating clubs, language clubs; all extra-curricular activities were banned from my life, and as I was practising five or six hours a day it was only at night that I could escape a little into a fantasy world. There was a streetlight that cast a beam onto my bed, and I would stay up into the wee hours reading exciting books by Jules Verne, Alexandre Dumas and P.C. Wren, Sienkiewicz and later, Tolstoy. It is only in retrospect that I wonder how I survived it all. Biddy was less fortunate: driving me hither and yon to lessons, arranging extra tutoring for me in certain subjects, and bringing me to competitions all over the province, as well as sitting by the piano and practising with me every day – all this began to take its toll. During my early to mid teens, she had several serious operations to remove suspected tumours and illnesses. One massive depression confined her to a hospital for months at a time. George was amazing, coping admirably, visiting Biddy every day, running the farm, cooking for me and being there for all of us. By this time, I had so much discipline instilled in me that my work barely skipped a beat. Besides, I knew that what would please Biddy the most would be if I continued working

as hard as I could. I missed her but it was also pleasant and relaxing to be just with my father, whom I adored. We would cook
together at night, go to concerts, and he would help me in the
evenings with my algebra and geometry homework. I remember those evenings with great nostalgia.

Around my sixteenth birthday I matriculated with honours
and the following year received my Baccalauréat and Maîtrise
in music from the Université de Montréal. And so it was that,
at the age of seventeen, I became a full-time musician without
having the slightest notion of what a career in music actually
entailed. I had not made any choices; it had all just happened.

But before I close this chapter on my school years, I must
introduce here a character who played one of the most important roles in my life.

DANA

It was shortly after Peter was sent to boarding school that Biddy
and I drove over to V.D. one evening for my Monday lesson.

When we arrived, a little girl was sitting on the piano stool
chatting with Soeur Stella in her studio. She was tiny, with arms
and legs like toothpicks, rich dark brown hair tied back in two
pigtails, big sparkling brown eyes and a mouth full of braces.
She was giggling and laughing. Her name was Dana and her
parents had sent her to V.D. from Buffalo to study with Paul
Loyonnet, the other "big" professor teaching at the school. For
a second, I was really put out by Dana's presence: I was supposed to be Soeur Stella's little girl and prize pupil. Who was
this usurper? My jealousy lasted about five minutes because
Dana was irresistible. And from that day on we became life-
long best friends.

Dana came from a dysfunctional family. Her father, who had
sung at one time in the Metropolitan Opera Chorus, seemed
to me to be peculiar, riddled with strange obsessions and habits. He loved Dana in his own way, but early on had decided she

was a genius and that he would do everything he could to see her become another Rubinstein or Horowitz. Dana's mother had had a rough childhood and was unsuited to having children of her own. She was certainly fond enough of Dana, but treated her more as one would a distant favourite cousin. She was a heavy smoker, a drinker and was clearly (and perhaps understandably) bored with her strange older husband. A good businesswoman, she travelled often for her job and had little thought or time for her daughter. Thus, at the age of twelve this English-speaking child who had never left home, who had been brought up Jewish like her father, was suddenly sent to Montreal to board with a French-speaking family and attend a French school run by Catholic nuns. It was her good fortune that she was put with Soeur Stella. But Soeur Stella was not able to be (nor was she permitted to even contemplate being) a surrogate mother to Dana, although she tried as best she could to fill the void. Dana must have been indescribably lonely, especially during her first few months away in the fall of 1963. I have a sad mental picture of her at that time sitting in front of the television in the students' lounge all alone, sobbing as she watched the news reports of the assassination of President Kennedy: a lonely little American girl far from home. I felt lucky to have a domineering mother and doting father who would never dream of sending me away.

Every Wednesday night Biddy brought me to V.D. to attend courses in counterpoint and acoustics. Dana would be waiting impatiently for us to arrive; I would go off to the classes and Dana and Biddy would have their "Wednesday night chats." She grew to adore not only Biddy, but also George, and would often tell me that she liked to pretend they were her parents.

That summer we both attended a three-week summer course at the school and boarded there for the duration. Although there were numerous classes and lessons, compared to what I went through during the winter at home it was a complete doddle and we had oodles of time to play and giggle and behave badly. We'd talk and laugh late into the night and when the supervising nun would bang on my door to see what all the commotion was about, Dana would quickly hide in the closet. I'm sure we fooled no one – I think the nuns were only too happy to see Dana, not to mention myself, carefree and having fun. One of our favourite pastimes was trying to sneak into the nuns' cloistered area. I never managed it but, for her birthday, Soeur Stella secretly allowed Dana to run through the cloister on the condition that she kept running and didn't stop to look.

Dana's talent was extraordinary. This tiny little waif was already playing pieces like the Brahms F-minor-sonata and the Chopin 1st Scherzo. A few months after she arrived, she won the Montreal Symphony concerto competition. When she met the conductor afterwards, he asked her which concerto she would like to play for the winner's concert the following year; "Beethoven's 4th," was her prompt reply. Soeur Aline feared this would be too much for her twelve-year-old protégée, but Dana learned the piece and performed it exquisitely. I recall being overcome with pride and emotion at hearing my friend play so touchingly well.

The following year William Tritt arrived. A "wunderkind" like Dana, with a sweet and loving personality, at age twelve he developed a huge crush on her, following her around like a faithful dog. To round off our circle of friends, there appeared a beautiful child named Marley Rynd, who played the violin as well as the double bass and whose mother, the archetypical Jewish mother, convinced that her daughter was being starved by the nuns, would bring over huge care packages from her local deli – bagels, cream cheese, lox, latkes, knishes – the lot. That summer we four were inseparable – a very happy group under the watchful eyes of the nuns and our highly involved (excluding Dana's) parents. And then, just as suddenly as she had appeared, Dana suddenly vanished, and Bill, Marley and I were left to mourn her absence. Her father had decided that the nuns and M. Loyonnet weren't good enough for his "treasure" and, just as she was finally settling in and had managed to create a whole new world and family for herself in Montreal, he yanked her out of the Vincent d'Indy School and sent her to New York to study with Nadia Reisenberg and to live alone in the Barbizon Hotel for Women. She was only fourteen.

The next time we had any news of her was when a telegram arrived from her father asking the nuns to pray for his daughter, who was dying. And how we prayed! It seemed unbelievable to all of us that this spunky, friendly little girl could be so gravely ill. Later, Dana told me that she had been feeling progressively weaker and dreadfully sick and had finally no longer been able to get out of her hotel bed. It was a reflection on her pathetic family relations that it never crossed her mind to call home to Buffalo for help. But, as Dana put it, somehow a latent maternal instinct prompted her mother to call her that very night for a chat. The next day Dana was flown to Buffalo and hospitalised. She was diagnosed with Hodgkin's disease. The treatments in those days were close to barbaric: radical surgery, which left Dana with terrible scars, and massive doses of radiation which left her with one lung in shreds and also resulted in repeated cancer episodes.

But Dana was extraordinary and, far from being defeated, she was back in New York within months. After she graduated from the High School for the Performing Arts, her parents asked her where she wanted to study next and she replied, "Paris," without hesitation, the city of her dreams. And so it was that she and I were reunited, this time as seventeen-year-olds in the City of Lights.

From the funny little girl with the big smile full of braces there suddenly appeared a beautiful young woman with long, gorgeous hair and a figure like a model. Having already been in Paris for a month, she was there to greet me and my parents when we arrived in September. She had already developed an exquisite Parisian accent and a great passion for Parisian life, and was savouring her every moment there.

But she also had a great need for human companionship and an even greater need for love and a home. Very soon she fell in love with a strange young man named Gérard. I never actually met Gérard but certainly heard all about him, or at least all that Dana deemed acceptable for me to hear! He was the first of a series of disastrous love affairs that plagued her life, although Gérard was one of the few who at least occasionally made her happy. Dana was one of the friendliest individuals in the world and one of the few people I have ever met who had had not an iota of prejudice in her. She was interested in people and wanted to be friends with everyone, whatever gender, race, size, colour, body-build, age, or religion they happened to be. It was quite natural for her to walk up to complete strangers and start a conversation … which is how she met Gérard. She had been standing on the Pont Neuf watching the Seine when he walked by. She asked him if he knew how deep the water was and they started a dialogue.

When Dana was in love, she gave herself totally over to the man she was with – subjugating her mind, her wishes and her desires to his. After a while she'd snap out of it, but in the early stages it could be a rather disconcerting process to watch, especially considering some of the men! Gérard felt that where she was living (a respectable boarding house with respectable bathrooms) was inconveniently far from him. He moved her to a garret near his apartment, with no running water and no toilet. As she was so caught up with her studies at the Conservatoire and with Gérard, and I of course was practising and living a little outside of Paris, we rarely saw each other. But when she did come (for a visit at Christmas or on a few other occasions), her first wish would be to take a long shower and wash her hair in my bathroom – always laughing and making fun of her predicament – always courageous.

She stayed in Paris for three years – I left after one. I believe that she tired of Gérard, who became quite obsessive, once even threatening her with a knife. I know he later turned up in New York looking for her, but eventually he disappeared.

I next saw Dana in New York in the Juilliard School cafeteria two years later, holding court with a strange looking assortment of friends. She had managed to get into the Gorodnitzki class where I had been a pupil since leaving France. Bit by bit, Dana had realised that she could never be a concert pianist, her health being far too fragile and, I think, also realising deep down that she didn't have long to live. Her natural talent carried her through Juilliard with the absolute minimum work. Mr. Gorodnitzki, one of the great disciplinarians of the school and a stickler for hard work, was transformed into an indulgent grandfatherly type every time she would walk into his studio. In fact, she would rarely even head for the piano, but would sit down on the visitor's couch while he sat in his big leather armchair, and they would have delightfully amusing conversations for an hour. This gave Mr. Gorodnitzki a pleasant and much needed break from the tensions of teaching ambitious and demanding students, and Dana found herself yet another possible father figure whom she adored. He was extremely kind to her, and gentle, but a week or so before the final exams of the year they both would wake up to the fact that she hadn't learned a single new piece all year long. In a panic they would throw together some old pieces, usually a lot of Bach, because he was her favourite composer and she played him well, and she would typically pass her exam with flying colours, albeit by the skin of her teeth!

Boyfriends came and went until she finally got involved with a particularly unsavoury fellow who ended up leaving her homeless, broken-hearted and with nowhere to go. This was just when I got my first apartment in New York all on my own, so I invited her to stay. She assured me that she only needed to come for the weekend and would find a place of her own within a few days. She stayed for five years.

We were certainly an odd couple, but I loved having her around and she was devoted to me. Every summer thereafter she would also come up to my parents' home in Canada on the Lake of Two Mountains; it was heaven for her. Dana would love to sit on the porch while I practised, sometimes playing scrabble with another visitor, or discussing world events with George, patting the dogs or helping my mother pick vegetables and flowers. She was my staunchest supporter and I remember clearly when, at the dinner table, someone mentioned that André Laplante would be playing the Rachmaninov 3rd piano concerto in Montreal – Dana, without hesitation, said: "Oh, Janina plays it far better than André!" Whereupon my father, understandably curious, asked her where she had heard André play the piece, to which, without batting an eyelid, Dana replied: "Oh, I never heard him play it, I just know Janina would play it better!" The remark was hilarious and totally untrue, but it demonstrates her utter devotion to me.

Her friendliness to the world in general continued undiminished, despite her unhappy love life. She simply seemed fearless when it came to people, always expecting the best from them. And she had an interesting collection of characters in her circle of friends – from an elderly Puerto Rican handyman to a Korean girl who spoke no English, a Chinese biochemist, a photographer who specialised in quasi-pornographic subjects, a nymphomaniac former Seventh Day Adventist, the innocent son of a Belgian millionaire, a kleptomaniac from Rhodesia and Arthur Ashe, the famous tennis star. I remember once waiting for her to arrive at Montreal airport. Among the early passengers to come through the gate before her was the actor/ big-time wrestler, André the Giant – someone easy to recognise. I instantly thought to myself that somehow Dana would emerge with a story to tell about him. Sure enough, André had spotted her on the plane and had come to sit next to her, starting up a friendly conversation and inviting her out when they got to Montreal. She said he was very nice and that she would most likely have gone out with him – all ninety pounds of her to his over three hundred pounds – had she not already been invited to our place.

One day, walking along the corridors of Juilliard, Dana heard a young boy speaking in a strange tongue over the payphone. She discovered that he was speaking to his mother in Turkish and had just arrived in Juilliard alone and bewildered. Dana took him under her wing and this early act of kindness was to have a far-reaching effect on her life. His name was Danyal (Danny for short), and he is a very talented pianist with a heart of gold.

She also soon made friends with my colleague and good friend Jeffrey Swann, although this relationship was always a bit strained as both considered themselves to be my best friend and I wasn't about to play favourites. One day, Dana and I were walking over to Jeff's, as we often would in the evenings, to cook dinner together. Dana suddenly and urgently had to go to the bathroom, and it was a mad dash to get to Jeff's apartment on time while I helpfully whistled Ravel's "Jeux d'Eau" along the way. We made it only to find that a friend of Jeff's, who we had never met before, was taking a bath. Unfazed, Dana marched right in, introduced herself and used the facilities. Then she stayed on for half an hour chatting away with her new friend, who was still in the bathtub.

And it wasn't only with people that Dana bonded so easily. Twice I returned home from concerts to find a stray cat ensconced in our apartment. I had no real objection, as I love animals, but it did become a bit of a trial as I am quite allergic to cats. These animals were constant companions to Dana and went with her whenever she flew to Buffalo or to France. There was also Morris the hamster, whom she would put in her pocket at the airport because she didn't really have the money to pay for the fares of three animals. On one memorable flight during the winter, she got on the plane, took off her coat and her winter boots, transferred Morris from her coat-pocket into one of her boots, and settled back to read one of her favourite books, usually one of three which she endlessly re-read: *À la recherche du temps perdu* by Proust, *Le grand Meaulnes* by Jean Fournier, and Thomas Mann's *Joseph und seine Brüder*. She was quietly reading when suddenly her neighbour, a nice elderly lady, started to emit little screaming sounds. Dana looked at her full of concern and the lady seemed to be on the point of fainting, her complexion as white as chalk. Gasping, she pointed to Dana's boot in horror. Morris, bored with hanging around in a dark hole, had climbed up to get some fresh air and was peering over the rim. Dana reassured the lady and calmed her down, subsequently collapsing with laughter as she recounted the story over the phone.

There was also the Christmas tree episode. We had bought a little tree for our apartment and decorated it simply but prettily. When Epiphany came around, I took down the decorations and started to remove the tree. Dana begged for me to leave it a little while longer as she loved it so much. By Easter, when all the needles had fallen off and only dry sticks remained, I finally threw it in the garbage while Dana was out one day, only to be accused of heartlessness and given great big reproachful looks upon her return. Mind you, she was laughing not only at me but at herself all along.

It was hard for me to refuse Dana anything. For one thing she was so disarmingly funny, and for another it was wonderful to have such a devoted friend. She honestly believed that I could achieve anything and treated every career triumph I had as her own. This was a woman who as a child had been a prodigious talent, yet she felt absolutely no jealousy towards me. I was at the start of my career and extremely insecure about it all; Dana, although frail and fragile, provided me with huge strength and support.

And then one day she went to apply for a job teaching French at a language school in midtown New York. Fearful that she wouldn't be hired because of her American-sounding name, she introduced herself using her middle name Patricia and invented a whole French background with a family living in Creteil outside Paris. For good measure she also lopped a few years off of her age. Her employer, François, was a nice young man with a handsome face and within a day or two they were "in love." The romance lasted for nearly a year before Dana found out that François' name was actually Saïd and that he was a Moslem from Morocco, and he found out that she was actually a Jewish girl from Buffalo, NY. But love can be a great builder of bridges, and for a while it almost seemed as though this could work. It didn't – there was a miscarriage, then some nasty scenes, and suddenly illness reared its ugly head again and Dana was diagnosed with thyroid cancer.

She recuperated for several weeks up at my parents' home and seemed to bounce back remarkably quickly, although she never could talk much above a whisper due to the damage to her vocal cords.

Back in New York she started up with François again only to come back to me soon after, distraught and in tears. For the first and only time in my life, I got quite furious with her as I heard her sobbing and being sick in the bathroom, having watched her not being able to eat for days. I stormed in and in an exasperated, angry voice told her that I was fed up with her – constantly getting involved with scum, breaking her heart and then coming back to me expecting me to pick up the pieces. To my total discomfiture Dana started laughing and laughing. She said that she had never seen me angry before and that I looked hilarious.

Shortly afterwards she upped and left for Paris where she had once been so happy. There she met a piano technician named Jean-Pierre, who had a certain Gallic charm and seemed harmless enough at first. She married him, had two delightful little girls and moved to Queens in New York, where Jean-Pierre got a job taking care of the pianos at Juilliard. But the marriage was doomed. She became ill again with breast cancer and a sick wife with two babies was simply too much for the weak and irresponsible Jean-Pierre. Their relationship disintegrated and Dana took the girls and returned to France where, never complaining, she had a dreadful winter. Jean-Pierre didn't send any child support and, unbeknownst to all of her friends, she could barely afford to feed her children or heat her apartment. I remember sending her cheques occasionally, but they were supposed to be for toys for the girls or an extra nice article of clothing for her. I never suspected in what dire straits she was living because her letters were always so upbeat and full of funny anecdotes. I admired her courage and stoicism, but sometimes it was misplaced and illogical. If only I could have helped; if only she had asked for my help.

Then, in February 1991, Danny got a call from France; friends of Dana's had taken in the two little girls and Dana herself was in hospital. She had been working as an accompanist in a small music school located far from her home, and it had meant walking several kilometres across town every day with her girls to get there, as she could not afford public transport or a baby-sitter. Her body had finally given out after so many years of disease and strain; she just collapsed. Danny and his partner Lou immediately flew over to France, collected Dana and the girls, and brought them home to New York. The night they returned, they celebrated Jessica's (her eldest daughter) fifth birthday, and the next day they took Dana to the emergency ward of the Memorial Sloan Kettering Cancer Center. I saw her there twice that week, in a room surrounded by photos of Jessica and Nathalie, the children whom she considered the greatest and most valuable achievement of her life. With these two beautiful little girls, Dana, despite all the horrors and suffering of her last years, found her ultimate happiness – the family and the love she had craved so desperately all her short life. While I was there, they were aspirating the liquid that had built up in her lungs – an excruciating procedure, but she showed amazing courage. And then a young resident doctor came in and gently told her that they were going to have to start massive chemotherapy as the cancer had spread extensively over her emaciated body. With her frail thin little voice, she begged him to do whatever he could: "I have to live, you understand, I have to live for them," and she gestured towards a photo of her children. Danny and Lou lovingly and devotedly watched over her and cared for the girls – shortly before the end they brought the girls to the lobby downstairs, arranging a little picnic there with their mother. I said good-bye to my best friend and told her that I'd see her again in two weeks' time. With a smile, she bravely said that she hoped she'd be out of hospital by then. I had to leave for Milano, where Jeff Swann and I were to play the Brahms "Liebeslieder-Waltzes" with the La Scala Choir. Two days later, Biddy called me at my hotel with the news that Dana had died; she was forty years old, and she left behind two little girls of five and four years old and literally hundreds of grieving friends.

As I write this, I cannot see the page for tears. So many years later, I still miss her: that indomitable spirit, that courage, that extraordinary humour. And, above all, I miss our rare and priceless friendship.

CHAPTER 3

The Sounds and the Scents
("Les sons et les parfums") by Claude Debussy

Returning to my own story, Anne-Marie Mangeot continued to have a great influence on Biddy, and it was on her advice that, the year I turned fifteen, I was enrolled in a summer course given by Yvonne Lefébure in Saint-Germain-en-Laye near Paris. Madame Lefébure was one of the most sought-after teachers in a nation that prides itself on its long and illustrious relationship with the piano.

The master classes took place in the charming eighteenth-century Pavillon de Noailles, owned by a Monsieur Guy, who was a great admirer of Mme. Lefébure and who donated his jewel of a house (which he had just acquired, and which was still unfurnished) for the duration of the course. Some students slept in camp beds right in the house. Others commuted every day from Paris and a few of us, myself included, stayed in the *pension* next door, where the simple French bourgeois fare was delicious.

Mme. Lefébure would appear two or three times a week to give master classes. Between times, we would all practise like crazy and be coached by one of her four assistants. The one I was assigned to was a capable and knowledgeable younger woman, with clearly burning ambitions of her own and very little tolerance or patience with the lesser students. Her better students adored her, but the rest spent their time fearful and generally in floods of tears. To me she showed only her most encouraging and rather artificially sweet side, but I was smart enough to realise that she was probably just hedging her bets with an eye to a possible good future recruit for her own class.

The fun began when Mme. Lefébure arrived. She would be driven into the courtyard like royalty, followed by a large retinue comprising her husband and various sycophantic assistants and admirers, each with their own function: one to carry her music scores, another her shawl, another her glasses case and another her umbrella. She was tiny, but with a perfect little figure and masses of hair of a rather determined shade of gold (she was sixty-eight years old at the time) tied back in a *chignon* from whence long wisps would escape and fly about dramatically while she played. She wore magnificent straw hats with brightly coloured ribbons to match her outfits, and tiny little shoes with the highest heels imaginable. Dreadfully short-sighted, she wore thick glasses with dark frames, and when she was pleased she would grin, showing all her teeth and conjuring up memories of Lewis Caroll and the Cheshire Cat. She had an aura of stardom about her, due primarily to her extremely strong personality and her conviction of her superiority to all of those around her. She cut a striking, quasi-Napoleonesque figure as she paraded through life, constantly surrounded by a coterie of devoted fans.

For the course I had prepared the sixth partita of Bach, the second Ballade of Chopin and Ravel's "Jeux d'eau". These were new pieces for me, but I had worked very hard on them under Biddy's supervision and was well prepared. Since nothing much was expected of a fifteen-year-old girl from far-off Canada, my playing surprised them and caused quite a stir. Mme. Lefébure enjoyed teaching me because I tried so hard and could understand and absorb what she showed me fairly quickly. Her star pupil at that time was Imogen Cooper. I was a little in awe of Imogen, who seemed so relaxed and professional and who played the fourth Ballade of Chopin and Debussy's "Reflets dans l'eau" exquisitely. She seemed to have so much more maturity as a musician than I had, although we were almost exactly the same age. There was a little rivalry between us, but nothing serious, as I already admired her and she, I think, was reasonably impressed with me. I lost track of her after this summer, only to meet her again after fourteen years in 1980 when she turned up backstage at my London recital debut; we have been close friends ever since and I continue to be in awe of her prodigious talent and profound musicianship.

Early on in the course, Biddy approached Mme Lefébure to ask her if she could take her photo. The reaction was swift: absolutely not, she wasn't prepared for such a thing – total horror at even the suggestion of such a bold request. Biddy was amused and thought no more about it until a week later when, sitting quietly in the garden reading during a break in the afternoon session, she was accosted by Imogen, who had come out of the Pavilion in search of her with the announcement: "Madame is ready." Biddy, a trifle taken aback, asked: "What for?" It appeared that Madame was ready to be photographed. And so it was that we have some lovely photographs of Mme. Lefébure standing in the garden of the Pavillon de Noailles all dressed up in her gold silk dress with bright purple polka-dots, her matching purple silk shoes, and a great big straw hat with a wide purple ribbon around it, looking as pleased as punch with herself.

In the master class she would sit in the front row near the performing student, her eyes closed as if in prayer, listening intently. When the pupil had finished, a feeling of tense expectation hovered over the company. Everyone watched Madame, not daring to utter a sound. Sometimes she would nod and say: "Bravo!" and then everyone would applaud enthusiastically and cheer lustily. But if Madame were displeased, the assistants would leap into action like a pack of jackals, tearing the poor frightened student to shreds. This was definitely not a playground for sissies, more like an ancient Roman arena. I was, luckily, one of the survivors.

As a result of this first encounter with Madame Lefébure, I returned to Paris a year and a half later to become her private pupil. She had resigned from her position at the Conservatoire de Paris just before I arrived, and it was generally thought that she had taken this step to dissimulate the fact that she was fast approaching seventy – the mandatory retirement age in France.

Biddy and George took a small apartment in Saint-Cloud, after two earlier brief occupancies in other locations where the neighbours complained so bitterly about my practising that we had to move. Even in Saint-Cloud I could only practise a couple of hours a day on a muted piano in our flat, and spent most of the time working either in an unheated garden-house owned by a local school, in which there was an upright piano, or in the basement of the Steinway dealer in Paris. The garden house was pleasant in the spring and summer but was cold and damp in winter; I had to work in my overcoat and was forever catching colds. Biddy was not very well at the time, and although she still attended most of my lessons, she had finally started leaving me alone while I practised, the cold in the garden house helping my emancipation enormously. However, I almost welcomed her presence at the lessons because of Freddy. Freddy, Madame Lefébure's husband, was very tall and as messy looking as she was neat, with long straggly hair and a face like that of a predatory bird. He was a source of general amusement amongst the students, except when he would find one of us girls alone, and then he was not so entertaining but downright lecherous. Biddy came in handy for this reason, although she herself was not exempt from his attentions, which seemed only fair as Madame had a huge crush on my father and would flirt with him outrageously whenever she had the opportunity. Freddy saw himself as a brilliant conductor, although none of us ever found evidence of his ever having conducted anything at all. However, when a pupil in the class was playing a concerto and someone had to play the orchestral reduction part on the second piano, he would position himself by the wretched accompanist and conduct very much in their face singing loudly. This could be rather disconcerting, as he spat a lot when he spoke or sang and would invariably be smoking as well, never flicking off the ashes but allowing then to fall gently all over one's hands or onto the keyboard. Amazingly, Mme. Lefébure, who rather endearingly lived in an enchanted world where only music existed and only her view of music-making prevailed, seemed oblivious to Freddy's shenanigans and quite tolerant of his deplorable behaviour. She was sometimes even influenced by his opinions, which always seemed strange to her followers as she was so much better a musician and brain than her husband. She once confided in Biddy that she was "*au fond, une petite bourgeoise*[1]" who liked to save her money but was invariably hard up because Freddy spent so much of her money on his *petites amies*. Rumour had it that Freddy was a frequent guest in certain Parisian establishments of ill repute. Freddy was also as short-sighted as she was, but would happily drive her all over Paris, paying no attention to traffic lights or parking restrictions or indeed anything to do with basic regulations. Once, when they came to our flat in Saint-Cloud for dinner, I happened to be watching out for their arrival from my bedroom window. There were three wide stone steps which led down from the parking lot to the entrance. Freddy, blind as a bat, never saw

---

1 Basically I am just a little 'bourgeois' lady.

the steps and blithely drove his old Humber car straight down them, deposited Madame at the front door, turned around, drove right back up the steps again and parked the car.

Mme. Lefébure's studio was a few blocks from her apartment. To reach it one walked down a sinister back alley to a derelict building (where a truly frightening woman would answer the doorbell and let us in, babbling nonsense and shaking her head a lot), up a staircase which looked ready to collapse at any moment, and then through an antechamber into a large, surprisingly pleasant room where Madame had her two pianos and held court. It was heated by a small coal stove, and in the winter was very dark but somehow quite cozy.

Every lesson was exciting and dramatic, and she would keep me sometimes for three or four hours at a stretch. I felt as though I were a character in a play or a Proustian novel – I was the nervous but devoted student anxious to glean every grain of knowledge I could from her superior mind, and she played the part of the revered, flamboyant teacher to perfection. The lessons were a mine of precious information, but they were also high entertainment.

Part of the great attraction was the anticipation of her occasional, totally outrageous personal comments. It was when I was playing for her the "Sonatine" of Ravel that she told me she had worked on this very piece with Ravel himself. She had also, apparently, given him pointers on how to improve on it, which she assured me he gratefully accepted and used. *"Mais naturellement, je n'étais qu'une toute jeune fille!"*[2] she added hastily.

And then the name of Dinu Lipatti came up one day and I mentioned how much I enjoyed listening to the recording of his last recital. *"Mais ma chérie,"* she exclaimed, *"les disques de Dinu Lipatti, eh bien, c'est moi!"*[3] and proceeded to explain that he had been very sweet and charming but had basically not a

2 But of course, I was just a very very young girl!

3 But my dear, Dinu Lipatti's recordings, they are all Me!

clue how to play the piano and that she had taught him every single note. Of course, she fully believed what she was saying, which made it all the more fun.

And there was the time when, exhausted after a day's work and suffering from the onset of arthritis in her arms and hands which clearly gave her considerable pain, she dramatically took Biddy's hand, telling her that she could confide in her because she was like her *petite soeur*;[4] then she added, her eyes misting over with emotion and speaking in a voice theatrically tinged with a sense of destiny and an unearthly, distant quality: "*Tu vois, ma chère Bridget, quand je passerai,*" here there was a tremulous sigh as she closed her eyes and bowed her head, "*il faudra que j'aie laissé quelque chose de moi au monde; c'est pourquoi je donne tellement à ces deux chouchoux.*"[5] The two *chouchoux* were myself and the English pianist, Martin Hughes, who was her special favourite. Martin had masses of temperament and fire and was ferociously committed to music and the piano. He was also highly amused by Madame Lefébure, although we were both devoted to her. She enjoyed pitting us against each other. When I first arrived, she would tell me in hushed tones, while he was playing, that he had only started playing the piano two years previously (totally untrue, of course) and that at the extraordinary pace he was developing, he was sure to surpass all his colleagues. To Martin, she said that I had learned Liszt's "Mazeppa" (a piece I had learned when I was fourteen and had worked on sporadically for the next three years) in exactly eight days. Both Martin and I eventually found out the truth, but not before we had suffered many days of despair at our own ineptitude and insignificance.

_____

4 Little sister.
5 You see, my dear Bridget, when I pass on, it is necessary that I leave something of myself to the world; which is why I give so much of myself to these two darlings.

There were wonderful times as well in that dimly lit room, when her four best students at that time would have lessons together. Imogen had already left her class to go to Vienna, but there would be Martin, myself, a beautiful Bulgarian girl named Roumiana Athanassova, who had a magnificent fluid technique and delicate musicality, and Ray Luck, a marvellous Guyanese pianist of Chinese descent, whom Madame Lefébure kept introducing to the world as Monsieur Ray Luck, "Bree-teesh subject," and poor Ray had to endlessly correct her, as Guyana had shed its colonial past several years earlier. The four of us would take turns playing, and the lessons would go on all night. Even though, in retrospect, there were musical ideas Madame Lefébure imparted to us that probably would no longer coincide with my own, she had such energy and such a passion for teaching and for music that her lessons were both irresistible and inspiring. She was immensely theatrical but could perform Bach beautifully, with an extraordinary facility for differentiating all the voices, and also play with tremendous intensity, which was most impressive in works such as the late Beethoven sonatas. But her approach to music was also rather intellectual, a bit cold, and her teaching dealt often in abstracts. Her sound had a crystal-like clarity, but there was no lushness to it, no particular warmth or lyricism. However, it was gripping, and she produced fantastically varied colours with wonderful textures and layers of sound. Her Debussy and Ravel were delightful, and she was compelling to listen to, whether one agreed with her interpretations or not.

I suppose what I learned most from that year with her in Paris was a level of dedication and respect for music heretofore unknown to me. What I also found in Paris during the 60s was that an artist who was mainly a teacher, such as Mme. Lefébure, was not only revered and respected by the music community, but also considered an essential and important figure in the make-up of French society. It seemed likely that Mme. Lefébure's name would be familiar not only to the upper classes or the educated bourgeoisie, but to the local shopkeepers as well. In North America at that time, a great piano teacher or concert pianist (other than Paderewski or Van Cliburn) was barely known outside of a very elite group and, even in that group, might be considered something out of the ordinary, a luxury or somehow a bonus to society. Mme. Lefébure showed me how, in Europe at that time, a musician of her stature was certainly treated like royalty, but no more so than a great scientist or doctor; the values of their respective professions were basically regarded as equal. I was also highly influenced by the level of intense commitment I felt around me in the class. And to this day when I perform certain pieces of French music, or even a piece like the Beethoven 4th piano concerto, I recognize certain important "Lefébure aspects" – voice differentiation, crystal clarity, intensity throughout and amazing fingerings – which were drilled into my subconscious so many years ago.

Madame Lefébure was also a delightful snob, and it pleased her no end that her pupil Gersende de Sabran, a lovely girl with a very respectable talent, was engaged to be married to one of the Comte de Paris' sons. For a people who had suffered through a gloriously bloody revolution, chopping off the heads of all the aristocrats they could lay their hands on, it was amazing to see such a passion for titles and such a preoccupation with the goings-on of the descendants of the various pretenders to the throne. Never was Madame happier than when young Jacques de France would show up at Gersende's lessons, and she would welcome him with the words: *"Ah! Mon petit prince charmant, quel bonheur que vous soyez là."*[6] Gersende, meanwhile, would roll her eyes heavenward.

Madame decided to put on a recital at the Salle Gaveau; we were all to play, and it would be entitled, with typical modesty, "An evening with the disciples of Yvonne Lefébure." Madame told us that she needed an opening piece because, even though

---

6 Oh! My little prince charming, what joy to have you here.

the concert was scheduled for 8:30 pm, and wouldn't actually begin until 8:55, she still feared that people would start turning up only around 9:00 (she was quite right; in fact, that was the accepted way in Parisian concerts at that time!). So Gersende and I were to open with the "Valses Romantiques" of Chabrier for two pianos, four hands, which was great fun. Then I was to play the Brahms-Handel Variations. Madame didn't like Brahms, (and she despised Wagner, although one wonders how much Wagner she had actually heard in her lifetime, and if this anti-Wagner stand was just a position certain French musicians of her era automatically took), but Martin and I were, at ages eighteen and seventeen, very attracted to the lush dark romanticism of Brahms; Martin was learning the d-minor concerto, which I used to accompany – marvellously passionate stuff. Anyhow, Mme. graciously allowed me to learn the Variations and at lessons, while she was demonstrating passages to me, she would become quite seduced by the music and moan in delight: "*O! La vieille Allemagne! Freddy, je joue Brahms tellement bien! Vraiment, je devrais le jouer bien plus souvent!*"[7]

Martin played the Schumann Fantasy superbly at the recital and then Roumiana played the Brahms-Paganini Variations followed by Beethoven's "Les Adieux" Sonata from Gersende and Liszt's Mephisto-Waltz from Ray.

There had been a terrible dilemma for the snob in Madame on the positioning in the program of the various sponsors of the concert. The biggest donors, by far, were Madame Bernheim and her son-in-law and daughter Marc and Miriam Stein. They were charming people who owned a gorgeous apartment on the Seine where they sometimes hosted "salons" or "house concerts" in which we would take part, and then they would regale us with *petits fours* from Fauchon. They were absurdly generous to Madame and to her pupils but they were Jewish,

---

7 Oh! The Old Germany! Freddy, I play Brahms so extremely well! Really I should play him much more often!

and in Madame's mind this caused a huge problem because the name Bernheim starts with a "B" and if she listed the names alphabetically, Bernheim would come first, ahead of Madame La Princesse "so and so" or Madame la Duchesse "such and such," whose names began with a letter lower down in the alphabet. I remember her airing this dilemma in a conversation with Biddy who, I am proud to say, was disgusted by the hypocrisy and said so in no uncertain terms to her face. There was a certain coolness between them after that but, like a spoilt child, Madame Lefébure felt that no one could possibly be irritated with her for too long, and she was right of course.

This childlike behaviour was never more evident than when it spilled over into her everyday domestic life.

It had been snowing in Paris all day, and by four o'clock the streets were dark and the sidewalks covered with brown slush. Christmas decorations glittered in the shop windows and there was a smell of burning coal and roasting chestnuts in the air. We had arrived early for my lesson, and the strange concierge had let us in but had forgotten to turn on the lights, so we stood waiting in the dark outside the studio in the chilly antechamber. Presently Mme. Lefébure appeared, complaining bitterly to Freddy all the way up the stairs, although she hadn't noticed that Freddy wasn't paying the slightest attention and was telling her that they should have dinner that night at *le petit chinois du coin.* Exasperated and wiping tears of frustration from her eyes with her little lace handkerchief, she said in a quavering voice: "*On aurait cru qu'ils m'auraient avertie; ma bonne était là, ma secrétaire était là, Freddy était là – personne ne m'a dit de me changer de souliers à cause de la neige!*"[8] Unthinkable! Such selfishness and lack of devotion on their part! It was hard not to start giggling, but she was evidently extremely upset.

---

8 You would have thought that they would have warned me; my housekeeper was there, my secretary was there, Freddy was there – no one told me to change my shoes because of the snow!

Then there was an occasion on which we were all to take part in a competition where Madame was to be a member of the jury (for starters, a peculiar situation to say the least). Exhausted with judging twelve hours a day, she nevertheless ordered us all to come to the studio in the evening so that she could review all our pieces one last time before the finals. Martin, Ray, Roumiana and I arrived in the little antechamber only to hear a Clementi Sonatina being played childishly and extremely badly in the studio. We stood rather surprised and had begun to speculate what the hell was going on, when Freddy rushed in telling us to keep our voices down: *"C'est la petite-nièce du General de Gaulle."*[9] We all had to wait at least another half hour, Madame's priorities striking us as being somewhat askew that day.

During my year with Mme. Lefébure there were other events occurring in Paris – trifles such as the May revolution and the fall of de Gaulle – but we were completely oblivious. Looking back, I feel nostalgic for that wonderful sensation of other-worldliness we had created and the total absorption we had in our music. Occasionally I did feel the single-mindedness a bit stifling, so followed, in my all too little spare time, some fascinating courses at the Institut Catholique on the plays of Racine and Victor Hugo. I needed some kind of balance, and this was a way of keeping my mind from atrophying. I also managed to do quite a lot of sightseeing both in Paris and in the outskirts – various fascinating *châteaux*, the cathedrals of Saint-Denis and Chartres, and Ravel's country home out in Montfort l'Amaury, which gave me a touching insight into Ravel, the human being. And, of course, I appreciated the restaurants and the food tremendously, growing to love Paris even more than before, if possible.

But Biddy had plans for me and they did not include another year with Mme. Lefébure. Instead, I was to return to and find a teacher in the United States where, in the 1970s, there was a

9 It is the grand-niece of General de Gaulle.

veritable plethora of pedagogical talent. Madame was not at all pleased by this defection and "betrayal" and kept repeating to me that Art languished in the United States and that one only went there to make money.

One of her best and most outrageous statements came after someone had played Debussy in a master class. First, she demonstrated how it *really* should sound and then, after all of her stooges had "oohed" and "aahed" and had exclaimed that no one could play French music as she did, she nodded pensively, acquiescing and in a voice full of the exhausted resignation of bearing such a heavy burden she said: "*Mais oui! Après tout, Gieseking – il jouait la musique française d'une certaine façon, enfin, pas mal; mais, avouons-le, ce n'était pas … enfin, vraiment, il ne jouait pas tellement bien. Mes enfants, au fond, il n'y a que moi!*"[10]

---

10 But yes – after all, Gieseking – he played French music in a certain way, actually not badly – but you have to admit – it wasn't – well, really he didn't play all that well. Children, basically, there is only me!

CHAPTER 4

A Maiden's Wish ("Zycenie")
by Frédéric Chopin

I left Paris with tremendous reluctance and regret. A year was far too short a time. The elegant streets and boulevards, the patisseries and charcuteries, the language so beautifully spoken, the little corner bistros, the old creaking metro carriages, the Parisians themselves, so opinionated and never at a loss for words, the smells of Gitanes, unleaded fuel, strong coffee and fresh croissants, walks in the Parc de St. Cloud, the disreputable, overweight dogs owned and spoilt by every concierge, the Jeux de Paume, bathed in Water Lilies, the Place Vendome, where Chopin breathed his last, the Seine and all its miraculous bridges, and my new friends and colleagues, Martin, Roumiana, and Ray, had all become very dear to me, and I felt bloody mutinous at being wrenched away from this city of loveliness to start again somewhere else.

In August of 1969 I flew down to New York City with Biddy to audition for Sasha Gorodnitzki, playing for him Beethoven's Sonata opus 109, the Chopin "Funeral March" sonata, the Brahms-Handel Variations, Ravel's Sonatine and the Bach Prelude and Fugue in E flat minor from Book I.

Without any obvious display of enthusiasm, in fact rather sourly, which was somewhat unnerving, he accepted me into his class. But my mother was unhappy about the idea of my living in New York so, after the relative freedom of Paris, I found myself once again back at home, in isolation, under her watchful – almost tyrannical – eye, flying down to New York every two weeks for a two-hour lesson alone with Mr. G. I didn't feel unhappy, but a certain tension was developing between my mother and me; she was reluctant to relinquish her

71

control over my life and I was longing for more independence. Certainly my natural shyness intensified during this period, and so I became totally withdrawn and alienated from the society of my generation. When not chained to the keyboard, I had for entertainment my father, with whom I would discuss current events and politics, my dogs, who acted as walking companions, and my books. I was too caught up in my work to contemplate how peculiar my life was compared to that of my old school contemporaries and, besides, I had a new goal: to participate in the famous International Chopin Competition, to be held in Warsaw in the fall of 1970. This was actually a dream of my father's which I had wholeheartedly embraced, and Mr. G., despite knowing full well that I was totally unprepared to take on the responsibilities of winning such a prize, reluctantly agreed to my pleas. A top prize at the Chopin competition in 1970 would have catapulted a young artist into a major concert career, and at nineteen I had neither the repertoire nor the performing experience to take on such a challenge. In the end, Mr. G. probably thought it would be a good learning experience for me, so we painstakingly prepared every piece for the competition until he was more or less satisfied with the result.

Warsaw in 1970 was very different from the vibrant modern city it has now become. It was grim, dark, shadowy and depressed, with cold coal smoke hanging in the autumn air, bright colours nowhere to be seen, shops and restaurants devoid of any personality or variety of wares, and the destruction from the Second World War's guns and bombs still very much in evidence. Perhaps as a result of these hardships, the city seethed with rebellion – like a pressure cooker about to explode. There was a terrible feeling circulating in the air that something powerful and violent was about to happen. The Poles, with Soviet troops breathing down their necks, were dangerously free in their ideas and their ideals; the churches, constantly harassed and persecuted by the government, were so full on Sundays that most of the congregations spilled out into the courtyards. The underground theatres, publishers and newspapers flourished, political satire was undercover but omnipresent, and the piano competition brought the entire country together for three weeks of passionate nationalistic fervour, fuelled by the Poles' love of Chopin, the genius whose music represents the soul of their country.

The concert hall was oversold for every single round; students, children, elderly people – everyone came from all over the country or listened at home on the radio. Everyone had an opinion, everyone had a favourite among the contestants. The atmosphere was electrifying.

I had flown over to Poland with my parents; this was an opportunity not only for them to hear me play but also to visit with my aunts, uncles, and cousins whom Biddy and I had never met. Naturally, the pressure on me to succeed was extreme and I wanted to, at least, make the final round of twelve. This was not an unrealistic wish.

Already weeks before, my appetite had all but vanished as I was caught in the grip of cold panic, terror of failure and the resulting nausea. Luckily for me, however, all the competitors were billeted together in the awful Dom Chlopa hotel (which no longer exists) and I was separated most of the time from my family. And when, one of the first evenings, there was a knock on my bedroom door and a sweet roly-poly boy stood there saying, "Hello, my name is Emanuel Ax; my teacher Mr. Munz heard you at the Juilliard entrance exams and told me you were very good – want to come and have dinner with us?" life perked up, and I was altogether much happier.

Such encounters with other young musicians made the occasional visit to an international competition, even an unsuccessful one, truly worthwhile. I was able to meet and, more importantly, hear pianists of my own age from all over the world: the strong Soviet contingent, always two or three of them and always kept prisoner in their embassy until it was their turn to perform; the ultra-serious French pianists, always on the lookout for the best restaurants; the hard-working, opinionated Germans; the brash North Americans who never really fit any category; and the very few (at the time) mysterious Japanese. In those days, before globalization, CDs, and YouTube, the different styles of playing were clearly marked and quite fascinating. In that sense, a competition was a revelation for an isolated pianist like myself.

In Warsaw we became a little pack; there was Emanuel, of course, but also Garrick Ohlsson, Jeffrey Swann, Diane Walsh and the German pianist Christian Zacharias. Very soon we realized that with our few dollars, and the comparative worthlessness of the Polish zloty, we could live like kings, so most evenings would find us at the Europejski hotel drinking champagne and eating at one of the only decent restaurants in the city. It was a thrilling emancipation for me. We were all so young, excited, nervous, but we also felt quite liberated, sophisticated, and wild with our sudden new wealth. We would order the most elaborate meals and drink many giddy toasts to the Russian pianist Yevgeny Mogilewski, reputed to be one of the Soviet Union's best, whose name and photo were in the competition program but who had never turned up – much to our relief!

The first round lasted for over a week and my turn to perform came during the morning of the fourth day. Having been so petrified for so long, I had the marvelous experience of completely shedding all traces of nerves as I stepped out on stage. I played better than I ever had before – everything fell into place and, amazingly, I even enjoyed myself. My parents, who had sat through most of the first-round performances, were extremely pleased, the newspapers were very complimentary and there seemed to be no doubt I would pass to the second round. So, for the next few days I practised my second-round program with relative equanimity. But then the results were posted on a wall at the Filharmonie, with the names of the competitors who had made it through listed in alphabetical order. At first, I thought that there must be a mistake and I kept reading and re-reading the names Ikuko Endo and Nathalia Gawrilowa – E and G, but no F, no Fialkowska – and I was flabbergasted. I felt as though the oxygen had been sucked out of my body and that somehow, I had been the victim of treachery and betrayal. That day I was forced to grow up a little and a first thin layer of cynicism found its way insidiously into my personality. Of course, it was all made much worse by my parents' presence as well as the presence of all the Polish relatives. Biddy and George were bitterly disappointed. The journalists provided some consolation, as they actually wrote articles decrying my elimination, and two concerts were hastily organized for me and another talented contestant, Mona Golabek, who had also seemingly unfairly been eliminated. So, I did get to play my second-round program and my concerto for sold-out and very partisan crowds. During the concerto performance, surrealistically, a corgi ran barking across the stage …

I left Poland with my confidence a little shaken but still intact and with a whole circle of new friends. The Warsaw experience, however, was not quite over. The juror who represented France, Mme Eliane Richepin, had been so outraged at my elimination that she organized a recital for me six months later at the Salle Pleyel in Paris. After the recital she held a lovely reception in her home with delicacies provided by Fauchon, and proceeded to show me all the marks of the various jurors. The highest possible mark was 25 and the five jurors from non-Communist countries all gave me marks above 22, the Japanese judge being particularly generous and awarding me a perfect 25. From the dozen or so other jurors, all from Communist countries, my marks were considerably lower, mostly below 15, and a Russian judge had given me a one. Only a couple of the Polish judges gave me normal marks of around 17 or 18. It was educational to see this – not shocking, as one had suspected something of this sort, but just a confirmation that competitions with a majority of Eastern European jury members were to be avoided. In those days, Canadians were rarely asked to sit on juries, so there was never anyone, if only by their presence, to put a halt to this sort of dishonest manipulation and criminal hanky-panky. So, it was easier for a juror from the Soviet Union, for instance, to eliminate a candidate from Canada than a candidate from the U.S. because there would always be a corresponding juror from the U.S. to safeguard the American contestants.

In hindsight, it is hard to put blame on the wretched Eastern judges. To give high marks to all the candidates from Communist countries regardless of their level of talent was a prerequisite and was their only way to be allowed out of their stifling countries – Poland, for instance, was a relative paradise compared to Bulgaria, Rumania, the Soviet Union or even East Germany. But the price they paid for this little bit of freedom was inordinately high, as it involved the loss of their artistic integrity.

In all honesty, in my case it all worked out well in the end. Garrick Ohlsson won the first prize, and it was well deserved. Yes, I probably should have reached the second round and might even have made the finals. But to win a prize and to start a career at that stage of my life would not have been beneficial. I was totally unprepared mentally, far too young and had far too small a repertoire even to contemplate concert tours. And so, back I went to the practice room, but not home to my parents. My *deus ex machina* had appeared in the form of a Canada Council jury, to whom I had applied for a study grant. This jury stepped into my life and provided me with the escape hatch I so desperately needed. Basically, they refused to "subsidize the airlines," as they put it and, with sensitive perception, felt that I would be much better off leaving Canada and living in New York, where I could not only study but also take part in chamber music classes and absorb all the marvels of the New York cultural scene. Biddy tried to fight their decision, but they made the move to New York their condition for awarding me the grant and they stood firm.

CHAPTER 5

Invitation to the Dance ("Aufforderung zum Tanz")
by Carl Maria von Weber

And so it was that in the fall of 1970 I set off for New York full
of ambition and preconceived ideas, mostly false, about the
modern music world. I was, for that rebellious and turbulent
time in America, a true outsider who embodied equal parts of
extreme innocence when it came to everyday life and a certain
sophistication from having already lived in Europe and grown
up in the midst of remarkably brilliant adults.

For the first few months I found a practice room close to
Mr. Gorodnitzki's studio on the 5th floor of the Juilliard school
in the brand-new Lincoln Center complex, and would spend
my days there from eight in the morning until six at night,
when I would board the bus and return to the East Side and
the Barbizon Hotel for Women where my mother had placed
me, feeling that I would be safe there. The hotel, where Dana
had lived during her ill-fated New York sojourn a few years
previously, was ghastly: poky, cramped rooms and a staff who
would have blended in perfectly in a prison camp. In such a
stifling atmosphere I felt dreadfully lonely and wrote voluminous letters home.

It was only after a while that I began to take notice of the
fellow who practised in the studio at Juilliard next to me. We
had of course met a few months before, briefly, at the Chopin
competition in Warsaw during one or two of those extravagant
dinners, so I knew who he was, but I was far too shy to make
any overtures of friendship. Luckily, Jeffrey Swann had no such
qualms. He, too, felt very much an outsider, coming to Juilliard
from Texas with a gigantic personality that frightened away
many of our colleagues. Still only a teenager, he had a curios-

ity and a passion for knowledge that knew no bounds and he desperately wanted to share all he knew, or had just learned, or was just wondering about, with anyone who would lend him an ear. He was quite brilliant and found in me an eager listener. I, in turn, had various attributes that could be of interest to him; I spoke perfect French, so he could practise his with me, I knew parts of Europe well, and I had a great love of literature. Our friendship was mutually beneficial and became very strong.

Juilliard in the early seventies was living its golden years. The professors (instrumental, vocal and theatrical) were revered and unique and at that time were considered worthy of admiration equal to that due their performing counterparts. The piano faculty alone attracted talent from all over the world, and the corridors were littered with the greats and near-greats all rubbing shoulders. Jeff was my constant companion, but Emanuel Ax, who already played like an angel, would be around for his lessons and classes and, whenever he managed to scrape together a few extra dollars from his various jobs accompanying for Mr. Galamian's or Mr. Fuchs' violin classes, would invite me to a nearby Howard Johnson's restaurant on Broadway to split our favourite: a Banana Royale. He was adorable back then. He still is, his amazing success not having changed him one whit. Garrick Ohlsson, another awe-inspiring young pianist, was also a great chum, but he appeared in the hallowed halls less frequently as his career was already on the ascendant, having won his great prize in Warsaw.

There were many others, of course, including the cellist Yo-Yo Ma, who was a young good-natured boy of fourteen at the time, astounding everyone with his phenomenal natural talent. The violin department was legendary, and it seemed as though all the great young violinists of the world were studying at Julliard when I was there; Nigel Kennedy, for instance, the future bad boy of the violin, who in those days, looked and spoke like a dear little choirboy. Of course, we had the colourful acting department with such future luminaries as Robin Williams, who held court in the cafeteria, Patti LuPone, and

Christopher Reeve, who attended all of Mr. G.'s master classes because he loved the piano. And in our German class, taught by a rather ancient and pedantic lady from Berlin who loved Goethe and whose wig was forever askew, a former chemistry major and future megastar named Barbara Hendricks used to liven up the tedious hour by singing Schubert Lieder to us quite gloriously. And the list goes on and on.

In those days, student tickets were cheap, and we went to every opera and concert possible: the incomparable Rubinstein, Serkin, Horowitz, Arrau, and Gilels were all still at the height of their powers and the young Ashkenazy, Argerich, Lupu, Perahia, and Pollini were just beginning to make their mark; we were thrilled by their wizardry. I recall a memorable week when Karl Richter and the Munich Bach Orchestra came to New York and performed the two passions of Bach, the B-minor Mass, the Magnificat and the Mozart Requiem over four consecutive evenings. Other high points for me were lieder recitals by Christa Ludwig, Janet Baker, Dietrich Fischer-Dieskau, Hermann Prey and Elisabeth Söderström; and of course we flocked to Carnegie Hall to hear Jacqueline du Pré, as well as Nathan Milstein, Henryk Szeryng, the Stern-Rose-Istomin Trio, the newly formed Guarneri Quartet, or to the Met, to be knocked out of our seats by Birgit Nilsson as Elektra or Brünhilde, the glorious Tatiana Troyanos as Kundry, Cherubino or Octavian, Nicolai Gedda as Don Ottavio, Jon Vickers' Otello and Sherill Milnes' Iago. Heady times for young musicians in New York, and we took full advantage. And it wasn't all just music; Jeff and I along with three other friends would meet once a week and read aloud from the Classics. We had marvellous evenings of Virginia Woolf, Thomas Mann, and Dostoyevsky, and our greatest achievement was the complete reading of James Joyce's Ulysses – even more exciting for me as, being the only woman in the group, I got to read all the juicy Molly Bloom parts! When the sessions were over, we would discuss and cook and eat and discuss some more and feel supremely alive. The hippie trends and drug culture of the seventies barely touched us, as we had created our own parallel world which, with all the confidence and conceit of youth, we deemed to be far more exciting and fulfilling.

After an initial period of tension when Mr. Gorodnitzki would constantly compare me unfavourably to every one of his many talented, female Asian students and had decided to make it his mission in life to rid me of what he would refer to as "all those terrible French habits," we adjusted to each other and got along famously. Honestly, I never really knew what those "terrible French habits" were. Certainly, the main thrust of the Gorodnitzki philosophy was to produce the beautiful but ubiquitous Russian sound at the piano with every note properly in place. He had heard Alfred Cortot – the inspiration and guiding light of all my teachers up until then – once, and had disliked the experience intensely. Cortot's visionary, wildly risky and overwhelmingly personal playing, which usually included fistfuls of wrong notes, would have been an anathema to the puritanical Gorodnitzki, and so my musical background worried him. It had been frustrating and difficult for me at first; I believed strongly in many valuable aspects of the French school, and I fought silently but determinedly for my previous interpretations. Eventually a compromise was achieved, and my playing was raised to a new level. A complete contrast to Mme. Lefébure's teaching, Mr Gorodnitazki's strongest emphasis was on the beautiful sound and long lyrical phrases of the Russian School, concepts he had inherited from his teachers Sergei Rachmaninov and Josef Lhévinne. He also took care that each student should pare every piece down to its most basic, purest form, only then superimposing their own (or if the student wasn't careful – his own) ideas and personality. Like Mme. Lefébure, he believed in hard work, and would often say that the sign of a great pianist was that he (or she) knew exactly what he was doing with every single note – not a single nuance or detail was to be neglected. Mr. Gorodnitzki was the ultimate perfectionist. I remained his pupil for five years and then became his assistant for another five, during which time

I first met my dear colleague Angela Cheng, younger than myself, who came into the class in the early eighties, becoming a great favourite of Mr. Gorodnitzki's and impressing everyone with her golden sound and remarkable musicianship.

Interestingly enough, I never gave a recital at Juilliard, although all of my colleagues did so regularly. Somehow, I was too frightened to play, even though I was, at that time, entering and sometimes doing quite well in international competitions. Finally, though, during my last year as a student, Mr. Gorodnitzki convinced me to learn the Rachmaninov 3rd piano concerto and to enter the school competition. Rachmaninov was a composer for whom I never felt much affinity, but out of loyalty to Mr. Gorodnitzki, who revered Rachmaninov and had known him well, I learned the piece and ultimately won the competition, suffering agonies of nervous sickness before the various stages. Mr. Gorodnitzki (who had been almost as nervous as I was) was overjoyed with our joint triumph and my student career ended with a flourish.

But perhaps the greatest emotional high points for me at Juilliard were my introduction to the music of Richard Wagner and the subsequent performances of his operas that I attended.

In the spring of 1971 the Chicago Symphony, under the direction of Georg Solti, was scheduled to give a concert performance in Carnegie Hall of Wagner's first opera of the Ring Cycle, *Das Rheingold*. Jeffrey Swann took it upon himself to educate me and prepare me. Already back then in 1971, he could play from the Ring absolutely breathtakingly for hours on end without the benefit of any score. His knowledge and understanding of this music were phenomenal.

"Don't you understand, this is going far beyond the concept of Leitmotiv!" he would exclaim, his teenage voice cracking with excitement while he enthusiastically and energetically attacked the keyboard. We were in his apartment at the Ansonia Hotel evening after evening, submerged in an orgy of Wagnerian magic, gold, heroes, gods, dwarfs, Rhine maidens and a great deal of chromaticism. "Listen," he would say excitedly, starting to play from the 3rd act of *Walküre*, "See how they are all interconnected? Loge's music is practically identical to the Tarnhelm, to Brünnhilde's awakening, to the Magic Portion in *Götterdämmerung* and is also closely related to the Magic Sleep as well as the Wanderer's music. All of these have to do with metamorphosis, disguise, transformation, illusion ..." I would listen transfixed, as he then skipped over to *Götterdämmerung* (the fourth and last opera of the cycle) and continued his stunning performance. During the day, the two-room apartment was occupied by a vocal coach; Jeff had the use of the piano and the rooms at night. The Ansonia at that time had fallen into disrepair and was incredibly shabby, only faint vestiges remaining of its glory days, when the likes of Caruso and Melba graced its halls. Even its wedding-cake exterior was crumbling and barely recognisable under the years of accumulated New York City grime. But it is only in retrospect, in my mind's eye, that I notice its awfulness. At the time I couldn't have cared less, because I was enthralled, indeed overwhelmed, and to this day, when I walk into an old derelict building and smell a certain decaying odour, far from being revolted, in true Proustian fashion I feel those old sensations of wildly youthful enthusiasm from the terrible pre-renovated Ansonia. A whole new dimension to the music world was opening up to me.

Maestro Solti and the Chicago Symphony had already stunned New York City with their Mahler performances the previous year and their concerts at Carnegie Hall were fast becoming cult events. The anticipation for the *Rheingold* concert was feverish. On the night, my heart was positively pounding with quasi-hysteria; it was my first time hearing the Chicago Symphony and Solti live, and my first Wagner performance. It was a powerful combination, and the fabulous performance did not disappoint. After it was all over, we felt as though we were walking on air, the resonance of those great E flat chords still ringing in our ears. We wanted to shout and scream and talk about it forever – the adrenaline rush was incredible.

I hurried out the next morning and bought the huge box set of Solti's recording of the Ring with the Vienna Philharmonic. Then I bought a subscription every subsequent year for the Chicago Symphony–Solti concerts at Carnegie Hall and would sit in the fourth row, (occasionally getting my ears blown off during a performance, such as the concert version of *Salome* starring Birgit Nilsson), and stare up at Solti and dream that maybe one day I might have the honour of working with him. Let's face it; quite apart from being a wildly exciting, intensely dramatic conductor who would particularly appeal to a young student, he was also extremely attractive with tons of animal magnetism. My inbred self-irony prevented me from becoming a total groupie – but it was a close call! My passion for Wagner and admiration for Solti continued unabated for years and it remains one of life's great pleasures to hear the magnificent Jeffrey Swann (who, in his spare time, now lectures on Wagner all over the world, including at the Wagnerian "holiest of holy" events in Bayreuth, Germany) play from the Wagner operas on the piano.

My first two years at Juilliard flashed by. They were filled with new experiences, emotional highs, very few lows, and considerable artistic growth. I soaked up as much as I could of the New York cultural scene, and I worked extremely hard. Six or seven hours a day, every day, I sat at the piano learning new repertoire ranging from Bach Preludes and Fugues to the Brahms B-flat concerto, to Ravel's "Gaspard de la nuit", to contemporary Canadian works, Schumann naturally, some of the Russians to please "Mr. G." – and always Chopin.

Mr. Gorodnitzki had now become more of a coach than a teacher, far less imposing, far more flexible, and a deep and satisfying friendship blossomed between us. Things were running along smoothly until in my twenty-second year I suddenly realised that I had plenty of ability and promise but absolutely no career or even a suggestion of a career. In fact the only professional concert I had ever played to that point was in Sherbrooke, Quebec (for four hundred dollars), where I had performed the Chopin E minor concerto with a young Polish conductor and a small, semi-professional chamber orchestra. Apart from having played the Brahms B-flat in the finals of a competition and the Rachmaninov 3rd at Juilliard, these three were the only concertos I had ever performed in their entirety with orchestra, and I had never played a professional recital. My success in competitions had been limited to an occasional trip to the finals and one big win, early on, in the National Canadian CBC festival. Sadly, my home province of Quebec and many of its musical organisations were not particularly interested in promoting someone with a non-French name, even though I was an authentic fourth-generation, bilingual Quebecker. Nationalistic feelings were running high during those years, which was unfortunate for me, and there were even a couple of occasions when the overt discrimination was downright humiliating. The rest of Canada barely knew me, or if they did, only as some lesser pianist from Quebec. The Canada Council had supported me very generously, but this support was also coming to an end, as my student days were numbered. There is no question that I am very attached to my country, Canada, and most particularly to my province of Quebec, but unlike any other country that I have dealt with, it had, during those early years, the hardest time appreciating and promoting its own young talent with any level of consistency. Americans supported Americans, the English supported the English, God knows the French, Germans, and Russians supported their own, but Canada was tentative.

It must be quickly noted here that attitudes in Canada have changed drastically and wonderfully since that time, and perhaps I may have had a little to do with the new-found pride we have in our young Canadian artists. But back in the 60s and 70s it was a rough ride for anyone trying to make their way in the concert world. We all had to leave Canada and somehow achieve fame in the international arena before the old, bureaucratic music organisations, based in Toronto and Montreal, would suffer even a minor acknowledgement of our talent. In those days, the West beyond Toronto was still young and would still look to the big Eastern cities for guidance, and, what with rampant nationalism in Quebec and a misogynist as the major power-broker in Toronto, my future as a pianist in Canada- indeed my career in general- did not seem too bright.

The 'coup de grâce' for me came when I entered the Leeds International Competition in 1972 and was eliminated before the finals. The fact that I was in excellent company (the marvellous future superstar Mitsuko Uchida was also ousted before the finals) did nothing to improve my mood. I was pole-axed by this turn of events and returned to Juilliard defeated, dejected, and lost. It was during this period that I was sharing an apartment with Yoko Nozaki, a very fine pianist and the future Mrs. Emanuel Ax. We had a lovely, quiet time together and her calm, solid friendship, her irreverent sense of humour, and her clear and perceptive outlook were all steadying factors in my life. But while I still worked as hard as ever and, in fact, my happiest moments were those spent at the keyboard, lost in my music, somehow the future, which had seemed so bright and obvious a year previously, was now murky and uncertain. Adding to this general malaise was the fact that my colleagues all seemed to be leaving me behind: Emanuel was busy concertizing all over the country, Jeff, even more spectacularly, had won the Gold Medal at the Queen Elizabeth Competition in Brussels, and Garrick, of course, was already set in a major international career. And I? Well, I had played one concert. This didn't bother Mr. Gorodnitzki in the slightest – as with Biddy, it was how you played that mattered to him, not how much. Perhaps – but a life of dependency on my parents was not something I envisioned with any enthusiasm.

And then, out of nowhere came the second *deus ex machina* of my life, in the form of Jacques Bertrand from Radio Canada. Of all the organisations in Canada dealing with music and musicians, it was the old CBC and its French counterpart, Radio Canada that were and have remained uniquely staunch supporters of my work. M. Bertrand telephoned out of the blue and asked if I would be interested in representing Canada at the first Arthur Rubinstein International Piano Competition, to be held in Jerusalem the following year. He said he had chosen me because he felt that I was the Canadian pianist most likely to succeed. He had heard me when I had won the CBC Natural Talent Festival in 1969 and had been an admirer of mine ever since. This was an extraordinary piece of good luck, since I had basically come to believe that no one in Canada had any interest in my talent. Radio Canada and the CBC would foot all the travel expenses in exchange for the rights to broadcast my performances there. I hemmed and hawed and refused to give an answer immediately. I had been badly bruised and hurt by the Leeds competition, but in the end, I succumbed to the greater temptations of perhaps having the opportunity to meet Arthur Rubinstein, the pianist I admired the most, and also having the chance to visit Jerusalem.

And so, with Mr. Gorodnitzki's help, I went to work. The program was quite substantial, challenging but also fascinating to prepare. In the first round I was to play the G minor Prelude and Fugue by Bach from Book II, "Feux Follets" of Liszt, the Chopin Etudes Opus 25 No. 6 ("in Thirds") and Opus 10 No.4, Debussy's Etude "Pour les arpèges composés", an Israeli contemporary work by Chaim Alexander, and two "set" pieces: the C minor Sonata by Mozart and Beethoven's "Waldstein" Sonata. The second round consisted of Beethoven's Sonata op. 111, the Liszt Sonata, Schönberg's Opus 11 and Beethoven's "Kreutzer" Sonata for violin and piano. For the finals I prepared Beethoven's 4th and Chopin's E minor piano concertos.

I tackled the project with relish but with no illusions as to the outcome. And then, suddenly and disastrously, on the Jewish high holy day of Yom Kippur, another Middle Eastern war broke out. Although the competition was scheduled for a few months later and although the Israeli victory was swift and solid, the competition had to be cancelled.

This was the final straw. I felt as though someone was trying to tell me that a career in music was simply unattainable. So, in April 1974, I had an interview with the Dean of the Faculté de Droit of the Université de Montréal. I was applying to the Law School way beyond the deadline for the upcoming scholastic year but, for some reason, my early good marks, my scholastic performance at Juilliard and the actual interview were enough for them to fast-track my application. Why law school? To this day I wonder why I picked this profession, which seems so unsuited to my personality. Rereading my diaries at the time, I can see how desperate, lonely and downright lost I had become. For nineteen of my twenty-three years I had devoted my life to the keyboard – happily, but nevertheless eschewing just about everything else in my pursuit of excellence and a successful musical career. And now I had to give it all up; I was a musician, for heaven's sake, who lived and breathed music and felt it through my fingertips. Opting for law school was a desperate act. I still cannot imagine why I didn't choose the more logical profession of medicine – and more specifically veterinary medicine, which has always interested me. But I suppose I was in a hurry and was looking for something that would need no preparatory years of study; after four years of law school, I could conceivably get a decent job that could support me and enable me to live independently. I just couldn't imagine living at home anymore. I believe I was vaguely thinking along the lines of doing graduate work in international law or entering the diplomatic corps, but my befuddled thoughts and emotions were in grave turmoil, and I realised soon thereafter that my heart was never in the law business.

Shortly after my interview with the Dean, word came that the Rubinstein competition was "on" again for September 1974. Within a matter of weeks, I received my acceptance to the law school, with classes starting also in September 1974. A few days later a phone call came from M. Bertrand of Radio Canada renewing his pledge of support. Everything was happening at once – I knew that if I went to Israel and made it to the finals, I would miss the registration and first three days of law school.

Ultimately the decision wasn't hard; Mr. Gorodnitzki and my parents had an easy time persuading me to go to Israel and give myself another chance, Mr. G. prophetically commenting that Rubinstein himself would be there, would like me, and would never stand for hanky-panky on the jury. My then sister-in-law promised to go to the university to register for me in my stead, and so, on August 28th, with a clear conscience, I found myself on an El Al jet, flying to Tel Aviv, with Emanuel sitting in the seat next to me.

Even though, for security reasons, our flight had been delayed over ten hours in New York, I was still feeling cheerful (albeit exhausted) as we landed in Ben Gurion airport. I had really nothing to lose and I was about to visit a new and fascinating country. The spirit in Israel at that time was one of great confidence and pride in their achievements. The cities were prosperous, the farms magnificent, the Arts were flourishing, and the mood was upbeat. The competition itself was also extremely well run, and even in the early stages we were treated with great solicitude. I played well in the first round and made it through to the second. By then we competitors had sorted ourselves into little groups. Mine consisted of Emanuel, naturally, but also our old friend Eugen Indjic, an American pianist whom we had also met at the Warsaw competition four years previously, and his lovely French wife, Odile. Arnaldo Cohen, from Brazil, would flit from group to group, keeping us all entertained with his clowning and marvellous nightclub act at the piano. He also, incidentally, played absolutely beautifully in the competition. Oscar Tarrago and Seta Tanyel were also very friendly to us, although they belonged to the tight little group of Dieter Weber students from Vienna. Then there were the Enrique Barenboim students, and I also found myself befriending the two French-speaking candidates, both fine pianists who have since made well deserved, outstanding careers: Pierre Reach, from France, and Evelyne Brancart, from Belgium, who was the youngest competitor and certainly one of the most talented.

Until the middle of the second round the atmosphere was pleasant and almost as though we were all on holiday together. I remember that the piano technician was particularly fond of me and allowed me extra time on the good pianos for practising. We had a bit of a problem adjusting to the practice times every day: 6 am to 2 pm and then 7 pm to 10 pm, plus the fact that on the Sabbath we couldn't work at all (probably a blessing in disguise). At first there had been side-trips to Bethlehem and to the Mount of Olives and fascinating walks in East Jerusalem, but by the middle of the second round, things had become deadly serious, and the piano ruled. After all, what happened to us in Israel would, quite literally, determine the course of the rest of our lives.

Arthur Rubinstein and his wife arrived for the second round, and he was to hold the non-voting position of Chairman of the Jury for the final two rounds. For all of us, his presence added a huge dimension of excitement and glamour. It was as though we were in the presence of the Piano God. Arthur Rubinstein radiated music, goodwill, good living, and generosity. We had already loved him through his performances. Now we had the privilege to meet and love the man.

It was evident early on that the first prize was a toss-up between Emanuel and Eugen. Both were playing extremely well, and both carried an aura of invincibility about them. I was just happy to have made it through the first round. Part of the second round was chamber music, and I remember hearing Emanuel play a truly stunning performance of the Brahms D minor violin and piano Sonata with Uri Pianka, concertmaster of the Israel Philharmonic. I also was present later when Eugen played a glorious Chopin 4th Ballade, a performance I can still hear in my head with great joy.

The tension was mounting. Next it was my turn. I have in front of me a letter I had written home to Biddy and George after that second-round performance. This was the first time they had not travelled to hear me play in a competition, and perhaps because of this, coupled with the fact that I truly had no expectations of victory, my attitude was far more relaxed than usual, and suddenly I wasn't sick anymore before the performances. It certainly helped not having my parents or teacher in the hall. My letter is full of excitement, astonishment, humility, and genuine happiness.

"I am terribly pleased, really. It went very well – much better than the first round. I really felt I was getting through and besides – Rubinstein was in the hall! I thought it would make me terrified but I knew he'd understand and I was really happy to be able to focus my attention on playing for one person – and such a person. The tape will probably sound messy in some places but I guess in the hall it sounded pretty good … so now I am hopeful, which is maybe bad."

That night there was a party with the jury members. The letter continues: "Later – I have absolutely never lived such a wonderful moment in my life. I don't care if I don't win a prize, but today Arthur Rubinstein told me that my performance of the Liszt Sonata had moved him to tears. And this for me is the greatest thing in the world."

Rubinstein had sought me out at the party and, warmly kissing me on both cheeks, had said that I was the only one who had touched him that day (Emanuel and Eugen were to play their second-round recitals the following morning) and he had been impressed by my chamber music as well. He'd felt I communicated real emotion to the public, and he invited me to visit him when he came to New York the following January for his annual North American tour. He then rather significantly asked me if I'd ever heard of the great "to-do" at the Chopin competition many years before, when a certain candidate named Michel Blok who, as a jury member, he had favoured, had been eliminated unfairly. I remembered the event well; it had been quite a scandal as Rubinstein had resigned from the jury and had not returned to Poland for several years, outraged by the shenanigans and deal-making he had witnessed. He said I was not to worry, and he promised that he would look after me. Little did I realise then in what an extraordinary fashion he would keep his promise.

That evening I was definitely the flavour "du jour" and I wrote
home that I was relieved my two friends (who were to play their
second round only the next day), had decided not to attend the
party, as it definitely would have made them nervous. Irony of
ironies, Dame Fanny Waterman, who had founded and who ran
the Leeds Competition, was there as an observer and sought
me out to invite me to participate in her competition the following year: "We need a strong woman candidate – Leeds has
never had a female first prize winner." William Mann, senior
music critic of the London *Times*, who was present to cover the
competition, told me that he would write in one of his articles
that my Liszt Sonata was THE Liszt Sonata. True to his word,
he also became my champion for years afterwards, continual-
ly giving me excellent reviews for my performances in London
and for my recordings.

Jacques Février, who I later saw often in Paris, Alexander
Tansman, Mindru Katz, Pnina Saltzman (whom my mother
remembered as a child prodigy in Paris at the École Normale),
Eugene Istomin and Guido Agosti (who later became a close

friend when I would perform in Rome) were all jury members and all came around to congratulate me. It was a staggering turn of events. Deep down I was expecting it all to be a flash in the pan – a fluke, a mistake, something lovely but brief – that soon I'd be "found out." Hence my last sentence to my parents, borrowing liberally from Thomas Edison's famous quotation; "We know that, in my particular case it is really one per cent talent and ninety-nine per cent perspiration but no matter. Can you believe this?"

Prize or no prize, that night I abandoned all thoughts of law school. I had desperately needed an indication that I had something to offer as a musician. An over-generous God had kindly sent me Arthur Rubinstein, and this was more than enough encouragement and incentive for me to take up the struggle again.

A side note: that afternoon as I performed my Liszt Sonata in the Jerusalem Theatre, a young immigrant from Lithuania was sitting in the audience. He was an exceptional physiotherapist who later moved to New York. His name was Shmuel Tatz and, 28 years later, our paths were to cross again under the most dramatic circumstances.

Frankly, after this glorious day in Jerusalem, the rest of the competition became rather unpleasant. The boys both played wonderfully the following morning, and we were supposed to find out who the four finalists were that evening. The evening passed, then the night, and all of the next morning. Finally at 3.30 in the afternoon of the next day, we were all bussed to the King David Hotel, where the announcement was made. Emanuel, Eugen and I stood literally clinging to each other, knowing that logically we should make the finals but terrified that we wouldn't; the agonising wait was taking its toll on our nerves, and we were crumbling under the stress. I remember noting that Rubinstein's face was quite pink and that he looked defiant and determined as he took his position at the centre of the jury. Much later he told me that, in fact, I had not had the requisite number of points to make the finals, simply because one member of the jury had given me a zero. Sadly, members of the jury who had pupils competing, even if they weren't allowed to vote for their own pupils, could still manipulate their marks to assist the advancement of their pupils, and this is what happened.

Of course, I was a perfect victim – unknown, from a country unrepresented on the jury, not expected to win first prize, and female. This one jury member had not counted on the determination of Rubinstein and, apparently, the outrage of many of the other jurors. Rubinstein threatened to resign and withdraw his name from the competition if I were to be eliminated. Two of the jurors, quite understandably, found this to be irregular and equally offensive and so the battle lines were drawn. For hours they fought, but in the end the majority was on my side, the rules were bent and I – together with Emanuel and Eugen – made it into the finals, with Rubinstein, as a compromise, giving his word that he wouldn't interfere in the final voting. But we, the three friends, of course knew none of this at the time and were busy being interviewed (the BBC was filming a documentary about the whole competition and there was a large presence of the international press), fêted and congratulated.

The boys had to play the next day. I was lucky; Seta Tanyel, a charming girl and a strong competitor with great appeal, and I were to play on the second night. The atmosphere had distinctly changed, and the boys were eyeing me warily. Eugen said that I was becoming far too dangerous, but he still managed to take the time to show me friendship and support the next day when I needed it during those nerve-racking moments right before my performance. Emanuel had become very quiet. At this point, we didn't speak much. Unlike the boys, I was happy just to be in the finals, to be the object of interest and of pleasant, respectful attention and, I admit, I enjoyed suddenly becoming a competitor who was considered a threat. Uri Pianka and his wife took me out to dinner the night the boys played, and I felt carefree and relaxed.

The outcome of the competition was fair and inevitable. Eugen, as unfortunately sometimes happens to sensitive artists, was nervous in the finals, but Emanuel played beautifully and was rock-solid. With my limited experience performing with orchestra, my concertos were clear and musical but, I fear, somewhat pale in character. I had yet to discover how one projects over an orchestra or how one uses the orchestra to enhance one's own performance. The conductor, Gary Bertini, was very helpful and did his best to give us the maximum support, despite the terribly brief rehearsal times. I tied for third with Seta Tanyel. Perhaps I was a little disappointed, having secretly begun to wish for a second prize, but, as he presented me with my silver medal, Rubinstein signalled to the audience, waving his index finger and mouthing the words: "My favourite!" This moment (precious for me) appears on the BBC documentary film. There was also an unexpected bonus for me that night: before the results were announced, the President of RCA Red Seal recordings offered me a contract.

So, it all worked out to perfection, at least for Emanuel – the winner – and for myself. Emanuel's career was launched, and he has never looked back, becoming one of the most beloved performers of our time. And I was given a second chance with a little extra time (something I desperately needed) to gain in experience and routine on stage. I was about to begin an extraordinary relationship with a living legend and was beginning to realise I would have to struggle and fight for my career and that, somehow, this struggle was necessary for my development as an artist and as a person. My friendship with Emanuel remained intact and only grew stronger over the years. Eugen lives in France; he is a truly exceptional pianist who came so close to victory, and naturally this "defeat" in Israel must have been very hard for him. He plays in Europe but, sadly, he rarely plays in North America. Seta Tanyel, now based in London, still plays marvellously, and has a considerable recording career.

Before the final gala concert in Israel (which I was to start with the Beethoven 4th piano concerto), Rubinstein hurried backstage to find me. In his white dinner jacket and with his wonderful mass of white hair, I couldn't help but think of the white rabbit from Alice in Wonderland as he dashed into my dressing room where I was warming up on the piano. He asked me, extremely politely, if I wouldn't mind him giving me a little advice. Sitting down at the piano, he played for me the openings of the first and third movements. He had taken a little speed off my tempi and he projected a world of beauty and emotion in those first chords – never hurrying – Beethoven's voice straight from the heart. Also, in the last movement, he slowed me down and gave me my first indications on how to project a marvellous sense of pulse and rhythm without sounding metronomic. The performance went well, and Rubinstein felt gratified that I had absorbed so readily at least a little of what he had advised. We parted warmly, and I truly never expected to see him again except backstage after his – presumably last – concert in New York a few months later. He was, after all, 87 years old when I first met him, a world figure with little time, I thought, to spend on a youngster like myself.

It was on a huge "high" that I returned to Montreal to start picking up the pieces of my life and plan my future. M. Bertrand of Radio Canada and many friends and members of my family gave me a rousing welcome at the airport. The only fly in the ointment was the reaction of the Montreal Press. Radio Canada had arranged a reception and press conference the next day at their downtown building and I had the opportunity to chat in an informal atmosphere with the gentlemen of the Press. In 1974 a Canadian placing high in a foreign, international competition was almost unheard of. Nevertheless, Claude Gingras in *La Presse* used the opportunity to start his thirty-year-campaign of gratuitous horror against me (some of my favourite Gingras headlines: "Fialkowska – Pourquois?"[11] Or "Fialkowska – Tristesse!"[12]). There were insinuations that I had probably only won my prize because, like Rubinstein, I was a Polish Jew, and

11 Fialkowska – Why?
12 Fialkowska – Sadness!

the main thrust of Jacob Siskind's article in the *Montreal Gazette* was that he couldn't understand why I, specifically, had been chosen by Radio Canada to represent Canada in Israel.

Why, I asked myself, and I still do, why be so unkind? More to the point, why be so rotten? A young girl from their home-town wins a prize and gains the admiration of a legendary pianist. Why not just report the facts and congratulate me? I was hurt by the petty cruelty of their remarks, but was also riding high on a curve of euphoria and managed to ignore them, more or less, perhaps helped by the fact that they tended to be nasty to everyone.

I moved back to New York, staying with Yoko until I found a place of my own, and two months after the competition I flew to Durham, North Carolina for Emanuel and Yoko's wedding. A few months later, Jeff Swann won the First Prize at the Dino Ciani competition at La Scala in Milan. The little circle of friends all seemed suddenly to be moving along the right track.

Rubinstein came to New York, found out where I was living and, on January 2nd, 1975, invited me over to the Drake Hotel on Park Avenue, where he had a large suite. This became the first of many such meetings at the Drake over the next few years. Arthur wanted to help me, but, being a wise old man, he also wanted to make sure that I could cope, indeed, that I really desired to pursue such a demanding career. I reassured him that it was something I wanted, but in a burst of honesty confessed to my uncontrollable sickness before concerts. His light-hearted, unconcerned, off-hand comment was that this display of nerves was really silly and that I should get over it. This little comment had a marvellous liberating effect, and funnily enough, except for one or two extremely stressful occasions, I've never felt sick before a concert since; nervous, for sure, but never nauseated. Rubinstein had a great deal of power over me, and I was very open to his thoughts and advice.

He then had me play for him – day after day. At first, I played him the pieces I had been working on: lots of Chopin, the Scherzo No.4, some Etudes, the B flat minor Sonata, also

Ravel's "Ondine" and a Mozart Sonata. He would then request the "other" Chopin Sonata and "Carnaval" of Schumann for the next day. I was young and inexperienced, and these were pieces I hadn't practised in a while. All night I sat at a friend's house (I didn't have a piano in my apartment until the following year, when Dana and I moved to a bigger place) working relentlessly to be ready to play for him the next day. Over the following weeks he requested more Chopin, more Beethoven, more Schumann. And each time after I had played for him, we'd have tea and he would tell me stories for hours about Cocteau and Pagnol, Diaghilev and Marie Curie, Proust and Sacha Guitry, Joseph Joachim and Sarah Bernhardt, Ravel and Rachmaninov, Stravinsky and Ysaÿe, Heifetz and Casals, Mascagni and Villa Lobos, Ronald Coleman and Gary Cooper, the Duke of Windsor and the King of Spain and so many more – all people he had actually known, and for each of them he had either a fascinating and/or witty anecdote. His energy was inhuman, and he would be still fresh as a daisy when I would be wilting from fatigue after a long afternoon and evening. He told me that he had another protégé at that time as well: the young French pianist François-René Duchable, who I was dying to meet, as Arthur said he was a marvellous pianist and a very nice fellow.

Then there was Arthur's performance with Daniel Barenboim and the New York Philharmonic – his final New York appearance. He played the Beethoven 4th piano concerto and the Brahms D minor. The Brahms, in particular, was unbelievably powerful, not even taking into account that Arthur was 88 years old. This concerto is, after all, the work of a very young man, and perhaps Brahms' only piano work in which he let his youthful passions rip. So, it was quite astounding to hear it played by Rubinstein, with all of his experience and knowledge, but still infused with an almost adolescent lust for life. After the concert there was a party back in his suite at the Drake with Emanuel and Yoko, Daniel Barenboim, and a young Australian couple who were friends of Barenboim, named Wolfensohn. James Wolfensohn later became President of Carnegie Hall and then President of the World Bank; he is also an amateur cellist and utterly charming. The last of the party was a young German who had just started up a company that was the first to make classical music videos and the first of them was to be a Rubinstein-London Philharmonic Orchestra-Bernard Haitink collaboration of Beethoven and Brahms concerti. This young man was practically turning cartwheels to please Arthur, who treated him kindly but rather the way one would a slightly hyperactive puppy.

Arthur told stories until four in the morning; there was a lot of laughter and we demolished eight bottles of Dom Pérignon and many pounds of beluga caviar and Scottish smoked salmon. At one point Arthur told us how a rumour had been circulating that he had converted to Christianity. It was all nonsense, he said, and was only because he had told Golda Meir that he admired Jesus Christ more than any man who had ever lived. But, he added, it was the Apostles, simple and uneducated men, who had turned Him into a God, and Paul had capitalised on it! Arthur said that he didn't believe in God, but he certainly had beliefs in the supernatural, inner strength and power.

At four in the morning, exhausted, we all got up to leave (despite his begging us to stay, his energy apparently boundless) as we knew that he had a nine o'clock flight to catch to Los Angeles, where his wife was recovering from an operation.

Concurrent with all this high living was my everyday life as a student at the Juilliard School. Unfortunately, Mr. Gorodnitzki was not amused by this turn of events, feeling that all this rushing around with Rubinstein was side-tracking me from practice and the search for perfection. To be honest, he was jealous of Rubinstein. Arthur, on the other hand, wondered aloud why I didn't stop having lessons with Mr. G., as he felt I was too old, at age 23, to still have a teacher who could potentially stifle my creativity. I was conflicted, feeling tremendous loyalty and love for my old teacher, but also fearful of displeasing my new mentor, so I finally arranged a meeting between them.

The Rubinsteins invited Mr. Gorodnitzki for a lunch "à qua-tre" in their suite at the hotel. Mr. G. was a powerful figure at Juilliard, but was also extremely shy; I think he was viewing the whole experience as an ordeal, and in the taxi driving over from Juilliard he was silent and tense. But Arthur greeted him warmly, with oodles of charm, and praised him to the skies for his work with me, and soon his reserve had melted and his own considerable charm surfaced. Since both men, perforce, knew many of the same great figures of the past, the conver-sation was lively and witty, and they got along so well that af-ter lunch Arthur pulled out a tape of himself that someone at RCA records had put together from old 45-discs. It consist-ed of short "salon" pieces such as Anton Rubinstein's "Valse-Caprice," Rachmaninov's Prelude in C-sharp minor and other flashy tidbits. Arthur had absolutely no recall of having record-ed these works and was delighted to find that his technique sounded so brilliant! We all listened and commented and had a marvellous time.

Suddenly I realised that Mr. G. had a lesson to teach at two o'clock, and it was already way past that time. I was taken aback when he telephoned the school to say that he wouldn't be back until four. This was unheard of, and a testament to Arthur's power to enchant. The Gorodnitzkis and the Rubinsteins did get together a few times after this memorable lunch, and I was able to relax a little ... but not completely. When, a year later, I was invited to play the Liszt E flat piano concerto for the first time with the Philharmonia Orchestra for my London orches-tral debut, Mr. Gorodnitzki was thrilled with the news and con-gratulated me heartily, but added in a worried voice: "But you must work this piece with me and not with HIM, dear – I un-derstand it better than he does!" And of course, ever trying to please, I worked it with both and then made up my own mind.

After a few months, having played for Arthur pretty well my entire repertoire, I decided to learn Stravinsky's *Petrushka* to surprise him when he was next in New York. He had told me that the piano version was a collaborative effort one summer between Stravinsky and himself while they were both holiday-ing in Biarritz. And, although it was before my time, I knew from many people that *Petrushka* had been one of Arthur's great "warhorses" with which he used to end many of his re-citals. Innocently, I thought it would please him if I learned the piece and then sought his advice on how to pull it off with maximum effect.

Petrushka is no easy piece and I had about two months, while he was in Europe, to get it to sound decent. I wasn't afraid he would feel it wasn't a piece for a young woman, as I had already played for him such (so-called) "man" pieces as the Rachmaninov 3rd and Brahms B flat concertos which he had accepted with-out demur.

He seemed quite thrilled when I told him (upon his return to New York) what I had done and briskly hauled his armchair over by the piano to watch me play. Then he lit his cigar and waited expectantly. The sure sign that my playing was cap-turing his attention was if the cigar was forgotten and extin-guished itself. But that day, as I huffed and puffed my way through the piece, not only did the cigar stay lit but I sensed that he was restless, tapping the ashes, lighting a new one, in-deed acting as though he were a bit bored. I ended with what I thought was a flourish and awaited the verdict. There was a si-lence, an indulgent smile, a melancholy shake of the head and then finally: "No – this is not a piece for you." He saw my face fall and, as we were still in the early stages of our friendship and he was still sugar-coating his criticisms, he explained that I was far too refined for a piece that needed to be played in a coarse, peasant-like manner!

The next day, full of injured pride, I sought out Mr. Gorodnitzki at Juilliard and asked him what he thought of my *Petrushka*, assuming he would take my side. "Janina, dear, I have thought all along that it isn't your kind of piece, but since you seemed so determined to learn it, I never said anything!" Bloody hell …

I learned a valuable lesson from this episode. Unless a piece of music is in one's blood and unless the idiosyncrasies – whether rhythmical, emotional, or analytical – of a composer are genuinely part of one's psyche, it really doesn't matter how much one likes a piece, or how well one can master the basic aspects of it, or even if one has tons of imaginative interpretative ideas about it; one will truly never be able to perform it successfully. And *Petrushka* – well, perhaps I will perform it in another life (I dearly hope so), but my personality really was not suited to it. My most natural affinity is to Chopin; I enjoy searching for lyricism, elegance, and the dignity of a polonaise or a mazurka; beautiful sounds, never harsh, an aristocratic atmosphere, gentle melancholy ... A far cry from the raw passion of the Russian!

CHAPTER 6

All Was Created by Him ("Par Lui tout a été fait")
by Oliver Messiaen

By mid-1975, Arthur had decided my talent was worthy of recognition and that he would actively help in the development of my career. He soon realised, however, that just asking managers to add me to their rosters, where I could sit unemployed for years, would be a futile endeavour, so he decided on a more aggressive strategy. Still feeling, at age 89, healthy and incredibly energetic, he decided to tour for one more year but made it a condition in each contract that he would only perform if I got the identical concert the following year. This turned into a tour of around fifty concerts in some of the great cities of Europe and North America. As well as these concerts obtained by this elegantly camouflaged arm-twisting, I had, on my own, garnered a few concerts in Canada and been invited to play with Zubin Mehta in Israel with the Israel Philharmonic. Suddenly, from nothing, I had a major career. Arthur also placed me with his agents: Hurok in New York, Van Wyck in London, Rainer in Paris, Johanna Beek in Amsterdam, and Annabelle Whitestone at the Quesada offices in Madrid.

My first concerts were in Tel Aviv, playing the Chopin E minor with Zubin Mehta. Fate had decreed I should start off my career with the very concerto and the very conductor involved in my life-changing experience in Montreal so many years before, only this time I was the soloist, not Arthur Rubinstein. The Chopin E-minor piano concerto is a work I had played as a teenager and the piece I have performed the most in my career, and have also recorded twice. An early work, it already contains all the hallmarks of Chopin's youthful genius and tantalizing hints of his future development. Highly virtuosic but also containing touching melodies that overflow with emotion and a rousing dance-like finale, this concerto can be a perfect vehicle for pianists of all ages and temperaments, the only prerequisite being a fluid technique, a good sense of phrasing, a bit of Slavic melancholy and a feel for Polish folk rhythms. I love playing this piece, and throughout my life it has been a constant but ever-changing companion.

In Israel there were six concerts. I had performed the concerto only twice before, so it was still a relatively new experience for me. Tentative at first, I grew into the piece through the six concerts. Zubin Mehta was a very sympathetic accompanist with an unusually profound (for a conductor) understanding of Chopin, so I learned a lot that week. I also enjoyed myself thoroughly as I stayed in the Israel Philharmonic Orchestra's comfortable guest house where, amongst other guests, the rowdy cast for a future *Carmen* production had gathered. I was far too excited to sleep and never really got used to the time change. The company was jolly, and we seemed to spend every delicious meal laughing ourselves silly. Uri Pianka and his wife took me out to exotic restaurants in Tel Aviv; partisan audiences, remembering me from the recent competition, gave me standing ovations every night and, all in all, it was a lovely first set of concerts in my professional life.

But things then went from the sublime to the ridiculous as the next concert, immediately afterwards in the Hollywood Bowl, was a bit of a farce. Zubin Mehta had hired me to play in Israel out of friendship for Arthur, but the Hollywood Bowl concert was the price the Los Angeles Philharmonic had to pay for having Rubinstein perform with them later on that year. Ernest Fleischmann, the powerful manager of the Los Angeles Philharmonic, decided, as the saying goes, to kill two birds with one stone, by taking the gamble of pairing me with a conductor of completely untested talent who was currently in the news.

She was an elderly lady who had been the music teacher of the famous pop singer Judy Collins. Ms. Collins, clearly a devoted and loyal soul, and also successful and wealthy, had made a documentary film about her teacher illustrating how this elderly lady had been discriminated against all her life by the male-dominated conducting world. The film had won many awards and made the old lady an instant Hollywood celebrity. The obvious next step was for her to be engaged by a major orchestra to conduct, since she would obviously be a box-office draw. So clever Mr. Fleischmann put us together to play Mozart's concerto K.467 on a fine summer evening in California. Rubinstein had forced him to hire me, and Hollywood had dictated that he hired this person. I think he just wanted to be rid of us both.

Sadly, the old lady was a very bad conductor, one of the worst in fact. Given that there were plenty of excellent struggling women conductors around at the time, it was a shame she was the one to get the concerts. But she had appeared in a film, and this was Hollywood. So "*le tout Hollywood*" attended the performance. It was quite awful. I wanted to feel sorry for her, but it was hard as she was rather arrogant and not very pleasant to me. The orchestra behaved rather well, I thought, as she took one funereal tempo after another and never knew when to bring them in at the end of my cadenzas. They helped her out by ignoring her and somehow Mozart limped to the finish line. We ended shakily but together.

Backstage afterwards the mood was mostly of embarrassment and trying to put the best face on things. I remember, of all people, the great music intellectual and Austria's premier pianist Alfred Brendel appearing from nowhere, finding me during the intermission (my Mozart was before the intermission, thank God, so I didn't have to stay for the second half), taking both my hands into his, gazing earnestly in my eyes and saying: "I was so sorry for you; this was a martyrdom and you played beautifully under the circumstances." And then he asked who had written the cadenza in the first movement and commented that he had liked it very much. I'm sure he had guessed I had written it and was only saying nice things because he was a good colleague trying to cheer me up! It was sweet of him, but I was not really depressed by the experience. I just accepted it and assumed this sort of thing happened often and I should learn to get used to it.

What I didn't realise was that this was quite a rare occurrence, and when I ran into Ernest Fleischmann many years later at a dinner given for me at the Garrick Club in London after a performance of the Szymanowski *Symphonie Concertante* with Libor Pešek and the Philharmonia Orchestra, he was still embarrassed about this concert. When Arthur heard about what had happened, he was absolutely livid, particularly as, by some coincidence, he had actually known this conductor in the past. He was furious with Fleischmann and, never one to hold back, articulated his rage in great detail, which also probably did me no good "*à la longue*." I have a letter from Arthur from that time where he describes my poor conductor as a "*vieille chipie*" (an old hag!). Because of this episode, he tried to persuade me to move to Paris, where he said he could keep a better eye on me and on my career. Some instinct prompted me to resist this idea, and, on many levels, I now feel that it was a good thing I remained somewhat apart, maintaining a modicum of my recent hard-fought independence.

But for all the tension of my new career and the pressures of living up to his vision of what I could or should become, we quite quickly grew beyond the mentor-protégé relationship and became, for lack of a better word, "chums." He was a legendary figure, a great intellect, one of the greatest musicians of the century, but thanks to his youthful, questioning mind and innate generosity of spirit, he treated me as an equal with only the difference in our ages marking any kind of inequality. Mind you, he was a very formal and old-fashioned Polish gentleman, who deplored bad manners and cheeky or careless familiarity. But, in spite of the formality, it was noticeable that he was at ease with any generation; small children adored him because he instinctively adapted to their level and outlook, sharing with them a childlike curiosity and wonder at the vagaries of our world. A case in point was a visit from the then eleven-year-old French prodigy Marc Laforet, who played for him rather beautifully the Schumann "Arabesque." Arthur was impressed, but ended up having much more fun just chatting with the little boy for an hour with lots of happy dialogue and eating of chocolate. The child was completely relaxed and left starry-eyed with unforgettable memories.

And so it was that I started to become increasingly a part of Arthur's life, and when he was in New York it was completely normal for me to spend most afternoons with him. Although his energy seemed unrelenting and boundless, he must have felt, at age 88, at least some of the incipient frailties of old age – the worst being that his eyesight was failing. And here was I, a young girl of Polish extraction, completely devoted to him and to everything he stood for in the music world: honesty, simplicity, refinement, generosity, humility, and a total sense of responsibility to the composers. He was also the most communicative performer on stage at that time, and from him I knew I could learn priceless things. He also knew it was in his power to help me in my development as a musician and in the development of my career. I had turned up at the perfect moment in his life as he made the difficult transition from world-beloved performer to wise, elderly retired gentleman.

I would come to the hotel around four and stand outside his suite listening to him practise. This was immensely amusing as he had such (outwardly) appalling practice habits. If he had a concert coming up, he would play through the program at full tempo in a rather desultory fashion; I sensed his mind was not on his work but on the amusing afternoon he was planning with me. Occasionally he would make a mistake and restart that particular passage, always still at full tempo. If he missed it again, he would try one more time and then, with an almost audible shrug of his shoulders he would leave it and carry on. He knew there was a 99-percent chance he would nail the passage in the concert that night because he did most of his practising in his head. Often, he would be playing pieces I had played for him the previous day or that I had promised to play for him that afternoon. He had an extremely open mind and would even tell me he'd learned things from my performances that he would incorporate into his own interpretations. Of course, if that was at all the case, the ideas most likely came originally from Mr. Gorodnitzki or Mme. Lefébure. But this was the remarkable nature of our relationship at that time.

He was not a good teacher per se. Mr. Gorodnitzki, for instance, could literally take an untalented, technically deficient piano player and after a few months turn him into a respectable musician. Arthur could take the same student and, with his overwhelming personality, inspire him for a few minutes to play way beyond his capabilities but, in the end, not change a thing, because he had no technical knowledge on how to develop another person's technique or taste or style over a period of time. For both of us though, the timing was perfect. Arthur was at the end of his career and searching for someone to inherit some of his accumulated wisdom, and I was wide open to receive his advice and suggestions. My technique was good, I had a solid base of good style, good taste, and good habits, but I needed confidence to unlock whatever hidden talent, unique to myself, I may have possessed. And we did have a profound musical bond, although in temperament and background our natures were far apart – he was the 'bon vivant' extrovert, legendary womaniser who adored society, parties, people and shunned daily practice, and I was the introverted, reticent, fanatically hardworking recluse. But he would often look at me, nod wisely and using that wonderful Proustian phrase, comment: "*Nous avons les atômes crochus.*" ("Our atoms are hooked together"). He felt that destiny had brought us together, and I believe he was right.

Standing outside the hotel room door, I would marvel at my good fortune and at the kind angel who had seen fit to cross my path with this great – and greatly endearing – man. Finally, I would knock at the door and invariably hear a huge sigh of relief, an exclamation such as: "Finally!" or "*Enfin!*" and a light patter of feet as he trotted over to greet me with enthusiasm. The afternoons would be filled with music and stories and wonderful food, which Mrs. Rubinstein, who remains to this day one of the best cooks I have ever met, would sometimes provide at intervals. Once, when Mrs. Rubinstein – Aniela or "Nela", but I always called her Mrs. Rubinstein – was in hospital about to undergo an operation and he was seriously worried about her, he suddenly turned to me and said dramatically that he must go to the piano because "*Dans mon désespoir, je vais me plonger dans le travail!*" This "drowning in work" lasted about twenty minutes and then he was back again chatting with me; practising long hours was simply not his forte, since life held too many interesting distractions.

And somehow during that first year I knew him, he also found the time to reread the complete *À la recherche du temps perdu* by Marcel Proust and *Der Zauberberg* by Thomas Mann. His mental energy was indefatigable, his conversation always fascinating, and, because of his love of literature and language, his choice of words and his phraseology were impeccable in seven languages!

It was during one of those Rubinstein visits to New York that I met the legendary Soviet pianist Emil Gilels. He had come for tea and cakes at the Drake and was the most morose person I had ever met, though, if possible, his wife was even worse. But I understood their depression; this was before the fall of the Soviet Union and Gilels' "minder" was stationed down in the lobby waiting for him, monitoring his every move. Officially, he told Arthur sadly that day, he received only two hundred dollars for each of his North American concerts from the Soviet authorities, a tiny fraction of what he earned and what was sent directly back to Moscow. Just so that he could have a little extra money, the Hurok office would pay him some cash under the table. Arthur had known him since he was a boy and, since he couldn't bear people around him feeling unhappy, he set about cheering Mr. Gilels up, at least for the afternoon. He told his most outrageous stories (which I didn't completely understand, because they spoke mostly in Russian, but which I could follow somewhat because of the hilarious accompanying facial expressions) and then all of a sudden he asked Gilels if he knew the Mozart String Quintets. No, Gilels didn't. Arthur had just discovered and had become addicted to a recording of the G minor Quintet played by the Griller Quartet and William Primrose, and he was dying to share it with anyone and everyone who walked through the door; I had already happily sat through it twice. So, we all went into the bedroom where the cassette-player was set up, sat on the bed and listened. It was as if we had given Gilels the greatest gift in the world – which perhaps we had. His face was transformed, wreathed in smiles – Arthur and Mozart had managed to give him a bright and happy afternoon.

It was in November of 1975 that Arthur's eyes, which had been troubling him (especially in the glare of bright stage lights), started to fail dramatically. Arthur, Mrs. Rubinstein and I were in Los Angeles. I played the first recital of my new career at the Ambassador College in Pasadena and they both came. My program was the Beethoven "Pastorale," Sonata Opus 28, the Liszt-Sonata, "Gaspard de la nuit" of Ravel, and a Chopin group. My old friend was very taken with the Beethoven and was pleased with most of the program but felt I had played the 4th Scherzo far too fast, as well as the Chopin Waltz that I had used as an encore. They both admitted that they had felt extremely nervous for me – I had certainly been nervous before the recital, but the lovely Beethoven was an amazing mental tranquillizer, apparently for all of us!

The next day Arthur moved me to his hotel, the Beverly Wiltshire in Beverly Hills. It was there that I made the acquaintance of an old friend of theirs, the Academy-Award-winning composer Bronislaw Kaper, in his late seventies at the time. Bronek was a great supporter of the arts, a fencing enthusiast, an inveterate womaniser, a teller of the most outrageous jokes – all this and he had a heart of gold as well. It was arranged that I would practise in his home, because Mrs. Rubinstein did not want me practising in their suite. Bronek was very kind to me, and his company was a welcome relief after the supercharged atmosphere of the Rubinstein ménage. Mrs. Rubinstein was extremely impatient and tense even during the less stressful periods of their lives, and at this time, when Arthur's eyes were failing and he had concerts to play, receptions to attend and visits with his son and grandchildren to fit in, I was not happy being around her. In fact, she bewildered me because I wasn't, as yet, used to her giant mood swings. After my performance, when the three of us went out to Chasin's, a fashionable restaurant straight out of their past, she was utterly delightful and treated me just as an over-indulgent loving mother would. Other times it was as if she resented my presence bitterly, and she became very unkind indeed. At those times I would keep out of her way as much as possible, only appearing when summoned.

Finally, early one morning, Bronek took Arthur to a famous optometrist for tests on his eyes and it was there he found out that his sight would only get worse, as the little arteries were drying out: advanced macular degeneration. Within weeks, if not days, he faced total blindness but for a little peripheral vision. It was here that the extraordinary character of the man was fully revealed. Mrs. Rubinstein and I were waiting in the hotel suite for their return. When the knock came on the door, we heard lots of giggling and laughing outside. Mrs. Rubinstein opened the door to find Arthur sporting a new pair of very dark glasses and holding on to an imaginary dog leash tied around Bronek's neck, with Bronek on all fours doing his best imitation of a seeing-eye dog out of control. Arthur thought it was hilarious and was laughing until the tears rolled down his cheeks. His situation was desperate but, somehow, he had us all roaring with laughter. Shortly afterwards, we proceeded to the Dorothy Chandler Pavilion where he rehearsed the Chopin F minor concerto and the Beethoven "Emperor" concerto with Zubin Mehta followed by a large reception and luncheon where Arthur delivered a witty speech. We then hurried back to the hall where Igor Oistrakh was playing Shostakovich for a matinee concert with the Symphony. On the program was also Brahms' 2nd Symphony, a piece Arthur adored. Brahms always held a special place in his heart, perhaps because his mentor had been Joseph Joachim, Brahms' dear friend.

After another reception, then a dinner, we finally piled into the car, Mrs. Rubinstein at the wheel, me sitting next to her, and Arthur in the back. We started to drive back to Beverly Hills. Mrs. Rubinstein and I were exhausted and, understandably upset over the terrible prognosis concerning Arthur's eyes. Arthur, in the back, sat smiling and humming Brahms to himself. It must have been already past eleven and he had a big performance the next day but, unfazed by the day's events, he suddenly cheerfully said: "Why don't we go to a movie?" Such was the indomitable spirit of the man. And the next day he played one of the best concerts I had ever heard from him. He told me later that, at first, he had difficulties seeing the keys, which made him excessively nervous. Soon, though, he had become used to it, and besides, he added, smiling, he never looked at his hands that much when he played anyway. The emotion in the hall was colossal, and when he finished the "Emperor" the cheers from the audience nearly blew the roof off. His first encore was the A flat Polonaise of Chopin magnificently played, then Villa-Lobos' "Polichinelle" and finally the Chopin D-flat major Nocturne, which left the entire audience wiping tears from their eyes. Backstage he was mobbed by adoring, relentless fans, but he was always gracious and patient with even the most demanding amongst them. We literally had to fight our way to the waiting limousine, where I was amazed to see a whole gaggle of screaming teenage girls waiting to get his autograph or just to touch him. It was quite a scene.

The party that night was held at Zubin Mehta's home in Brentwood, and Zubin's wife Nancy had made a wonderful Russian feast with lovely black breads and chicken Kiev. The star-studded guest list included the legendary Russian cellist Gregor Piatigorsky, the dancers Valery and Galina Panov, Mrs. Nathan Milstein, widow of my favourite violinist, Bronek, of course, Ginger Rogers, Danny Kaye (who had been at my Hollywood Bowl debut and who spent the evening teasing me about it when he wasn't doing outrageous imitations of Piatigorsky's thick Russian accent and Zubin's father, the conductor Mehli Mehta's Indian-English accent) and so on. The storytelling went on late into the night and there was never a mention or hint of Arthur's impending loss of sight and the probable sudden end of his career.

Back in New York it did not take long for the phone to ring and for me to be told by my representative at the Hurok agency, Walter Prude, that since Arthur was now blind and would clearly be unable to complete his tour, which was to provide me with all of my engagements for the next year, I should consider entering the Leeds or some other prestigious piano competition. Arthur was quite put out when I relayed this to him and made me promise that I would never enter another competition. In turn he promised me that, blind or not, he would finish all his contracted engagements.

And so my career began in earnest: a recital at the Kennedy Center followed by my debut in Paris in January 1976. Attending the concert were Biddy and George, dear Mademoiselle Mangeot, the Rubinstein entourage – which included many members of the Rothschild family – and of course Mme. Lefébure, who turned up with Freddy at the reception given by the Canadian cultural attaché. They had missed the actual performance because Freddy had driven down a one-way street and had had difficulty backing out again. Mme. Lefébure was in fabulous new straw hat with a magnificent emerald green ribbon to match her green silk outfit and she instantly became the centre of attention, quite ignoring me and amusing Arthur mightily by flirting with him shamelessly all evening. Mrs. Rubinstein was not amused, but I was glad to see that Mme. Lefébure was still true to form, still a 'force of nature', and still putting on the best show in Paris.

The concert was well received, but probably the most significant aspect of the evening was that I made friends with the young conductor from Japan, Kazuhiro Koizumi, who had just won the Karajan competition and who was also making his own Parisian debut. Arthur came to the rehearsals and, without being too intrusive, gave us both very helpful suggestions. The next year Koizumi was named music director in Winnipeg, where I suddenly became a frequent visitor and built up the special relationship that I have to this day with this unusual Canadian city.

After Paris came my first concerts in England, beginning with Liverpool, where I worked with a rather unpleasant Dutch conductor. The experience was otherwise a good one, though (this was when I visited the School of Tropical Medicine and saw where my grandfather's African expeditions had been planned and launched). And, after one of the three concerts, I was introduced to the Dutch conductor's young manager, David Sigall. This would turn out to be a most fortuitous meeting with long ranging consequences.

Many of Arthur's concerts were in major cities, but others were in smaller towns such as Huddersfield and Farnborough. His fee was extremely low, even by the standards of the 1970s, as he firmly believed he should not be paid more than what could be raised at the box office. Right from the start I loved touring in England – perhaps because I am so fond of the English countryside and, in those days, British Rail was a divine way to travel. England was followed by a tour of Spain where I met a gorgeous Englishwoman, Annabelle Whitestone, who was the backbone of the Quesada agency, my management at that time. The Rubinsteins came down for the Marbella concert – it was just after Arthur's final concert, which had taken place at Wigmore Hall in London. He had developed stomach ulcers from the strain of performing with fast diminishing eyesight, and I think he was actually relieved to stop concertizing and get on with the next phase of his life. There was a big party after my recital with a guest list filled with Baron this and Count that – Europe's jet-set aristocracy who had all recently discovered the delights of Marbella. Mrs. Rubinstein was happy in this milieu and for once was pleasantly relaxed. The next day I flew off to Alicante and she called me in my hotel there to tell me how much she already missed me and that I was like a daughter to her. She was very dear that evening and I thought that perhaps we could always remain on such friendly, close terms with no more tensions. It was important for me that she knew the relationship I had with her husband was one of great friendship and nothing more, and I thought she had at last realised I was no threat to her marriage but just wanted peace between us and to be a support and help to her.

In the fall of 1976, I played my Philadelphia Orchestra debut with a young American conductor also making his debut, Leonard Slatkin, who has since gone on to become one of America's finest conductors. In the audience for one of the performances was the marvellous Japanese conductor Kazuyoshi Akiyama, who, the following year, invited me to play with his orchestra, the Vancouver Symphony, and go on a West Coast tour with them.

In Cleveland I played the Beethoven 4th piano concerto with Lorin Maazel conducting. I was warned that he could be rather formidable and grand, but he couldn't have been nicer. The concert went rather well, and I was completely in awe of his stick technique and control of the orchestra. Together they provided such a stellar and pristine accompaniment that they inspired me to play well beyond what I expected of myself, and the event caused enough of a stir for me to be immediately re-engaged. Lots of friendly support came from my colleagues Malcolm

Frager, who was in Cleveland to perform the Beethoven Triple concerto later that week, and Israela Margelit, who was married to Maazel at the time. I had met neither of them before but was touched by their solicitude and encouragement. What I learned from this, and I admit it surprised me greatly, was how very nice concert pianists are to one another. In fact, I cannot think of any other profession where the competition for so few jobs is so intense and yet the protagonists are so invariably kind, supportive and generally enthusiastic about each other. If there are exceptions, these people stand out like sore thumbs. Only one pianist among the fifty or so with international careers whom I know personally has been, shall we say, less than honourable towards his colleagues. And while I try to adopt a noblesse oblige and "do not sink to his level" attitude, it does amuse me mightily when I hear that my family and friends, upon seeing one of this scoundrel's CDs prominently displayed in a record store, will carefully remove it and find it a new home (usually among the Rap CDs, but the back of the Country Western section is also considered an excellent depository). My performance in Cleveland was broadcast over National Public Radio and a surprising number of people heard it and sent me compliments. A distant cousin of mine whose family had been our neighbour in Canada for three generations also heard the broadcast and telephoned Biddy to congratulate her. He also asked her where I was living and, hearing that I was in New York, suggested I visit him and his wife in their home in Connecticut. This cousin was the great actor Christopher Plummer, and, with his wife Elaine, he was soon to become a major player in my life.

And then there were recitals in Chicago, Houston, San Francisco, Montreal and Vancouver (ah yes, it took a Rubinstein to really get my career started in Canada!), orchestral dates in Detroit and in the famed Mormon Tabernacle in Salt Lake City; but it was in London, England, oddly enough, in that great barn and acoustical nightmare, the Albert Hall, that I had the first real epiphany of my adult life. It was the Chopin E-minor concerto, the conductor was Bernard Haitink, and the orchestra was the London Philharmonic. Haitink was already a major figure in the music world, and I was nervous about meeting him and working with him. All fears were dispelled, though, when a soft-spoken, unassuming, gentle man, a true gentleman, came to my dressing room prior to the first rehearsal and introduced himself as Bernard Haitink, saying how delighted he was to be working with me and actually sounding as though he meant it. The orchestra adored him, and there was a pervasive calm serenity throughout the entire experience. It was during the second concert that suddenly I felt completely transported into another world. I felt as if the orchestra and I were floating, suspended in a bubble high above the clouds, and all that mattered was the pure, pristine music. It was the first time I felt so close to the soul of Chopin himself. It was eerie and other-worldly and filled me with indescribable joy. Funnily enough, when I have subsequently had these rare experiences, I realise that it hasn't necessarily meant that the audience has joined me on my supernatural trip. Sometimes, yes, for sure, but if I don't make the extra effort to project what I am feeling to them, or if this effort is unsuccessful, the audience can be completely left behind. It is a tricky business, but, luckily for me, on that particular night it all came together and Haitink himself was impressed enough to voluntarily offer to help me look for a new English manager, as my current one was due to retire. It was also particularly gratifying to find myself invited to play with his orchestra, the venerable Concertgebouw in Amsterdam, two years later.

For my Paris debut, the Rubinsteins had invited me to stay in their Paris home, located in a secluded square of the Avenue Foch. Their house was surprisingly small (the bedrooms were tiny), but wonderfully comfortable and quiet. The front garden was minuscule and dominated by the outline of the great Steinway concert grand standing behind the glass French doors that led into the salon. On the piano were photos of his best friends: the violinist Pawel Kochanski and the composer Karol

Szymanowski, a photo of himself with Albert Schweitzer, another with Pablo Picasso, and a photo with a lovely dedication from Arturo Toscanini. In the bookcase nearby was a photo of the Spanish King Juan Carlos and his family, and next to it, displayed in a glass case, was the Arthur Rubinstein tulip dipped in gold, a gift from Queen Beatrix of the Netherlands. Arthur was very proud of his relationships with the various European royal families. He really was a bit of a snob, but recognized this "faiblesse" and often laughed about it. There was a gorgeous Chagall over the mantelpiece, and he also owned several works of Picasso, including a huge piece of painted pottery and the famous Picasso sketches of Arthur himself. For some reason, the stereo system, instead of being in the comfortable salon, was located in the draughty entrance hall, where we always had to wear scarves and drag in chairs on which to sit. Since Arthur had started to spend more and more time listening to recordings, it amazed me that a more suitable arrangement was never contemplated. Thanks to Mrs. Rubinstein, we ate magnificently well and often, with no stinting when it came to butter or cream. It was also a global cuisine, not just Polish or French, but it was rich and after a week I always managed to have quite acute pains in my overtaxed liver; however, the Rubinsteins clearly thrived on having three or four meals a day, unfettered by any kind of healthful restrictions!

Arthur always complained that I practised too hard, but I was able to persuade him to let me work undisturbed all morning. I was shy at first, feeling that everyone was listening (and they were), but soon I became used to it and was quite happy banging away on the great man's piano (a gift to him from the Israel Philharmonic). Often, that first year, he would have to go away, out of Paris, and play a concert himself, and I would be left alone in the house with the servants. This was heavenly for me, as I had just started to read Proust and Stendhal on Jeff's recommendation, and would revel in being in that beautiful little Parisian house submerging my brain in all those glorious words. Between chapters I would take lovely walks, appropri-

ately in the Bois de Boulogne, or just around the neighbourhood and also, having recently discovered the music of Gustav
Mahler, would listen to his symphonies by the hour.

We were also huge fans of the English television series
Upstairs Downstairs. Once, in New York, I had even been under strict instructions to get the television in the suite set up
on the correct channel for when Arthur returned from a matinee in Philadelphia. Atypically, he rushed through the reception after his concert, urged the chauffeur to drive as fast as
he dared back to New York, and dashed into the hotel sitting
room exactly on time for the start of the program. Still in his
concert attire and overcoat, he sat cross-legged on the floor
close to the screen so that he could see it with his peripheral vision, delighted anticipation written all over his face and
a bar of Lindt Bitter Chocolate ready for consumption in his
hand. Then some nice fan of his gave him the whole series on
video (since he had missed so many episodes) and I would have
fun watching them alone in Paris when the Rubinsteins were
on tour.

Princess Grace of Monaco, who lived in the house next door,
and who actually came to our door once to borrow a cup of caviar (Well, why not? Some neighbours borrow sugar – others
caviar), was also a big *Upstairs, Downstairs* fan and spent several afternoons in the Rubinsteins' sitting room watching the
tapes with her younger daughter Stephanie, then only a little
thumb-sucking child. Since I was the only one in the house
who knew how to operate the machine, I was duly assigned by
Mrs. Rubinstein the task of taking care of her Serene Highness.
She was charmingly down-to-earth, so the job wasn't onerous,
although I was a little irritated at having to waste two entire
afternoons watching re-runs.

Other visitors to the house included many of their friends
from Poland, amongst them the author Jaroslaw Iwaszkiewicz.
There was also the French author of *Belle du Jour*, Joseph Kessel,
and the legendary Soviet pianist Sviatoslav Richter. His playing was a top favourite of both of Arthur and mine, although

sometimes we were puzzled by his interpretations (but certainly never bored). The brilliant and gorgeous French writer Jean d'Ormesson, who was at that time editor of the Parisian newspaper *Le Figaro*, turned up occasionally and of course there were always musicians dropping by – both aspiring young ones and established famous ones.

For me, the greatest fun was when Arthur's "other" protégé came to spend the afternoon. François-René Duchable was at that time an extremely serious young man of about twenty-two, who almost physically trembled from the power of his great passion for music. He had marvellous, flawless technique and could sight-read anything, much to Arthur's delight, especially when one day Arthur felt like hearing again the Chabrier "Pièces Pittoresques" and François dashed them off like nothing at first sight. François also adored Chopin, but his special, extremely French approach to this music was challenging for Arthur, as it was quite different from his own interpretations. But François is a strong and convincing personality at the keyboard and elicited much admiration from Arthur and from myself. I also happened to like him personally very much; he was kind and loyal, intensely religious, and quite devoted to his widowed, colourful Italian mother. He was also petrified of air travel and would only play concerts in cities he could reach by car, train, or ship. His dedication to his music and profession was absolute and almost frighteningly intense. I was never happier than when the three of us would spend long afternoons together, listening to and making music, then discussing all the problems of the world (Sadly, I lost touch with Francois after Arthur died since I am only sporadically in Paris, and he never comes to North America. However, not long ago I read an interview in a French newspaper where he decried the current state of the music world and stated that as a protest he would burn his evening clothes at his next concert and have his grand piano dropped from a helicopter into lake Annecy …).

Another frequent visitor was Isaac Stern who, at that time, was arguably the greatest powerbroker on the North American music scene (if not the entire world). It was understood that if a violinist did not have Stern's approval, he or she was not likely to make a career. Along with his satellites (young conductors and musicians who owed him a great deal), he wielded almost as much power in the piano world. Thus, it amused me no end to witness Arthur's reaction when he espied Stern's rotund little frame purposefully entering the square and heading for our front gate. "Oh my God, it's Isaac! Quick, let's hide under the piano." Then he would look at me sheepishly and say plaintively: "It's just that he can be so boring, always after me to champion some cause or other." Jokingly and with mock heroism I would tell Arthur that I would stand by him and support him when Stern had worn him down. And then Arthur would spend the entire visit, which was usually around teatime, trying to make me giggle. I think he was basically quite fond of Stern, but it was such a relief to me to find at least one major musician so totally unimpressed and unconcerned by Mr. Stern's powerful reputation.

My own personal relationship with Isaac Stern, if you could call it that – it was better described as a prolonged acquaintanceship somewhat akin to a chronic case of hives – began at the Rubinstein home in Paris where he ignored me to the point of rudeness. In all fairness, I was probably rendered insignificant in his eyes by my shyness. Why am I trying to excuse him? Am I still fearful of his power from beyond the grave? But no, he was definitely rude to me. Anyhow, this "relationship" was shadowy and based on an unpleasant blend of fear, awe and mistrust on my side and barely disguised disdain on his. There is no denying he achieved great things during his lifetime. In his youth he was an extraordinary talent and performer, a fine musician. He almost single-handedly saved the venerable Carnegie Hall from demolition, and he discovered, nurtured and promoted the careers of many worthy young musicians, half a dozen of whom developed into superstars and are arguably amongst the finest violinists of our time. I am the first to applaud and cheer when senior musicians take the trouble to help their younger colleagues. But recommending and promoting young talent is one thing – even forceful persuasion is permissible and may be necessary in our ever-shrinking, competitive classical world … after all, who am I to complain when my career was jump-started this very way? What made the Stern method unsavoury was that he took the process not one but two fairly reprehensible steps further. Not content with just persuading various tame presenters and conductors to hire his new discoveries and give them repeated chances to prove themselves, he began over the years to fall in love with power and accumulating more of it, until it consumed his whole life, much to the detriment of his performances, which suffered increasingly due to lack of attention and practise. This hunger for power turned a charismatic, great musician into an oftentimes petty, prejudicial, and bad colleague. Not content with just ignoring young musicians who were of no use to him, he would actively block the careers of aspiring artists whose advancement he feared might get in the way of his own protégées; even worse, he would sometimes make sure they would not be hired, by spreading false and negative information. And the worst of it was that his information was rarely based on first-hand experience of their musical talent – Mr. Stern would never voluntarily attend performances of those who didn't interest him.

His kingdom was New York City, and his playground was ICM Artists Ltd. (the agency that also happened to manage my North American career), where his relationship with the successive Presidents was strong, personal, and very forceful; after all, with his vast number of connections he wielded an amazing amount of clout, something the management was smart enough to recognize – they certainly knew on which side their bread was buttered!

So how did all of this affect my own fledgling career? Taking the long view, the adversity wasn't so bad; many of my colleagues were badly scarred by the Stern machine and, tragically, many even destroyed. Yes, I was a female from Canada of Polish-Catholic descent and, even less attractive to Mr. Stern, I was someone else's protégée and this someone was Arthur Rubinstein, which must have infuriated him. At that time, Mr. Stern was heavily promoting a young and highly gifted Israeli pianist. He had the youngster play for Arthur, who was generous and charmingly polite to the boy, but not overly enthusiastic; the boy had flawless, high speed virtuosity but a still very under-developed level of imagination and intensity, and this always annoyed Arthur. So, he was polite, encouraging, but clearly preferred my playing (or François's or Eugen's or Emanuel's) and was not about to recommend the boy everywhere, at least not until he could then gauge how or if the boy were maturing. Not used to having his opinions overruled, Stern became exasperated, even infuriated when Arthur praised me to him, which was entertaining and highly amusing to observe.

Another interesting side-effect was that many of the lower echelon at ICM – the bookers, the PR people, some of the secretaries and assistants – got a little tired of the Stern machine constantly forcing certain artists down their throats. This, for me, was somewhat of a boon for, in spite of the pressures put on them, they would rebelliously champion my cause. I was probably overlooked for many of the more "important" opportunities that would present themselves over those early years, but I survived in fine fashion with the help of John Anderson (now President of the Barrett agency), the late Jim Griggs, and others as well. Because of these friends, I rarely felt left out or ignored and eventually progressed to the point where my career started to run itself.

Still, Isaac Stern had great charm and he was a truly towering figure in the music world, so it did rankle that he steadfastly continued to ignore me. I always had the feeling, naïve perhaps, that if he could just hear me play once, perhaps he would change his tune. Well, lo and behold, I was suddenly granted my wish!

ICM called me up, asking if I could play a mini recital at a benefit dinner at the Waldorf Astoria Hotel for an archaeological project based in Jerusalem. Teddy Kollek, the charismatic mayor of Jerusalem at that time and a close friend of Arthur's (perhaps this was why I was invited) was the guest of honour, but Isaac Stern was to be there as well. I chose my short program with great care and was determined to impress or at least to make a valiant stand. It was a glittering, high profile crowd, and the pre-dinner conversations were lively and intense. After a while everyone settled down. Only an errant waiter still silently hovered about, and there was an occasional clink of wine glasses. I began with the lovely Poulenc Intermezzo in A Flat, followed by a Chopin group, and ended with a very flashy piece by Karl Tausig. From the moment the first note was struck, someone in the front row began to speak, carrying on a nonstop monologue not in a whisper but in rather stentorian tones. It was maddening and extremely distracting, and in the middle of the Poulenc I managed to look up to try and glare at the offender in an attempt to silence him, convinced that it was an ill-mannered, high-society airhead or a desensitized politician. Imagine my shock when I saw that it was none other than

Isaac Stern, totally turned around with his back to me talking to someone seated behind him. I nearly fell off my bench. As God is my witness, he never stopped talking until the last chords of the Tausig were played. Puzzled at first and hurt, I continued playing, refusing to allow this strange behaviour to alter my performance, and must have succeeded, for I was warmly applauded and later cheered up by some pleasant conversations with Mr. Kollek and also with Guy de Rothschild, with whom I had become acquainted through Arthur. Stern, who had been on his way out, noticed that I was on familiar terms with Monsieur de Rothschild, suddenly turned around, pushing his way over to where we were chatting, dismissing me with a curt "you played well very well under the circumstances." This was all he said before turning his back on me and cutting me out of the conversation. This behaviour finally forced me to accept the fact that he would never treat me with any kind of respect and that it was no use whatsoever attempting to create a rapprochement; I gave up and moved on.

It was during one of my early visits to Arthur's home in Paris that I made my first recording with RCA France, a Liszt recording featuring the B minor Sonata and some shorter works. I had seen the state-of-the-art RCA studios in New York by that time, so I was a little mystified to find myself, the morning of the first session, being driven far out into the countryside to a nondescript little church standing next to the courtyard of a big farm. Monsieur le Curé came out to greet us and then the session began. I was well prepared, and the piano was good, so there were no real problems, but occasionally I had to do a re-take because the microphones had picked up the sound of a rooster clearing his lungs and crowing lustily in the fresh morning air, or the patter of rain on the roof was too noisy. But the conundrum as to why we were there was solved when we stopped recording and went for lunch.

I was in France, so of course the most important reason for doing anything, anywhere, was the close proximity of a first-class restaurant. In this we were not disappointed. It was a little country *auberge* with the most marvellous *hors d'oeuvres* of fresh, crisp crudités, garlicky sausages, and sardines silvery in olive oil. Then a *roti de porc*, perfectly cooked with wonderful roasted potatoes, little onions and grilled fennel, and an *ile flottante* for dessert, light as a feather floating on a silky rich golden crème anglaise. When I came home and told Arthur about it, he immediately wanted to plan an excursion out there. Musicians the world over are quite obsessed by food; good music and delicious meals seem to complement each other, and besides, there isn't much else a lonely artist can do on tour other than play the concerts and eat.

It was obvious that, as his eyesight failed, listening to music became more and more important to Arthur. Current events also fascinated him, and I often had the pleasure of reading the newspapers to him in the morning; also, as I was the only one in that multi-lingual house who, other than Arthur, had a knowledge of German, it fell upon me to read to him his voluminous fan mail and correspondence from Germany. Answering the phone at the Rubinsteins' was also something of an adventure, as it could easily be Roman Polanski or Golda Meir or Douglas Fairbanks Jr. or Van Cliburn or any number of celebrated world figures at the other end of the line, with whom I would have the opportunity (albeit minimally) to chat.

In fact, life was always exciting with Arthur, and never more so than at breakfast, when he was full of energy and anticipation and would suggest lovely plans for the day. There were concerts and films at night, impromptu afternoon visits to Angélina's on the Rue de Rivoli for delicious teas or hot chocolate and their incomparable Tarte aux Myrtilles, lunches at Fouquet's or Prunier's, where we once met the legendary film star Jean Gabin, and one time, on the spur of the moment, he took Annabelle Whitestone and myself to Lasserre, which still had the Michelin three-star rating in those days and where most people had to reserve months in advance. We arrived "à l'improviste" at two in the afternoon and were shown magically to the best table, whereupon Arthur started to order without even consulting a menu. It was a glorious spring afternoon, and the streets of Paris were glistening from a gentle morning rain shower. Our lunch – a delectable duck concoction and an even more delectable chocolate creation for dessert – was heavenly, and when the coffee was served, the entire roof of the restaurant was rolled back and the sun poured in.

Arthur was definitely impressive in restaurants as he would, for instance, order a lobster and, if he liked it, simply order another one! Waiters and chefs adored him, and they were not the only ones; wherever I went on tour, I never heard anything but wonderful anecdotes about him and how he touched people's lives with his art, his generous nature and his consummate professionalism. When touring he never made a fuss or unreasonable demands, and he kept his good humour in spite of fatigue and sometimes less than ideal conditions. This forbearance and strict professionalism were unshakable axioms that he taught me, in addition to the two mottoes by which he lived: "*Nie dam się*" which, translated from Polish, means, "I will never give up" and "Never ask for anything, make people want to give to you."

In a way this could have been an ideal and magical time for me, and to a certain extent it was. But I could not handle with equanimity Mrs. Rubinstein's strange hot-and-cold attitude towards me. She would write me the most loving letters, inviting me to stay and telling me how much she missed me. She would cook especially for me a wonderful lemon tart that I adored or buy me lovely clothes. But then, just when I was thinking all was well, she would have an extraordinary change of mood, turning on me quite viciously at times. I learned, for instance, to avoid her like the plague on the days of my concerts when, seemingly deliberately, she would set out to keep me from relaxing and concentrating on the evening performance. She would send me on errands and abuse me verbally, turning me into a gibbering wreck and then, like the turning off of a tap, her good mood would return after the concert, and all would be forgotten. I don't think Arthur was aware of what was going on. His hearing was not very good and for him to understand what people were saying, they had to speak clearly and with elevated volume. I also think that, after forty-odd years, he was used to her shenanigans and perhaps didn't realize how difficult she made my life.

I could have overlooked and forgiven all, because I felt she was trying to cope with stresses and obsessions beyond my understanding, but she was also unbelievably rude to my parents, and this went too far for me.

Biddy and George took the opportunity to come to Paris whenever I performed there, and after my debut with the Orchestre National de Radio France at Le Théatre des Champs-Elysées in 1976, the Rubinsteins invited them to lunch. I wasn't at all nervous, because this was an occasion when I knew Biddy and George would shine; my parents were eccentric, but they were also undeniably charming, civilised people. Mrs. Rubinstein had made Flaki, a Polish tripe dish which I had mentioned was an old favourite of George's. All was going very well; Arthur was enchanted and having a good time, and Mrs. Rubinstein was enjoying talking about Poland with George, as they were roughly the same age and had even spent a summer before the war in Zakopane at exactly the same time. However, Arthur had to take a train to Strasbourg for a concert later on that afternoon and, all of a sudden, Mrs. Rubinstein slipped into one of her terrible, impatient, irrational moods, accusing Biddy of not having brought me up correctly and almost literally throwing my parents out of the house. Biddy and George held their tongues and tempers out of deference to Arthur, who was most apologetic and dreadfully embarrassed by her behaviour, but it was a nasty moment.

And the next year, when I gave a concert at the Canadian Cultural Centre in Paris, there was a similar unpleasant scene. I, of course, was staying at the Rubinsteins' and naturally assumed that we would all drive together to my recital. Half an hour before we were to leave, Mrs. Rubinstein suddenly announced that she didn't want to go with me and that I should take a taxi. Of course, it's next to impossible to find a taxi in Paris at 7.30 in the evening, so Arthur put his foot down and sent me off with the chauffeur and their car to the concert. The chauffeur was to deposit me and then come back to pick them up. With the heavy evening traffic, I arrived slightly late and was completely strung out. The organiser of the concert held the curtain for twenty minutes in deference to the Rubinsteins, but as they still hadn't shown up, I started to play my opening piece – the Mozart Sonata K. 310. The first movement, a dramatic almost operatic piece in the minor key, passed by in a flash; it was terribly hard for me to focus. I fared better in the second lyrical slow movement and took my time over it, seduced by Mozart's long melodic lines and the tension-building middle section. The Rubinsteins arrived in time for the last movement, Arthur looking mortified. At the reception afterwards, Arthur apologised to me and, with great charm tried to smooth things over with the Embassy people. But the coup de grâce came when Mrs. Rubinstein, spotting Biddy, dashed over to her and accused her of ruining the evening as she (Biddy) should have arranged my transport from her (Mrs. Rubinstein's) house to the Centre. Biddy, God bless her, inwardly livid at the rudeness, responded with great dignity, which irritated Mrs. Rubinstein even more. And then, an hour later sitting around the Rubinstein's kitchen table eating ice cream, just the three of us, she was completely calm again and quite sweet. It was very hard to handle.

Back in New York I got a call one winter's day from a friend who had heard on the radio that Arthur was in hospital in Paris with pneumonia. At age 90, this could be a frightening situation. I found out his telephone number at the hospital and minutes later was speaking to him. I should have known that, typical Arthur, he was having the time of his life, saying he felt better than anyone in the room and that he was enjoying the attention of all the nurses who had crushes on him. He regaled me with all his latest hospital jokes, adding: "I will be out of here next week – why don't you come and see me?" I was free at the time and when he passed the phone to Mrs. Rubinstein,

I tactfully asked her if she would mind a visit from me to help with the patient. She seemed very reluctant at first, so I quickly dropped the idea only to have her write me a day later warmly inviting me for a week's stay. So, I flew to Paris for a six-day visit. All seemed to go well at first. Arthur looked thin and pale but was in tearing spirits, full of jokes and fun. I played for him by the hour, we listened to music together, and I told him about my latest adventures on the road; I had just been to Salt Lake City and had some good stories to tell about my strange new Mormon acquaintances and their odd habits. François came over for a few marvellous afternoons. Annabelle was also there, as was Roman Jasinski, an old friend of the family, who was visiting from Poland. Roman was a very quiet, rather nervous, extremely educated man with a wide knowledge of unusual piano pieces. We seemed a very merry party and I did a lot of playing for them all; Chopin Etudes and Impromptus, Schumann's "Davidsbündler Tänze," "Miroirs" by Ravel, Liszt Etudes, and the Rachmaninov transcription of an excerpt from Mendelssohn's *Midsummer night's Dream*. Arthur and I had a battle over a Chopin Polonaise that I was working on at that time. He was exasperated by what he felt was my too metronomic sense of rhythm. I tried and tried to please him, and we'd laugh a lot, and he would apologise, and I would apologise. He even demonstrated the steps of the Polonaise for me, and I would think and listen and try some more, until something finally twigged in my brain, and I played it for him once again, and finally we were both satisfied. Then, he started to make plans for a trip that we would all take to Italy so that he could show me Venice. He was also excited about our upcoming summer in Marbella together. And when Mrs. Rubinstein invited me to spend the morning with Roman and herself at the Louvre, I was happy to accept and enjoyed myself thoroughly.

All seemed harmonious until a tea party the day before I left. Baron Alain and Mary de Rothschild were the guests. Everyone was in a good mood, although Arthur was having a hard time hearing Mary de Rothschild who was telling, in her quiet melodious voice, a long and involved story about a charity concert that she was organising. I could see he was getting bored (since his deafness cut him out of the conversation) because he started impishly making faces behind her back, looking exasperated and very naughty. Roman, Annabelle and I were having a hard time keeping straight faces when, without any warning, Mrs. Rubinstein went on the attack, making dreadfully sarcastic and vicious remarks in an undertone about her husband. Arthur, luckily, couldn't hear, but the rest of us were sick with embarrassment. To change the subject, Mary de Rothschild, always the gracious lady, turned to me to ask what had brought me to Paris. I started to answer that I was just visiting and hopefully entertaining the recovering patient, when Mrs. Rubinstein cut across my reply to say that the only reason I ever came was to get free piano lessons. This was hard to take, especially as she would always manage to attack speaking softly so that Arthur couldn't hear. I began to feel physically ill and had to excuse myself from the table.

For Arthur's sake I nevertheless still tried hard to get along with his wife. Perhaps I shouldn't have bothered. All my life I have loathed and feared conflict and would do anything to avoid it. My mother had a frightening temper and my parents, although devoted to each other, never backed away from a fight. It used to terrify me. Raised voices, verbal abuse and lost tempers are things I simply cannot abide. The situation was becoming difficult and unpleasant for me.

CHAPTER 7

Nights in the Gardens of Spain ("Noches in los jardines d'Espagna") by Manuel de Falla

During the summer of 1976, my father was diagnosed as suffering from the symptoms of diabetes. He had just returned from an exciting trip on the Nile and at first, we all thought he had caught some dreadful tropical bug. The symptoms were serious, and he was hospitalised for a while. With the presence of this unpleasant disease in our family, relationships and dynamics changed. My mother transferred almost her entire focus onto my father and to keeping his sugar-level balanced. She watched him like a hawk, followed him everywhere, cooked special meals for him and phoned me daily, not just to remind me to "practise hard" – this habitual refrain became almost amusing when I wasn't too tired – but also to express all her worries. If my father had had an insulin reaction, which he did frequently in the early adjustment stages, she would describe it in frightening detail.

My father, courageous as ever, essentially set out to control the disease and then to continue his life as before, minus all the lovely chocolates and sweets he so loved. But Biddy's over-protectiveness ran up against his independent spirit, as did the fact that the disease led to exhaustion and curtailed some of his more vigorous activities. He also missed going on his solitary adventures to exotic places. However, despite the friction between these two powerful characters jockeying for supremacy and control, he managed to live with diabetes for another seventeen years and, although the trips were now mostly to Europe or somewhere in North America, he did manage to drag my poor frantic mother to the Middle East once, and on a trip to Kenya, where her fears were realised when he ended up spending nearly a month in a Nairobi hospital. Since there is much of my mother in my own character, I admit that at first, I too felt tremendous, obsessive anxiety for my father's health, especially when I heard of episodes during insulin reactions when he would get lost in downtown Montreal and wander aimlessly for hours. Although he soon learned to identify the signs of an oncoming reaction, I still remember spending many a sleepless night worrying about him and making many extra visits home to cheer up the atmosphere. Peter, my brother, was marvellous at dealing with George, and I was the one who dealt with Biddy.

This was also the first summer that I was invited to spend a month in Marbella on the Costa del Sol with the Rubinsteins. At first the magic of the place overpowered me; the brilliant, harsh colours of the Spanish countryside and the little mountain-side property, in whose garden glistening lemons, pungently fragrant oranges, and tomatoes of a red so deep as to be almost the colour of blood, ripened harmoniously under the hot Andalusian sun. At night, when the arid soil relinquished its warmth and a slight cool breeze would unobtrusively drift through the air, the intoxicating smell of rose and jasmine would fill our nostrils, and the stars, their silvery light reflecting in the pool below the terrace, were so bright in the dark, ink-blue heavens, one felt one could grab great handfuls of them and toss them around to create our own meteorite showers, all sparkles, ice-cold. And, always in the background, providing a relentless accompaniment to our days and nights, the monotonous grinding sound of the cicadas.

The house itself was built high up on the edge of the mountain, where the air was dryer and fresher than down in the more populated beach area. The views of the Mediterranean were breathtaking and, unlike many of the palatial homes in the district, the Rubinstein house and studio next door were very simply decorated – the furniture, solid Spanish provincial, was attractive and comfortable, the floors were beautifully tiled, and the walls were white-washed. There was a long terrace filled with bright-coloured flowers in big ceramic pots, roses the size of cabbages, and jasmine running wild over the walls and the roofs.

One afternoon we were lazily chatting after a large meal when we decided to turn on the radio to find out how the Polish volleyball team was doing at the Montreal Olympics. They were supposed to be meeting the Russian team in the finals that day. As we fiddled around with the channels, we came across a performance of *Die Walküre*, seemingly live from Bayreuth with the young newcomer, Peter Hofmann, as Siegmund. I was thrilled, and as Arthur was indulgent towards what he called my "Wagneritis" – as he referred to my love of Wagner – he sat with me until the end. Emboldened by our first Wagner experience together, particularly after I heard him late into that night playing passages from *Walküre* on the piano, I hauled out the recording of *Tristan und Isolde*, with Furtwängler conducting, that I had found stashed away at the back of a cupboard. Again, he indulgently listened with me, but *Tristan*, an opera overflowing with lust, sex, love and death, was probably not the wisest opera to play to an old man (however vibrant and energetic) and after a while it was clear that he wasn't sharing my unbounded enthusiasm – because he started to tease me. The Wagner opera Arthur still loved was *Meistersinger*, even though he would invariably tell me that Wagner was a nasty man with a nasty mind, and that obviously Eva should have married Hans Sachs in the end and not the *poseur* Walter! In revenge for my having, as he would impishly put it, forced him to sit through "that endless Tristan," there was a day in Paris, months later, when he decided we'd listen to all of his recordings of *Meistersinger* and compare them. Solti's overture won as the most exciting, but we preferred Knappertsbusch's Eva and overall preferred Eugen Jochum's version, which Daniel Barenboim had thoughtfully brought over the day before for Arthur's amusement. Three Meistersingers in one day! It was enormous fun, although we were exhausted by the end, and Arthur laughingly pointed out that he now had his revenge: this would teach me not to force him to sit through performances of *Tristan*!

It had been a few months since Arthur had played his last concert and he was settling into his new life admirably. He had no more concert tours to plan or to prepare, but he did have the second volume of his memoirs to tackle, and for this he had hired Tony Madigan, the young grandson of an old friend, to help. Arthur would dictate and Tony would transcribe. Tony was energetic, fun, easy-going, bright, and couth. We got along like a house on fire and, when I wasn't working or Tony wasn't writing, we would have a lovely time together, swimming in the pool or wandering around Marbella itself, window-shopping, watching the fishing-boats sail into the little harbour, or eating "Jamon Serrano" and grilled sardines amidst the bustle of the daily market. Tony was studying the flamenco music of Spain, earnestly practising his guitar many hours a day and, several times during the summer, we all trooped down to a restaurant in the port where, late at night, he rather shyly performed with his more experienced colleagues. Having him there that first summer of 1976 helped ease some of the tensions that had been building up in Paris and gave a touch of holiday spirit to my stay. And Marbella was delightful in the 70s, still retaining its authentic fishing village charm. It is true that the hordes of insanely wealthy nouveaux riches, with the pencil-thin women wearing improbable make-up, ultra-peculiar hair styles and world-weary expressions, and the men stinking of cologne, with shirts open to the navel, sporting huge gold chains resting on masses of black sweaty chesthair, were beginning to make their presence felt. But somehow it wasn't spoilt yet, and the houses that dotted the hillside were generally owned by long-time residents who had migrated to Marbella to seek a quiet retreat in the sun; old families, old money, old titles, older artists, and good taste still prevailed.

Tony and I kept Arthur busy, and I think he was enjoying himself at first quite a lot. Apart from his ulcers, his health was excellent, and he had even bought himself, upon the recommendation of his masseur, an exercise bicycle on which to work out every morning. Mind you, he soon tired of it, but two mornings a week, whenever he would hear the approaching footsteps of the masseur, he would dash over to the bicycle and do a grand imitation of a Tour de France participant, complete with agonising facial expressions and heavy breathing, pretending he'd been riding for hours – completely fooling the poor man and amusing himself mightily. I believe Arthur could have been a great actor.

Music filled our time during the day – I would practise all morning in the studio, happily surrounded by priceless Picassos and objets d'art, and then Arthur would come and either listen secretly on the terrace outside the glass doors or, more formally, would have me play for him.

I was working on the Chopin "Barcarolle," and we had long sessions together searching for the perfect sound, the perfect phrasing, the perfect tempi. Both our interpretations of this, one of Chopin's greatest masterpieces, fluctuated from day to day, a satisfactory result always remaining elusive. It was fascinating and frustrating and utterly absorbing. To project, to com-municate, to question, to search, to never be absolutely sure, all of this, I was learning, was the artist's glorious burden, and I was also receiving extraordinary lessons on how to become a conduit between the geniuses of the past and the public of today.

We also worked on Liszt's "Au Bord d'une Source," which Arthur quickly made me re-think as a delicate, lyrical, almost impressionistic work, rather than the more virtuoso showpiece I had originally presented to him, and the "Petrarch Sonnets" which delighted him. And then, of course, there was the Rachmaninov 3rd piano concerto, which I was to play at the Kennedy Centre in Washington D.C. just a few weeks after my departure. Arthur had once learned this piece and had even planned on recording it with, I believe, Fritz Reiner in Chicago, but typically never felt like putting in the endless, arduous hours of practising all of those thousands of notes, so the project was never complet-ed. However, we had fun working on it together, as it wasn't the kind of music to provoke deep philosophical discussions or, more to the point, deep divisions between us. The outer move-ments he more or less left up to me, but we sang away together the big phrases of the slow movement, adding layer upon lay-er of lushness and romanticism and a controlled build-up to the final climax.

After a particularly productive morning, during which I had finally given a seriously good performance of the Rachmaninov, Mrs. Rubinstein announced she had had a telephone call from a Polish pianist of excellent reputation who was holidaying near-by and who desired to come and pay his respects. The usually ultra-social Arthur was uncharacteristically grumpy, as he had already planned an afternoon with Tony and myself, listening to music and then going down to the town for hot chocolate in the early evening. I, on the other hand, was quite curious to meet this fellow pianist and presently he turned up with his wife. Arthur was rather formal with him, and the poor fellow was extremely nervous and over-awed. What soon became evi-dent, though, was that he was working himself up to ask Arthur for lessons sometime over the next few weeks. He was shocked to find me already there, seemingly as Arthur's student.

Mrs. Rubinstein prepared a delicious tea. Our guest and his wife sat next to Arthur and spoke to him in excited Polish, desperately trying to win his approval. I was at the other end of the table chatting with Tony and Mrs. Rubinstein when I realised that Arthur was looking at me and obviously speaking about me. The poor fellow had finally felt compelled to ask politely who I was, and Arthur was singing my praises, telling him how I could tackle anything at the piano. Some cruel God prompted our guest innocently to ask if I played the Rachmaninov 3rd piano concerto, upon which Arthur devilishly hailed me from the other end of the table and wickedly asked me: "Nina, do you play the Rachmaninov third?"

"Er, yes, I do," I replied briefly, not sure what role I was supposed to be playing.

"Come on, then, our guest would love to hear you play it!" And then he got up, interrupting our luscious tea, and dragged us all over to the studio. "Play the slow movement!" which I did, and of course it went beautifully as we had just nailed it that morning.

Our guest crumpled; even Arthur began to feel sorry for him and pressed him to play for us. The wretched fellow had been on holiday and hadn't practised for a few weeks and the last thing he wanted to do was to play that day for Arthur, especially after my performance. He started on a Chopin sonata but stopped after a few bars and doused his sweaty hands with talcum powder, apologising frantically. Then he tried a few bars of a Beethoven Sonata which also ended in disaster. Finally, he played quite delightfully some mazurkas. At this point, we were all suffering so much for him that the relief of hearing him get through anything was overwhelming and we lavished praise on him.

Arthur, perhaps feeling a touch guilty, was particularly kind, but he still couldn't quite extinguish the naughty glint in his eyes. Our guests stayed and stayed and when at last they left, we all collapsed in a heap. Suddenly Arthur started laughing and presently we all joined in. Wiping the tears from his eyes he said: "I suppose I was a little cruel, but he was so pushy, and he really just wanted lessons from me."

And so it went. I continued to play for Arthur every day, Chopin, Liszt, Mozart – and Mrs. Rubinstein prepared divine meals using the wonderful local produce, our own vegetables, and fish straight from the Mediterranean: merlusa, salmonettas, San Pedro, dorade, sole, and those delectable sardines. Her paella was magnificent and her tarts and cakes *sans pareil*. We ate at least five meals a day and the food was rich – luckily, I swam a lot in the pool to save myself from total obesity. Arthur loved his food and particularly loved chocolate. One afternoon, when Mrs. Rubinstein served us vanilla ice cream with mounds of excessively rich warm chocolate sauce poured all over it, he dipped his spoon into the scrumptious concoction and, his eyes raised heavenward, exclaimed "Vanilla ice cream with chocolate sauce: it's ... it's ... Beethoven!"

About halfway through my stay, the atmosphere soured. Arthur, Tony, and I had our own little world of music, literature and fun, from which Mrs. Rubinstein seemed involuntarily excluded. The feelings of jealousy and resentment that had manifested themselves in Paris began to surface again. So, in an attempt at peace-making, Tony and I made a point of leaving them together, when we were not working, to give Mrs. Rubinstein a break from our – or, more particularly, my – presence. This tactic proved counter-productive, as we would come home to find that either Arthur had been left all alone most of the afternoon "bored to a stiff" as he put it (since his blindness precluded most unaccompanied activities) while she had gone off shopping, or they had had a blazing row leaving her agitated and miserable, banging pots and pans in the kitchen or watching television, while he would be sitting in his studio with violent stomach cramps.

I tried another tack: since I truly was impressed by her extraordinary talents in the kitchen, I begged to be allowed to assist or at least observe. This didn't work either because, however willing I was, she became impatient and irritated by what she considered my total ineptitude. The only thing that did work, somewhat, was when I expressed an interest in playing Scrabble with her in the evenings while Arthur was still dictating to Tony. She enjoyed this game, and it became a regular pastime for us every night. The tension subsided a bit, but only temporarily. I understood her frustrations but felt unable to help. It was evident to me that, although she was the daughter of a famous conductor and the wife of a pianist, music was not a great passion of hers and that listening to music all day drove her crazy. And here was Arthur, who was just bringing home what his life had always been, except that instead of travelling and performing, he was now staying at home and listening. They were suddenly discovering that they really hadn't much left in common and that Arthur's vision of old age and how to live it proactively was far from her own. Arthur was definitely not ready to sit back and live with memories.

Poor Mrs. Rubinstein decided it could help her cause, and dilute Arthur's interest in my career and future, if more young pianists were invited to stay. She would cook for everyone and have lots of new Scrabble victims and reclaim some of the attention she so desperately needed. Ironically, I would have been thrilled to have more young colleagues about and said so – but Arthur would only have me there. He was determined to help me prepare for my first tours and he desired with all his heart that I should be a success. He certainly didn't want the distractions of other, eager, young pianists during those few weeks. Mrs. Rubinstein was not pleased. It didn't help matters when, at lunch one day, he announced with mock drama that he was suffering from terrible writer's block and laughingly added: "I think this book will just have one sentence: 'There is this pianist called Nina ...'" We all laughed, but the tension rose several notches.

And then I played the Schumann "Fantasy," a piece about which I felt extremely strongly and one I had already performed a great deal. For me it signifies the ultimate in romanticism and I sense its passionate power right to the very tips of my nerve endings. This is Schumann in love, pouring his obsession for Clara Wieck into the keyboard. Arthur had had a shouting match with his wife directly before I played it for him and his stomach was causing him pain. The first movement rather impressed him although we worked a little on tightening the structure but, when I played the second movement, the skies fell in and he was furious with me. It was a question of rhythm and a sense of nobility, which he felt were lacking and, since I wasn't immediately able to understand or correct it, he became both exasperated and livid. Somehow, the more I tried the worse it got and he stormed out, leaving me silently dissolving into tears. And then suddenly Mrs. Rubinstein appeared, showing the sweet, kind side of her nature that I had thought I would never experience again – coming in and rescuing me, inviting me to swim with her, making me my favourite lemon tart. These people were becoming far too complicated, and I started to long for home.

But Arthur was a true friend and the next day when we were alone at breakfast, he apologised magnificently for his outburst of the day before: "I was angry with my wife and took it out on you and this was unforgivable – besides, who am I to tell you how to play the Schumann "Fantasy"? – you should be giving 'advices' to me!" I forgave him readily and we returned to our epic struggle without any bad feelings.

On July 27th, the Rubinsteins were to celebrate their forty-fourth wedding anniversary and a sort of truce was achieved, mainly because Arthur adored a good party and a chance to see a lot of old friends; also, Mrs. Rubinstein loved to give parties and do all of the cooking herself, so, for a change, she was happy we were all occupied and not in her way. The guest list was a throwback to pre-Revolutionary Europe and peppered with titled aristocracy. Estrella (Tony's grandmother), Tony, his sister Sheila, and I were naturally all invited, plus a few of the local resident artists, decorators and couturiers – but we

142

commoners were in the minority. The bulk of the guests carried names and titles which recalled a time long past: the Duke and Duchess de la Rochefoucauld, Guy de Rothschild and his wife Marie-Hélène, the Duchess of Alba, the Duke and Duchess Romanones, Marques Luis and Marquesa Nena de Salamanca, the Count and Countess Larisch, Baron and Baroness von Pantz, and Prince Alfonso von Hohenlohe.

After a wonderful dinner the music, carefully chosen by Arthur, Tony and myself, began with a recording of Arthur playing the A major "military" Polonaise of Chopin. During a lighter moment the night before, Arthur and Mrs. Rubinstein had taken the trouble to teach Tony and myself how to dance the Polonaise properly, so it was with confidence that we took our place in the long procession that danced its way through the house. Waltzes and tangos followed; Arthur invited me to dance a waltz with him early on, then Tony took care of me for the rest of the evening. Another guest was the enchanting actress Deborah Kerr, who was clearly smitten by Arthur, as were all the women present. He charmed them with ease: he had such a witty manner, and he made everyone feel so comfortable in his presence. The champagne flowed.

In the early hours of the morning, during a lull in the dancing, we heard music coming from the kitchen. There we found the servants, many of whom had been hired just for the occasion, having a flamenco party of their own. We were soon joined by Arthur and Deborah Kerr. The singing was savage and primitive and the rhythms relentless; it was the music of gypsies, raw and wild. Sparks were flying, colours flashing – we were inside the great heart of Spain.

The next day I had to leave for America, as the Washington, D.C., concert was fast approaching. Mrs. Rubinstein seemed truly sad that I was going, and we parted with affection. Arthur and Tony were more demonstrative and before the taxi arrived Arthur showed me a photo of myself he had put on his desk so that, he said, with a twinkle in his eye, I could inspire him every morning when he wrote his book. Tony wrote me the next week to say that Mrs. Rubinstein had removed the photo. Clearly, she felt threatened, but I simply cannot imagine she ever suspected I was having an affair with her husband. Even if I had wanted to, which I categorically did not, the logistics were simply too complicated. More likely, I think, she was annoyed that he was so attached and interested in someone who was neither his wife nor his own child.

I spent the following winter on tour finishing the engagements that Arthur had secured for me. With the predictable exception of Montreal and a mixed reaction in Detroit, the newspaper coverage for all the concerts and for the first recording (the Liszt Sonata) were all excellent, which was a big relief for me, for Arthur, and for the agents. Tony had left Arthur's employ after a few months because he was beginning to feel trapped and unhappy in the stressful atmosphere. His place was taken by Annabelle.

In January of 1977, the Rubinsteins came to New York with Annabelle in tow, and faithful Bronek Kaper flew in from California for a visit. As often before, we had a few pleasant evenings but then, like a recurring nightmare, Mrs. Rubinstein's jealousy reared its ugly head. Annabelle, Dana, and I had planned a dinner together at Trader Vic's restaurant. Naturally, this was right up Arthur's alley, not to mention Bronek's, but, since they were unable to join us, they suggested we stop by the hotel after our meal to say hello. Apparently, this plan enraged Mrs. Rubinstein, and she told Arthur that if we were to come she would refuse to offer us anything to eat or drink. Naturally we didn't know any of this so, having eaten a huge meal and drunk far too many of those lethal Polynesian drinks called Scorpions, with orchids floating on top and tasting innocently of soda pop but packing a colossal alcoholic punch, we arrived at the suite happy and a little bit intoxicated.

Bronek and Arthur were delighted to see us, as they had seemingly spent the evening just chatting while Mrs. Rubinstein watched television. Mrs. Rubinstein completely ignored Dana, even refusing her proffered hand when introduced, and then ostentatiously turned her back on us and raised the television volume so we could hardly converse and Arthur had trouble hearing Dana, whose voice, minus a vocal cord, was very soft. I was furious at this display of rudeness towards my friend, who looked so frail and ill at that time. As usual, though, Arthur sensed what was important to me and brought out his secret hoard of chocolate and spent the rest of the evening directing his entire attention to Dana, telling her his most wonderful stories and making her feel an honoured and appreciated guest. Bronek added a lot of humour to the conversation, so we had fun. Mrs. Rubinstein, however, sat alone in her personal hell, her back, in silent protest, turned firmly towards us. I was surprised to realise I felt tremendous pity for her.

A few days later we celebrated Arthur's 90th birthday in the hotel suite. Mrs. Rubinstein, three of their children and one grandchild were there, as well as Bronek, Annabelle and myself. Arthur was thrilled to be 90 – he thought it was a rather distinguished age, with a good ring to it. He enjoyed beginning sentences with the phrase: "At 90, I now feel that ..." He kept the party energised and outwardly cheerful. But there was also an air of forced jollity that distressed and enervated me. Undercurrents of tension and hostility seeped into the conversation, making my skin crawl, and I was vastly relieved when the evening was over.

The next day I flew to San Francisco to begin my West Coast tour. I telephoned Annabelle and, to my dismay, found her in floods of tears and at the end of her tether. I had assumed she was as tough as nails and could handle the tension and the abuse directed towards her by Mrs. Rubinstein far better than I could. We talked a long time and I strongly advised her to leave immediately and to go back to Madrid. I remember saying to her that Arthur was a survivor – that he'd already lasted in this awful marriage for 44 years and that he would manage fine if she left. Luckily for Arthur, she didn't take my advice. By the time I telephoned again a few days later from San Diego, she had pulled herself together and decided to tough it out. It was now out-and-out war between her and Mrs. Rubinstein. Annabelle adored Arthur with a constant and very deep love and was quite willing to devote the rest of her life to making him happy, whatever the consequences. She was young, beautiful and, above all, her interests coincided precisely with his. She was more than happy to listen to music all day, to live out of a suitcase and to arrange his social and professional life without a hint of strain or impatience. Her knowledge of chamber music was encyclopaedic, and this was a subject that fascinated Arthur. She understood and appreciated the strengths, foibles, and weaknesses of musicians, having dealt with them her entire adult life, and she was strong-willed, yet self-effacing when the occasion demanded. She came from a good upper-class English family and her sense of humour and fun could be equally English and outrageous. Hotel life held no terrors for her, and she fit into Arthur's vast social circle without any fuss but with flair. In fact, she was perfect for him. However, I believe he might not have eventually ended his marriage had Mrs. Rubinstein been clever. Arthur was a great deal older than her, and at 90 was not going to change. But Mrs. Rubinstein, in her early 70s, was still a relatively young woman, and it seemed obvious to me that with just a few modifications she would have been able to hold on to their relationship. However, this was not to be, though the marriage continued for a while, albeit with increasing tension ...

I continued my tour to England and Portugal. I was in touch by phone with Annabelle most of the time and would write friendly, uncontroversial letters to Mrs. Rubinstein.

While in England, I received a surprise call from Mrs. Rubinstein inviting me to Paris for the weekend. She sounded so relaxed and nice that, against my better judgement, I accepted, even though it was a weekend that landed between two important concerts. I knew that Arthur and Mrs. Rubinstein had just been to Israel for the second competition in his name, and hoped that their having been close together for a while might have ameliorated their tense relationship somewhat. Poor innocent fool that I was!

The weekend was a nightmare, except for the few moments when I could practise and lose myself in my work. Arthur, for the first time ever, looked truly old and worn out. I couldn't sleep and caught a cold, and it was around that time that I started waking up in the morning feeling horribly ill and suddenly getting horrific chest pains during odd moments in the day. That the pains were clearly psychosomatic did nothing to lessen them. Arthur tried desperately to make my stay happy, but with all the shouting behind closed doors and the unpleasant, sarcastic remarks at mealtimes (which Arthur mostly never heard), it was hard. Mrs. Rubinstein suddenly realised the stress I was under when I appeared the last morning, green in the face and unable to eat my breakfast. All at once she became adorable and concerned and, yet again, I felt I must give her another chance.

Everyone assumed I was coming to Marbella again that summer. But I kept having to change my ticket as Arthur was manoeuvring his schedule so as to have a week away from his wife. I was beginning to dread the whole thing and seriously thought of cancelling. But I told myself it was only for a few weeks and, whatever happened, I always learned a great deal (not only about music but sadly about certain unsavoury human relationships). Also, I looked forward with joy to being welcomed every morning at breakfast by this great man whom I loved so dearly, his arms held out wide, then giving me a great hug and kisses on both cheeks. Affection (and preferably demonstrative affection) is something I have always craved, and I rank it higher than just about anything else – and Arthur certainly gave me plenty of affection. He wanted me to be in Marbella, and it seemed as though his wife did as well. I owed them a great deal, so I went.

I found I was not to stay in the main house "La Rueda" but in their guesthouse or the Casita, which was on the other side of an adjacent field. It was a charming little house and was where Daniel Barenboim and Jacqueline du Pré had spent part of their honeymoon. Annabelle was already ensconced there, and I was delighted to have her as a companion. There was one problem: the Casita was filthy. A thick layer of dust on every surface, spider webs in every corner, and strange creatures in the bathtub. Annabelle was all for toughing it out and doing some cleaning ourselves, but for some reason I felt this neglect was intentional. I spoke to one of the maids at the main house, who informed me that the *señora* had told them not to bother with the guesthouse. Feeling I should take a stand, I told Arthur and he was mortified. Six servants were instantly dispatched to clean the place and Mrs. Rubinstein was irritated.

The days settled into a sort of routine. Arthur would walk over to the Casita in the morning and have a second breakfast with us, and then I'd leave him and Annabelle to work on the second volume of his autobiography while I walked over to the studio to practise. In the afternoon we would listen to music, or I would play for Arthur, and occasionally we would go into Marbella to pass the time in a pleasant café. In the evenings I'd play Scrabble with Mrs. Rubinstein.

But as the time went by, the rows grew more frequent, and the tensions increased. Despite constantly suffering from stomach pains Arthur tried to put a good face on the situation. Once, as I sat waiting for him in the studio, feeling horribly embarrassed since he and Mrs. Rubinstein were shouting at each other in the main house next door, he finally joined me, looking haggard, and sat still for a moment. Then he winked at me, smiled, and started to sing from the film *Mary Poppins*: "Chim, chimney, / Chim, chimney / Chim, chim, cher-ee / A sweep is as lucky / As lucky can be!" and we settled down to work. Another time instead of *Mary Poppins* it was *My Fair Lady*: "I'm just an ordinary man ..." he would say in his best Rex Harrison imitation.

I had the illusion that the household I was living in was straight out of an Ibsen play. Even so, there were magical times: I gained extraordinary insights as I worked with Arthur on the Chopin "Fantasy on Polish Airs," as well as the Tchaikowsky 1st piano concerto and the Mozart concerto K.449. We had a wager in the Tchaikowsky that he would give me ten dollars if I could play the whole piece through without bending my back or leaning forward, making unnecessary, "Glenn Gould–like" motions – which I never did, although I did sway back and forth. Arthur exaggerated to make his point. Of course, I won amidst a lot of joking and merriment.

Adding to the surreal quality of the household, there were two other eccentric guests staying. One was an elderly Polish lady, a distant cousin who lived in Switzerland, whose name was Nina Raue. She was a wonderful character, extremely frail, with a very clever mind but, sadly, she had lost much of her short-term memory. Her great love was Arthur's son Johnny, who was her favourite of Arthur's four children, and had been an enchanting child. Three or four times a day she would ask Annabelle or myself if we had ever met Johnny and would launch into some complicated story about how he had visited her in Geneva and had had a party where his friends had danced naked in front of the windows and the police had been called in. The other thing she always asked was whether we knew if the Spaniards drank milk. But she was also an entertaining, perceptive lady and a little wicked too, as she was well aware of the frictions in the household, and quite enjoyed them, often making sharp, witty and provocative comments about it all – which would help me deal with the tension. I grew fond of her and enjoyed seeing her health visibly improve as she sat on the terrace reading and resting every day or listening to music.

The other guest, whose first name was Jan (I never knew his surname) was also Polish, but he still lived in Poland and was a cousin of Mrs. Rubinstein. We all dubbed him Cousin and that become his official name thereafter. He was always trying to please, jumping up to obey any command, and was highly nervous, especially around Mrs. Rubinstein, who bossed him mercilessly. He adored Arthur and loved listening to music and, at age 72, still spoke of his own father with an endearing, child-like devotion. He would describe endlessly how his father played the violin magnificently, and it became rather a joke among us, because whatever piece of music we happened to be listening to, be it a piano concerto, a Schubert lied or a Mahler symphony, there would be a brief pause at the end and Cousin, his eyes misting over with emotion, would softly whisper to us that his father used to play that piece beautifully. We loved Cousin because he was a genuine innocent and a gentle character and sometimes, when he calmed down, he could be very interesting, especially one starry night when he gave me, rather shyly, a long and fascinating lecture on astronomy and the different constellations.

Our little party relished occasionally going into Marbella to our favourite café at around six in the evening. Arthur loved the thick, rich hot chocolate and drank without any qualms two huge cups, plus the little accompanying *churros*. Nina R. and Cousin were thrilled just to walk around a little and then sit, watch the world go by, and listen to Arthur's marvellous stories. Mind you, Annabelle and I felt a little like nursery governesses trying to keep everyone together. Arthur, completely blind, but refusing to let on that it was any kind of a problem, would ask us if there was anything in his way along the sidewalk. When told it was clear for at least thirty yards, he would stride off, leaving us scrambling to keep up. Cousin was always bouncing off and getting lost, and Nina, frail and wobbly, also needed a sharp eye on her, as she tended to forget where she was. But it was worth the slight anxiety because we were such a merry party.

Mrs. Rubinstein would try to keep us from going to the town. Why did she want to deny these nice people such an innocent pleasure once or twice a week? Some days she was adamant and quite frantic that we shouldn't go; it was ridiculous – she could make just as good hot chocolate as the café. What she didn't understand was that the hot chocolate was only an excuse for three elderly people to have an adventure in a foreign country and enjoy feeling free and young again.

One day we were all invited to Guy de Rothschild's house for lunch. It was hot and sultry by the Mediterranean, but they had a beautiful home, and the lunch was exquisite. I sat next to Madame la Baronne Cécile de Rothschild who, Mrs. Rubinstein told me in a loud whisper, was allegedly a notorious lesbian and I should be careful! I didn't see what there was to be careful about, and enjoyed her company greatly. Guy and his wife Marie-Hélène both had little dachshunds who sat on their knees at table and ate with us. I was very amused when Marie-Hélène sent back her dog's little plate of food, complaining that it wasn't cooked properly. Marie-Hélène had two young men in tow that summer whenever we saw her – "lovers," whispered Mrs. Rubinstein, "and one of them is the brother of the husband of the Queen of Denmark!" I wasn't sure how much of this I could believe, especially as I found our host and hostess utterly charming and hospitable and Guy, especially, even as an elderly man, was still extremely attractive. The so-called lover (who was probably just a hanger-on with no royal connection) was the epitome of sleaze, but the young royal-by-connection was pleasant. The only other people there were a young Brazilian couple, obviously extremely wealthy and full of South American joie-de-vivre. The wife was beautifully turned out, very attractive and bronzed, with wonderful gold bangles and exotic jewellery and she absolutely fell for Arthur, flirting with him madly all through lunch. He was having a lovely time.

And then suddenly Mrs. Rubinstein had had enough and decided it was imperative we all leave immediately. Why we all automatically obeyed her is beyond me, but I guess it was to avoid a scene. Because we were a large party, we had arrived in a car and a taxi. Mrs. Rubinstein didn't want to wait for a taxi, so she insisted that we all pile into her car which she was driving. The scene was hilarious – on one side the ultra-sophisticated, super-chic, super-polite hosts waving good-bye, on the other this circus act with Mrs. Rubinstein hysterically shouting at all of us to hurry up as we squeezed into the car onto each other's laps, then roaring off at top speed. Yes, we were living in an Ibsen play, but the stage direction was all Goldoni and commedia dell'arte.

Arthur's vulnerability was now making its appearance more frequently. One afternoon, he asked me earnestly if I was his friend – his *real* friend – to which I replied, yes, he was my best friend, and his eyes filled with tears. He gave me a hug and said he was very happy and very honoured. One of the many admirable things about Arthur was that he never, ever, took things or people for granted.

Another day, when we sensed a terrible row brewing, Annabelle and I escaped to the couch on the terrace of his studio and waited anxiously for him to appear. When he finally showed up, he settled himself down between us and said: "Ach! I love it here between you two. I somehow feel so safe here – I feel that nothing can get at me, can hurt me." Then, after a pause for reflection, his irrepressible comic nature surfaced and he added: "If I were thirty or forty years younger, I'd put my arms around both of you and squeeze and see how far I could go before getting a slap in the face!" There was a silence, so he then began chuckling and said: "Deep silence; you are both thinking, no, we really wouldn't go that far and slap the old man in the face!" He then had me play the Chopin B minor Sonata, then we listened to a lovely performance on the radio of Joseph Krips conducting the Mozart G minor symphony as we sat side by side on the couch, with our six feet lined up in front of us resting on the coffee table and conducting the symphony in beautiful synchronisation.

But then there would be another meal to face, and at this point they so upset me that I often excused myself the minute coffee was served and escaped to the terrace. Scrabble games at night had become almost a martyrdom. Arthur and Annabelle would be in the next room working, and sometimes Arthur would be so infuriated with his wife's behaviour at dinner that his voice became a little too loud and we could hear him say things like: "She is really becoming absolutely intolerable." So I'd start singing loudly, any song I could think of, or force myself to tell Mrs. Rubinstein long stories as we played. She became increasingly hyper and, because she lost interest in the game if she wasn't ahead, I had to make sure that she was winning. She was a good player so this wasn't always necessary, and things improved somewhat when we found a French Scrabble board and Cousin (who spoke fluent French) could join our game.

And then there was a day when the weather suddenly turned unbearably warm, and a hot wind blew over from Northern Africa. Nerves were on edge so, in the late afternoon, we decided to cheer ourselves up by listening to a rousing performance of Beethoven's ninth symphony with Szell conducting. When it was over Arthur started to talk about Beethoven and the "Heiligenstädter Testament" and suddenly he burst into tears and began to sob. It was sympathy for Beethoven, but we recognized it was also a huge release from pent-up emotions, so we let him continue uninterrupted. Cousin looked bewildered and poor old Nina started to get teary-eyed herself, so at that point I briskly rounded them up and marched everyone to the main house for tea. Unfortunately, Mrs. Rubinstein was in a frantic mood and, worried that we would all want to go down to the café in Marbella, had made her own version of the sickly-sweet hot chocolate – sadly, the last thing we felt like drinking on such a hot day. Arthur insisted on tea for himself which provoked a wild harangue from his wife on his selfishness, which he chose not to hear and continued sobbing quietly.

Suddenly in the middle of all of this Cousin piped up brightly saying: "My father used to play Beethoven's symphonies with me." And he started singing something which, for the life of me, sounded like Bizet's *Carmen*. In the meanwhile, Mrs. Rubinstein had left the room and we heard her on the phone shouting at her neighbour Estrella, Tony's grandmother. It was all over some fish that Estrella's cook Pepito had offered to get and cook for the Rubinsteins' anniversary party the next day (yes, they were going to go through with it and have their yearly party). Suddenly I heard Mrs. Rubinstein scream into the phone: "Janina is none of my business – arrange it with her yourself!" And she slammed down the phone as Cousin continued singing, Arthur continued sobbing and Nina R. asked me if they drank milk in Spain. I told Annabelle we'd better go and see if Estrella was alright. Outwardly she was a tough old society lady, but there was a genuine old "softie" underneath. When we arrived, we found her crying, with Pepito patting her hands, trying to console her. All she had asked, she told us between sobs, was if she could come and hear me play one day! She adored music, she said; I'd been there ten days and she had missed me because Mrs. Rubinstein hadn't allowed her near the house; Mrs. Rubinstein had insulted Pepito and Pepito's fish as well. Then there were more floods of tears. We suggested to Pepito that perhaps something cool to drink would restore our spirits, whereupon he went and made us fresh lemonade. I then assured Estrella that she should just show up any time at the Rubinsteins' and Arthur and I would see to it that she would get her concert. So she dried her tears and we stayed a bit longer making inroads on the lemonade and hearing some of her more juicy bits of local gossip and pithy remarks about the Rubinstein household. Later, Annabelle and I had a nice, quiet afternoon walking in Marbella and buying some presents for our families and friends back home but then, on the way back up the mountain, as the sun was setting, we suddenly saw Cousin hopping across a field looking quite mad ... and there was another evening of Scrabble to face.

The anniversary party, with most of the same guests from the year before, was unpleasant for me. The sleazy friend of Marie-Hélène de Rothschild followed me around for the first part of it and I just couldn't get myself into a party spirit – it all seemed so hypocritical. Arthur was distracted, Mrs. Rubinstein drank a great deal and, less sensibly, called me a "Judas" in a loud voice. There was still an entire week before I could leave and go home. I had developed terrible migraines, lost my appetite and wasn't sleeping. In desperation, I told Annabelle I couldn't take it much longer. She spoke to Arthur, who came to find me the next afternoon as I lay in his studio with a blinding headache. He apologised and apologised, and I explained that he was not at fault but that I just couldn't handle the tension anymore. "Please stay, Nina," he implored. "Don't you see, when you are here, everyone at least has to try and be polite." And then he added: "I should miss you too much." So I stayed.

CHAPTER 8

"Marche funèbre" from the B flat minor
Sonata by Frédéric Chopin

"If a way to the Better there be,
it exacts a full look at the Worst."
Thomas Hardy

Neither frustration nor anxiety nor fatigue from a terrible journey could diminish the thrill I experienced when I stepped out of the station in Venice in September 1977 and saw the Grand Canal for the first time. It was a view I had dreamed about and read about so often – but for all the scenes painted by Canaletto that I had admired, and all the photos, travel-books and television documentaries I had seen, nothing had really prepared me for this enchanting sight, this feeling of walking through an invisible screen and finding myself in the 16th century – the colours of the Renaissance at sunset in the slightly misty autumnal air, the sounds and the smells of a bygone era, a uniquely magical civilisation, frozen in time. For a few seconds I was so overwhelmed, I could hardly breathe, but then pragmatism surfaced, and I began to wonder how the hell I was going to find the Palazzo Mocenigo at the vaporetto stop of San Samuele (this being the only address I had).

By this time, I had made the important and comforting discovery that if I stood long enough, and looked lost and pathetic long enough, someone would invariably come to my rescue. And so it was that I was directed to the Vaporetto (the Venetian water bus) which I rode, utterly entranced, until I saw the sign for the San Samuele stop. My suitcases were heavy and the streets deserted. I started to walk aimlessly, knowing only that the palace was on the Grand Canal. A lady in a hurry, laden down with bags of groceries and a yard of bread under her arm, came towards me and I desperately asked her for directions. She looked puzzled but then pointed me down an alleyway. As I trudged through it, my footsteps echoing, feeling a little teary and very tired from the journey that had begun 24 hours earlier in New York, a handsome and stylish young man walked past me, then retraced his steps.

"Are you by any chance Miss Fialkowska?" Bless him, he even pronounced my name correctly! He was the magnificent Italian violinist Uto Ughi, a resident of Venice and a great friend of Olga, the Marchesa de Cadaval, who was to be my hostess for the week. They had been waiting and worrying about me all day, and he quickly took charge of my luggage and directed me just around the corner to an impressive wrought-iron gate.

The Marchesa de Cadaval was extraordinary, even within Arthur's wide circle of notable friends. From an ancient aristocratic Venetian family that descended from the Doges (one of their typical hats lay on display in a glass case in the entrance hall), she had married into an equally aristocratic Portuguese family and consequently divided her time between her terraced estate dripping with flowers of every possible colour in Sintra, Portugal (where I had already stayed a few months earlier and where most of the deposed royalty of Europe congregated) and her historic Palazzo in Venice. She was tall, autocratic and imposing, and her comportment bore the self assurance that only centuries of belonging to the ruling classes could achieve. She was secure in the knowledge of her social superiority, but was also a true guardian angel to poor or displaced musicians, turning her home in Sintra, with its magnificent Steinway, into a sanctuary for those fleeing communism. It was with her that pianists Vladimir Ashkenazy and Fou Tsong found refuge when they defected from Russia and China respectively, and at any given time her house was home to three or four young musicians needing a place to stay and to recuperate from their arduous tours, people such as Martha Argerich, Nelson Freire, Jeffrey Swann, Tamas Vasary, and many others. And despite providing sanctuary for those fleeing Communist oppression she also managed, some-how, to maintain excellent relations with the Soviet Embassy in Lisbon, perhaps because she would also host all the Soviet musicians such as Emil Gilels and Sviatoslav Richter as they passed through Portugal. In fact, she was so well respected that when Portugal underwent its nasty and traumatic revolution (known as the "Carnation Revolution") in 1974, a few years after the death of the long-time dictator Salazar, she was completely un-affected, while many of her titled and large landowner neigh-bours suffered severe losses. The only problem that did arise was that her Portuguese servants, determined to show at least a little rebellious spirit, suddenly refused to make the biannual trip with her to Venice. However, as she noted rather smugly, this action backfired, as their lack of presence in Italy didn't bother her in the slightest but the servants, on the other hand, sudden-ly realised that they missed their Italian jaunts. So, for Venice, the Marchesa had a young English art student cooking for her and her concierge doing the cleaning – it was all very peaceful.

The Marchesa had been at the Rubinstein competition when I had won my prize and was a very close friend of Arthur. When it was reported that Arthur had wept during my performance of the Liszt Sonata, she made the priceless remark that, although she was very impressed with my playing, unlike Arthur, "*Je n'ai pas la larme facile!*"[13] When I was later engaged to play in Lisbon, Arthur asked her if I could stay with her. She agreed and we got along well, having long conversations together, mostly about the Rubinstein family situation (she truly adored Arthur), but also about politics and literature. As a result of my recital at the Gulbenkian in Lisbon, she became a partisan fan of mine and threw me the most wonderful party ... and also invited me to stay in Venice whenever she was in residence there. Which is why, dishevelled, tired, and on the verge of tears, I turned up on her doorstep that evening.

---

13 My tears don't flow easily.

My room in the Palazzo was magnificent, and over the appropriately massive and ornate bed I could stare up at a Tiepolo fresco on the ceiling. My windows opened onto the Grand Canal, and Lord Byron himself had stayed in that very room and would, so the story goes, jump out of the window on a whim to swim all the way to the Lido.

I was to play a recital at La Fenice, but it was no ordinary recital, since I was sharing it with Arthur. He was to give a little lecture for the first half about his philosophy of life, recounting some of his experiences, and I was to play in the second half. The big surprise was that Mrs. Rubinstein had not made the journey and, when I walked over to the restaurant next to La Fenice to meet Arthur for dinner, I found him looking radiant and incredibly pleased with himself, and sitting next to him was an equally radiant Annabelle. I gathered that, since Marbella, there had been some horrific rows, and that Arthur had actually suffered from heart palpitations. But it seemed that Arthur had finally left his wife and here they were, completely relaxed and having the time of their lives. Poor Mrs. Rubinstein – when she had telephoned the Marchesa to complain bitterly, even that lady had showed her scant sympathy, bluntly remarking that Mrs. Rubinstein should be grateful to Annabelle for making Arthur so happy!

My initial reaction was one of tempered relief. I was happy for Arthur – he had taken a giant, rather courageous, step and, for him, as well as for Annabelle, it proved to be the right one. It also made life a whole lot easier for me as it put a stop to my always being in the middle of impossibly unpleasant situations. But I also knew that Mrs. Rubinstein had once cared for me, and she now appeared to be the tragic victim of her own complex personality. No doubt she was suffering greatly, and for this reason it was hard to rejoice wholeheartedly.

The following morning the Marchesa walked me over to La Fenice to practise. How fortunate I felt to play all alone in that jewel of a theatre, filled with so much history! Annabelle and Arthur eventually came to fetch me, as Arthur was determined that he should be with me when I first saw the Piazza San Marco. As we passed the church of San Moisé and entered the last little alley before reaching the square, he made me take his hand and shut my eyes. We walked a little further and then he said: "Now!" I opened my eyes. And there it was: the Basilica of San Marco, with its domes and mosaics and, above the central portal, the marvellous four horses. Over to the side, the bronze Moors aloft on the Clock Tower were striking the massive bell at that very moment. And there was more: the glorious arcades, the strangely out-of-place Campanile, Café Florian's with its cheerful awnings, chic patrons and waiters scurrying between tables, balancing trays over their heads filled with brightly coloured, pre-dinner aperitifs – luscious Bellinis and Tizianos, made with freshly crushed peaches and grapes. And all this was accompanied by an orchestra playing nostalgic tunes at the rival café across the square, with the winged Lion peacefully looking on. Little groups of tourists, huddled around their leaders, stared intently into their guidebooks; children dashed about screaming lustily, playing soccer, and pigeons were everywhere. The old man waited, his hand gripping mine tightly as he watched my expression expectantly: "It's quite something, isn't it?" And then I realised that even though he had seen it a million times before, it still inspired a feeling of great emotion, and this whole "mise en scène" of having me arrive at just the right angle, at just the right time of day, with my eyes closed until I was in the perfect position, was his generous attempt to share with me this feeling he treasured. It was a heavenly moment.

For the recital the next day, there was something extraordinarily romantic about arriving at the theatre with the Marchesa in a boat. Surprisingly, Arthur was extremely nervous, so I kept well away from him backstage. But his speech, half in French, half in Italian, delighted the audience, who cheered him for so long that I began to wonder if I was ever going to get to play. A definite anti-climax, I nevertheless earned a standing ovation and the opportunity to offer four encores. Afterwards, at a huge party in a neighbouring restaurant, to which it felt as if the entire audience, not to mention the entire press corps of Northern Italy, was invited, I sat next to Arthur and basked in his reflected glory until the wee hours of the morning.

I was intending to spend the next day with Annabelle and Arthur, who were staying at the Bauer-Grünwald Hotel, but then it dawned on me that perhaps they would prefer to sight-see alone as this was, after all, a sort of honeymoon for them. So, we had lunch together, but the rest of the day I roamed by myself, visiting the Accademia and as many churches as I could before collapsing with fatigue.

In the evening I had a friendly meal in a little local family restaurant with the Marchesa. The weather was cooling off and it was very damp and cold in my palatial room. The week before, Yehudi and Diana Menuhin had been staying there and, having also suffered from the bitter chill of the damp, cold marble, had bought two electric heaters for the room. The Marchesa scoffed at them, but I was secretly very grateful.

Annabelle and Arthur left the next day for Rome. I spent my final day in Venice looking for the Palazzo where Wagner died (which I eventually found; it is now the Venice Casino!), visiting the Ca'd'oro, touring the Doges' palace, and laughing at the marvellous lions in front of the Arsenale. In the late afternoon, I took a boat out to the Lido and, as the sun set, had a true "Death in Venice" moment as I sat on the beach in front of the Hotel des Bains watching beautiful young Italian boys play a game of volleyball. I felt a hollowness inside; such terrible loneliness. I needed someone. I had no one. I was filled with a sense of oppressive emptiness. The celibate life I had been leading was not something I had wished for nor sought for myself. I was filled with the desires and needs of any normal young woman, perhaps more so considering my temperament. But, in my heart of hearts, I knew a long-term relationship at this point was not an option, and casual affairs were of no interest. I had just been witness to a horrendous marital breakup. My own parents, although they loved each other deeply, spent their time fighting, and the unhealthy relationships of my closest friend Dana had done nothing to encourage me to pursue a serious romance. I was having trouble just keeping my nerves steady enough to build my career, which was suddenly taking off. I didn't need more emotional turmoil. I needed a supportive partner, but I simply hadn't met him yet.

That night, wrapped in several layers of clothing, with the sound of the water lapping against the walls of the old palazzo, I spent a long time at the window just looking at the magnificent buildings opposite and the Gondolas going by, the church bells mournfully marking the hours. Mentally exhausted, I had a sleepless night and left at 6 the next morning for Venice airport. The Marchesa, wonderful lady that she was, rose early to see me off.

As for Mrs. Rubinstein, I saw her several times after that – in Paris, and for a lunch in New York. She was understandably bitter, had taken up chain-smoking again, and was accusatory and even more hyper than before. These meetings were tremendously unpleasant and, however hard I tried to soothe and/or placate, I really didn't know how to deal with her. During my subsequent troubles, she never showed the slightest sympathy or interest, only resurfacing in my life in 1987, when I played for the Chopin Society in Miami at a recital commemorating Arthur's centennial. She was the guest of honour, and it was a far nicer experience, almost like the good times we once, sporadically, had together, and I am happy that our last meeting was one of pleasure, not of rancour and enmity. She still, unwittingly, plays an important role in my life as, to this day, I regularly use her fabulous cookbook, published shortly after the break-up of her marriage.

After Venice, my troubles began to accumulate. One by one the original managers with whom Arthur had placed me were either going bankrupt or retiring. I was lucky enough in America to be able to transfer over to ICM Artists from the Hurok company. A former Hurok vice president, Walter Prude, who had been my personal representative, had moved over to ICM himself and, in all innocence, I called him up and asked him if I could come along as well. Such a simple approach would be unheard of nowadays – my poor young colleagues must win three or four international prizes before a top manager would even begin to consider acknowledging, let alone speaking to them! – but it worked back then, and I remained at ICM for over twenty years.

In France, my relationship with Michael Rainer fizzled when he and the Rubinsteins had a falling out. Johanna Beek, our Dutch manager, retired, and of course Annabelle had left Quesada in Spain. This left England, where Van Wyck wanted to retire, and I wanted to leave him anyway as he was elderly, irascible, and rather unpleasant. First, Bernard Haitink tried to help me find someone in his own management, Harold Holt, and then Arthur tried with his old friend Ian Hunter, also at the Holt office. They politely declined. Arthur was very sensitive to the fact that since he was no longer performing, a lot of these people in the music business were no longer interested in listening to his opinions. I believe it was hurtful and shocking to him (it certainly was to me) and just around this time, Annabelle very tactfully let me know that I should try to avoid troubling Arthur with my career difficulties.

Concerts followed in Bonn, Germany and in England. In Germany I was ill the whole time, and this developed into a 'flu by the time I reached England. In Bonn, I played the Rachmaninov 3rd piano concerto, and for the first time in my life I performed (what I considered to be) very badly. Certainly, I had played uninspired concerts before, but never concerts where I missed handfuls of notes, and was basically out of control. The concert surprisingly received rave reviews from two of Germany's leading newspapers. It was another lesson: one can play beautifully and get panned, but the opposite is also possible. As Arthur said, never believe a review; never believe two reviews; but if three or four start criticizing the same thing, start paying attention.

As the New Year approached, I found myself unusually apprehensive over the upcoming tours. Back in Canada, George was again adjusting his insulin levels, trying in vain to "conquer" his disease, but ending up ill and depressed. Biddy had to go into hospital for tests, so I was summoned home to take care of things.

The month of January passed, and I was feeling increasingly distraught. For the first time I was asking myself: did I really want to go on with this career? Would I be able to continue handling the pressures it involved? Mornings were now agony and I found myself having frightening anxiety attacks whenever the thought of upcoming concerts crossed my mind. I lost my appetite, I started falling asleep at odd times during the day. My brain, overloaded with tension, was shutting down.

I played two concerts in Calgary with the Philharmonic where my dear friend Marley, from the Vincent d'Indy days, was now in the double bass section. She drove me out to Banff on my day off and made me take a long walk for exercise and tried to get me to relax.

I was now preparing my London recital debut and my German recital debut in Munich. The German recital was extremely important to me, as I had obtained it purely on my own merit with no connection to Arthur. A twelve-concert West Coast tour with the Vancouver Symphony was also coming up, plus recitals in Chicago, Cincinnati and San Antonio, and a big tour of Great Britain. But before all of these I had to play the Chopin "Fantasy on Polish Airs" and the Szymanowski "Symphonie concertante" with the Montreal Symphony. The young American conductor had requested Rachmaninov 3rd, as we had worked on it together once before elsewhere, but the symphony (with my full approval) felt unusually daring and programmed the lesser-known works. The conductor was furious and, although he was very pleasant to me, made it quite clear that he loathed the Szymanowski and had barely bothered to study it. The rehearsals were rushed and unsatisfactory. I could no longer swallow food and could barely see from the blinding headaches I was experiencing. The days of the two concerts were complete nightmares and I very nearly cancelled. Somehow, once on stage, I was all right, but before the second performance I could hardly move and finally fell into a hysterical sleep which my mother had to shake me out of before I went on stage. The following morning, I was to fly to Munich. Biddy came to wake me up and found me paralysed in bed. I lay there crying silently for hours, unable to move. Biddy cancelled Germany and England and telegraphed to Arthur and Annabelle, who were to fly over and hear me in London.

What triggered this collapse? Many factors were involved: physical exhaustion, the pressures of performing, living up to Arthur's expectations, my beloved father's recent diagnosis, and yes, the temporary loss of Arthur as he started to build a new life for himself with Annabelle. But perhaps the most significant factor was the question invading my mind like some malignant tumour: was I worthy of this career? Or was it something I had just fallen into over the years, without any decisive choices on my part?

However, after a few days I thought that I felt better, particularly after some extraordinarily comforting conversations with Mr. Gorodnitzki, who told me that he had been through the same sort of crisis once and that I just needed a lot of rest. He actually told me to stop practising and to take a holiday in the Caribbean; I was very touched by his solicitude. Shortly thereafter I flew down to New York to see if I could get back to normal. Dana and Jeff surrounded me with loving attention; Mr. Gorodnitzki gave me a superb lesson and I was actually elated for a while. But then the horror returned, the nightmarish sensation that my mind was no longer my own, but under the control of some dark, evil power – something that I now recognize as massive anxiety attacks. And when I was out walking with Jeff, I suddenly thought it would be so much easier to end it all, so that when we were about to cross West 66th Street near Juilliard and a large bus approached, I stepped off the curb, simply not caring any more. Jeff's strong arm reached out and pulled me back. That afternoon I took the next flight back to Montreal and the next evening I started psychiatric treatment with Dr. Carlo Bos, one of God's angels sent to earth to do good.

He began by spending considerable time convincing me that there was nothing wrong with me; rather, by having pushed myself far too hard, I was having a nasty but logical reaction, and, in self-defence, my body had cleverly developed a phobia about going out on stage. He prescribed rest and elimination of tension, combined with an attempt to re-balance my body chemistry with an assortment of tranquilizers and antidepressants. Psychiatry was very much a developing science in those days and was often a hit-or-miss kind of thing. The hospital where I was treated was on the cutting edge of this research and Dr. Bos was the head of the department. A huge, bear-like man with a razor-sharp mind, eyes like a wise owl and the gentlest manner imaginable, he inspired such calm and reassurance that I began to look forward to my weekly sessions with all the desperation of a prisoner waiting for his meagre, life-sustaining weekly rations.

Most of the time I was too tired to be frightened and would sleep fourteen or fifteen hours a day – an unsatisfactory drug-induced sleep. My concerts were cancelled until the beginning of the next season in September. Mr. Van Wyck in London was furious and demanded compensation for the lost revenues. It was also at this time that one of the London newspapers ran a story confusing me with Annabelle and describing me as the "other woman" who stole Arthur away from his wife, commenting on the disparity in our ages and on my obvious career aspirations. Van Wyck protested to the newspapers and the editor said he was sorry, but no retraction appeared in print. This article was a big setback to my career: my engagements in England suddenly dried up, and I heard about it all as I lay in a tortured stupor at my parents' home. Annabelle (who kept in close touch) and Arthur, true to form, saw only the comic side of my tabloid scandal and couldn't understand why I was so depressed.

At first, none of the drugs seemed to work. I hated taking them, feeling weak and cowardly and that I had let everyone down. Dr. Bos, who had been born in China, and who was fascinated by the Eastern philosophies, talked to me about the Hindu thread of life, which was never straight but continued on with ups and downs. Some of the drugs gave me huge highs which lasted an hour or so; some were quite hallucinatory: others, he explained to me, recreated the same effects on the brain as were achieved by the Yogis in India after a lifetime of training and meditation. Both versions were equally addictive, he sternly warned me.

There were days when every muscle in my body felt as though it was locked in some huge cramp, and I could barely move. Other days, I perspired so terribly I had to change clothes every few hours. And finally, there were the days when I would shake uncontrollably, but the pill to counteract put me in such a death-like state that I decided the shaking was preferable. Often my head was exploding with pain and constantly crammed with black thoughts of losing my sanity and ability to function as a normal human being, panic, terror, misery; what I self-diagnosed as madness.

In May, when the world was crumbling around me, my beloved childhood friend Dana was diagnosed with cancer of the thyroid. Somehow, I flew down to New York to be with her. I spent two days with her, and we both managed to laugh and to help each other. Neither of us could sleep much, and when we did, we both had nightmares. The last morning, Dana said: "You know, it really would be too cruel if I should die now." I remember thinking: "If only I could exchange places with her." Life had so little meaning for me.

I returned to Montreal, and in July, after her operation at the Sloan Kettering, Dana came up to Canada to recuperate. I loved having her there; she could make me laugh so well. After she left, Biddy suddenly decided that I should meet eligible young men and urged me to *go out more*. I couldn't have been less in the mood, although to keep the peace I did go out a few times, but on the whole felt more and more defeated. Mr. and Mrs. Gorodnitzki continued their solid, loving support; Jeff telephoned daily; Dr. Bos adjusted the pills; and, in spite of the aches, cramps, shaking, and hallucinations, I continued to go the piano every day and practise.

And then in August a giant step: I flew to Switzerland to visit with Arthur and Annabelle. I was actually feeling too ill to travel and was phobicly fearful of leaving my parents' home. But Arthur telephoned me personally and persuaded me to join them in Lucerne, where they were holidaying. He even sent me a round-trip first-class ticket, promising me that I would be met at the Zurich airport by a chauffeured limousine.

"You must come," he said, "Solti will be conducting at the Festival and I will introduce you to him. Besides, I'm a poor old man and I need some 'advices' from you." When I arrived at the Palace Hotel, he was waiting in the lobby to welcome me and took me up to my room, where he had placed two dozen roses, chocolates and fruit. He merrily checked the taps in the bathroom, flushing the toilet just to see that "everything is in order"! He was incredibly kind: knowing the fragile state I was in, he made every effort to ensure this time in Lucerne was memorable for me, even telling the hotel people, in my presence, that I was a great pianist and his special friend and that they were to pay extra-special attention to me.

Arthur and Annabelle's suite, which overlooked the lake, had a lovely balcony and Arthur would enjoy standing on it and, full of mischief, flicking his cigar ashes onto the people having breakfast on the terrace immediately below, then quickly stepping back into his sitting room before he could be found out as the perpetrator of this childish prank.

He had a hard time dealing with my illness, as I appeared outwardly completely healthy and, never having experienced anything remotely like a depression or a phobia, he had no idea what I was going through. He teased me, calling me "the Lord Cancellor" and that he would have to call in a priest to exorcise me. But he was also concerned and did everything possible to give me back my confidence and my happiness. Knowing my love for Wagner, he took me out the first day to the Wagner Museum, a few kilometres away in Triebschen, and we spent several hours there with the curator looking at and examining everything. Arthur even played a few phrases from "Meistersinger" for me on the piano.

We had long walks by the lake, Arthur, Annabelle and I, and ate memorable meals at the hotel or in town. He had a piano in his sitting room, and I played for him Schumann's "Faschingsschwank aus Wien." Enthusiastically, he declared that I was playing like a different person, that there was a new, greater freedom and that obviously all of the suffering had been worth it. Very sweetly, he added that, now my playing was free, he was sure that the rest of me would become free as well. I played for him the Chopin F minor concerto that I had just learned, and the Chopin B minor sonata and a Bach-Liszt prelude and fugue. Without consulting me, he invited his friend Mieczislaw Horszowski (who at 87 was still performing at the festival) over to the hotel and had me play for him. This turned out to be a delightful experience for me, as both elderly gentlemen were utterly adorable, supportive, and enthusiastic. Then, the next day, he had me filmed (playing the Schumann) by a television crew that was making a 13-part "Life of A.R." miniseries. These actions of his, getting me to perform again, were amazingly beneficial and restored much of my confidence.

One morning as I practised the piano in his hotel sitting room, he left with Annabelle, ostensibly to buy fresh fruit (one of his great passions), of which he could eat an enormous bowlful in one sitting. When they returned, he rather shyly presented me with a very beautiful gold watch he had just purchased.

We had marvellous talks late into the night, the three of us, often in the hotel drawing room where a young man, understandably paralysed with fear, played the piano to entertain the guests. Arthur called him over and was so complimentary and kind to him, showing such genuine interest in his life that unfortunately the young man was emboldened to start playing less light and much more serious music, which was a bit of a disaster; but Arthur smiled throughout and listened and applauded and made him feel important.

And then the great day arrived when the Karajan family came to the hotel (Karajan was to conduct the Verdi Requiem at the festival). We had already been delighted by the company of two of the soloists, Mirella Freni and Nicolai Ghiaurov, who were big fans of Arthur's and who exuded charm and warmth towards him. But Karajan was quite different. Arthur was, of course, almost completely blind at that time, so Annabelle and I had to give him a running commentary on what was happening over at the Karajan table, which was adjacent to ours. Karajan was sitting with his wife and two daughters and remained totally aloof from all of us, not even acknowledging Arthur's presence with a civil nod. The rudeness was quite astounding, although Arthur didn't seem to care, since his opinion of Karajan as a man was rather low. The fun part occurred whenever Karajan left the dining room, because the second he was out of sight, his wife and daughters would rush over to our table, and we all had a hilarious time together. Arthur was in fine form, flirting and telling some of his most outrageous anecdotes to an admiring, all-female audience. We would laugh at his jokes until we cried, and he would keep us entertained for hours, never repeating himself, although we'd sometimes beg him for a reprise.

The next day the Karajans were gone – his photo, which had hung prominently in the hall lobby, was taken down, and Solti's was put up at its place. All through lunch Arthur teased me, sensing that my heart was aflutter at the thought of finally meeting Solti: "I think you had better fix your hair, there is some mayonnaise in it," he said, or "Quick, swallow your food I think he is coming," or "Are you sure you shouldn't change your dress? I hear that he hates the colour green." And so on. We were laughing ourselves silly when suddenly Solti dashed in (he didn't walk, he dashed everywhere) and embraced Arthur heartily, saying how wonderful it was to see him.

"Maestro," said Arthur, "I'd like you to meet a young pianist who absolutely detests your conducting!" There was a stunned silence – I turned beet red and Solti was a little shocked. Then Arthur wickedly added "No – actually she is crazy about you, and I am jealous!" So, of course, I turned four shades deeper red.

At the concert that night my beloved Chicago Symphony played the glorious Brahms 3rd and 4th Symphonies. The performance was everything I had wished for, and in my vulnerable state it was impossible to keep the tears from flowing, so shaken was I by the power of these magnificent scores.

The next morning, I had to fly back to North America to resume my career. Arthur, Annabelle and I had breakfast together and Arthur, ever the happy entertainer, was giving his imitation of Popeye while he drank his Tonic, when he suddenly turned to me and said that he was being silly and that he had to clown around because if he didn't, he would start to cry, as he knew that he was going to miss me. He was very dear to me and, still worried as well as confused by my illness, he quite wisely suggested that I ask Dana to travel with me for my first comeback concerts. He then added that if I started up again with my "extravagances" he would tell her to beat me.

In fact, Dana did travel with me to my first recital a week later in Lawrence, Kansas, but she herself was still recovering from her bout with thyroid cancer and, although she enjoyed the time in Kansas, the exhausting plane-rides home were too much for her and she felt ill for a few days after. This, of course, made me feel dreadfully guilty and I never asked her to travel with me on tour again, determined to tough it out on my own.

Over the next few months, I was in Winnipeg, Vancouver, Tuscon, Cincinnati, Thomasville, Georgia, and Portland, Oregon. Between concerts I would rush up to Montreal for sessions with Dr. Bos, still utterly dependent on him and on the medications. The concerts themselves were pure agony and I felt ill all of the time, unable to eat because of constant nausea, and exhausted from the battles going on my brain; I refused to give up, but could I realistically continue suffering from such phobias, with my nerves stretched like piano-wire, and manage such a demanding career?

In November of 1978, I flew to Amsterdam for my debut with the Concertgebouw Orchestra and the Soviet conductor Kyril Kondrashin. Kondrashin was a grim, taciturn man with a morose expression who was constantly followed by nasty little officials from the Soviet Embassy. One of them caught me backstage after the rehearsal and started to question me about Kondrashin: Did he have dinner with me the night before? Did I speak Russian with him? Did I have family still in Poland? Normally I am a most passive creature, but, in this case, I was furious and bluntly told the man to go to hell.

We played the Liszt E flat concerto, and I got no sense as to whether or not Kondrashin enjoyed working with me. I spent the days surviving panic episodes, terrible sweats, chest pains and black thoughts, but I did find some quiet pleasure when I visited the Rijksmuseum and also when I went to an Indonesian restaurant and ate Rijstafel: all those marvellous and fascinating culinary delicacies.

The first concert was in Nijmegen, and for the two-hour drive Kondrashin was silent, staring broodily out of the window. The next day the skies were gloomy and damp heavy snow covered the ground. But my concerts were a success, and the review couldn't have been better if I had written it myself. It even congratulated Rubinstein on having personally promoted me.

And yet there were moments when I felt I would crack with tension and fatigue; as well as a horrid, scary feeling of simply not being able to relax, I desperately hated taking the pills, which made me feel nauseated and didn't seem to be helping much.

Arthur and Annabelle made the trip up to Amsterdam for the last performance. Backstage was buzzing with excitement at their imminent arrival. Even silent Kondrashin kept asking the orchestra manager where Arthur would be sitting. It turned out he was sitting dead centre in the second row, where I could see him the minute I stepped onto the stage and, as usual, derive a huge sense of partisanship and support from his presence. I wasn't the slightest bit nervous for the concerto and Arthur bounced back at intermission, gave me three big kisses and hugs and said a resounding: "Good girl!" With an extremely naughty smile, he added: "Why, it could have been me playing!" He said this loudly to give me pleasure but also, I'm sure, to impress Johanna Beek (our soon-to-retire manager who, incidentally, was so crazy about Arthur that she asked Annabelle if she could have one of his socks as a souvenir!) as well as the Concertgebouw people and Kondrashin. He then went off to hear the second half, whispering in my ear that, as it was Rimsky-Korsakov's "Sheherazade," he would have a nice nap to feel fit and refreshed for the reception and the dinner afterwards.

At the reception in the Amstel Hotel, Kondrashin sat and chatted with Arthur intensely in a corner. It turned out that he did in fact like my playing after all but had many other things on his mind that week. Gidon Kremer and his then-wife Elena were also at the reception, anxious to make the acquaintance of Arthur. I was tired and glad when just Madame Beek, Annabelle, Arthur, and I went out to dinner at the Excelsior afterwards and Arthur introduced me to the delights of smoked eel in a green sauce. It was an extremely pleasant evening and Arthur kept the conversation light and congenial. But as they saw me home, he suddenly turned to me in the taxi and said: "You know, last spring you really let me down; you should not have cancelled those concerts." Annabelle, sitting next to me, froze; she understood how damaging such a statement could be to someone in my neurotic state. Arthur really didn't completely understand; he still believed that on a certain level, my cancellations were the result of a silly whim or temperamental weakness. Since to him I appeared just the same as always, even playing better than usual and with no evident signs of illness, he thought I had been unprofessional. This little remark sent me into a tailspin which lasted quite a while but, as I had learned from bitter experience, all things do pass, and I soon understood his remark for what it was and moved on.

The next day on the plane going home, I read in the *Herald Tribune* that Kyril Kondrashin had defected from the Soviet Union and had gone into hiding somewhere in Holland with friends ... which certainly explained his strange behaviour. He had fallen in love with a Westerner; it was as simple as that!

The following year passed by in a grey haze. Through sheer willpower, I played a great many concerts in North America and even enjoyed visiting some of the new places. I also played in Poland and in South America. My London manager situation was finally resolved when young David Sigall, who had heard me play in Liverpool years before, enthusiastically took me on at Ingpen & Williams, where I remained for thirty-five years. It was typical of David that he judged me by my performance of the Chopin concerto in Liverpool and not by all the ugly, erroneous rumours that still floated around me. In New York I played my debut recital, garnering a grudgingly good review from the New York Times. I had invited Christopher and Elaine Plummer to attend, since Christopher had always telephoned Biddy after hearing performances of mine on the radio and was always so complimentary. They couldn't come to this particular recital, but subsequently invited me to their home in Connecticut for a long weekend. I was enchanted not only by their lovely property on the water, so close to New York and yet so free of the pollution, noise, and anxieties that plague city life, but also by their wonderful generosity and ability to entertain in the most agreeable and relaxed fashion. This was the first of many visits.

My London debut recital had been re-scheduled for February of 1980. It was nearly two years after my initial breakdown, but I was still suffering from its effects and was still on medication. Two days before the recital I performed a Mozart concerto with Andrew Davis and the London Philharmonic Orchestra at the Festival Hall. Something snapped in me at the reception following the concert and I felt as though I was falling once again into that nightmarish abyss. I stopped being able to eat. My dearest friends in London, Linn and Jack Rothstein, in whose home I always practised whenever I was there, tried in vain to get me to swallow some food. I was losing my grip on life, and, in desperation, I telephoned Dr. Bos, back in Montreal.

The morning of the recital was a nightmare. My cousin Dane came over to the hotel to try to force at least a cup of tea down my gullet. I made myself go for a walk around Mayfair and into Hyde Park, but I felt so awful that I finally telephoned David Sigall at home and told him that I thought I might not be able to play the recital.

"Just a second, I have some bread baking in the oven and have to take it out – hold on," he said in such a calm, matter-of-fact way that I started to believe that perhaps he could save the situation. He returned to the phone and quietly asked: "Can you get yourself to the hall?" I replied in the affirmative, albeit somewhat shakily. "Good ..." he said, " ... then I'll get you on stage."

Linn and Jack drove me to Queen Elizabeth Hall, chatting all the way, getting me to laugh and helping me to recover some of my poise. David met me at the backstage door and, chatting to me quietly, mostly about nonsensical things to keep my brain distracted, true to his word and with a final shove, he got me out on stage. Once there I was all right and played a decent recital, which was clean and musical but probably restrained and a bit pale. After it was over, I telephoned home to put my family out of their misery of anxiety.

Dr. Bos, unbeknownst to me, had sat by his telephone the entire morning without moving, waiting for Biddy's call. He was apparently ecstatic at the news that I had played. So much for professional detachment!

Inevitably, life started to improve for me. The London experience had perhaps been the most traumatic yet, but I had survived it and bit by bit this knowledge comforted and reassured me. In the summer, I started to cut down on the medication. This process was excruciating and often I felt my brain was about to explode with pain, to the point where I would find myself banging my head against the wall.

From this time stems my disgust toward recreational drug use by educated people. I had begun to consider the drugs that I was injecting into my body as pernicious poisons and viewed them with hatred. To this day I debate with myself over the need to take even a minor headache tablet, and it's hard for me to comprehend those who actually enjoy drugs. I wish I hadn't had to take so many pills for all of that time, but would never have been able to return so quickly to the stage had I not. The lessons I learned from these years of torment were invaluable. I'm convinced that through this experience and the self-knowledge I gained from it of my limitations, both mental and physical, I have been spared later episodes of uncontrollable depression and torment.

Shortly after, Arthur was diagnosed with prostate cancer and the operation he had at the New York University Hospital left him weakened and in great pain. During his recovery period I would visit him in his suite at the Waldorf Towers and play for him, at first just Chopin nocturnes and then, as he became stronger, more varied and demanding repertoire, including the Chopin 3rd Ballade, which always made him think of an Aubrey Beardsley drawing he particularly enjoyed, depicting a woman on a horse! He often used mental pictures to assist in the understanding and interpreting of works, mostly, but not always, dealing with flirtation and courtship. He told me hilarious and imaginative stories about the different little pieces in "Carnaval" of Schumann, not to mention Schumann's "Fantasy," Ravel's "Valses Nobles et Sentimentales" and even Mozart and Beethoven concerti and sonatas. One of the things that set him apart from most pianists was this extraordinary imagination and the unique range of emotions, thoughts, dynamics, and colours which he could present to the public with such intensity and ease. And he was fearless – willing to take all sorts of risks to prove his points and encouraging me to do the same. It was the degree of his inner convictions that sealed his success. He was also living proof of my conviction that, although artists should be treated with understanding and tenderness due to the obvious stress in their lives, they should in return behave with grace and consideration. Tantrums and unreasonable displays of temperament played no part in his life on tour, and I have tried to follow his shining example.

Although not a natural piano teacher, he nevertheless taught me things of immeasurable value. Because of him, I understood the importance of communication, consequently beginning my lifelong study of projecting beautiful sounds from the instrument, and in so doing, attempting the near impossible: sharing the genius and innermost soul of the composer with the public. Arthur had perhaps the greatest talent of the twentieth century for this art of communicating from the stage. He also understood the structure of every piece he performed – the high points, the low points, the exciting points and the restful ones – and could tie all the elements together and make them sound completely and organically sane. There was tremendous wisdom and logic to his playing; his audiences were never worried or uneasy, for even when he missed passages (usually due to lack of practice) they still knew he was in total command of the situation, not only in the broader sense, but also in every last tiny detail. His sense of rhythm and pulse were, of course, "non-pareil" and he told me that, as Picasso had once told him he painted from his stomach, he, Arthur, felt the rhythm of a piece in his stomach. No one had a more natural delivery of the disparate rhythms found in mazurkas, polonaises, tangos, waltzes ...

His Chopin was always what touched me most – perhaps because Chopin is the composer I love best. Somehow Arthur impregnated every note with such meaning, beauty and vibrant lyricism and yet, miraculously, managed to keep the long lines and phrases, as if singing them all in one breath.

And it was under Arthur's influence that I began to develop my own theories on the choice of tempi. It eventually became clear to me that the tempo of a piece was actually the last decision I should make. Unless one is performing with an inflexible machine, the metronome markings sometimes given by composers are merely helpful hints and general guidelines. Richard Wagner, for instance, once tried to have a conductor adhere to his metronome markings and was absolutely appalled at the results! It would be ridiculous (and counterproductive) to always play a work at the exact same tempo. There are so many variables that can affect the speed one finally chooses – the size and acoustics of the hall, the mood of the audience, the touch of the piano, the weather, the time of day, even current world events. For me, the correct tempo of a piece is the one that feels perfect at that particular moment, and which allows me to express everything I feel I can and should express – again, at that particular moment – and my lifelong experience should keep me choosing something outrageous. Metaphorically speaking, a tempo is like an overcoat which is donned after one has washed and done one's hair, put on make-up and then chosen one's concert apparel. The overcoat must not only fit, but also match the rest of the outfit and suit the weather, the occasion and one's mood.

A few weeks after his operation, Arthur – now well into his nineties – was feeling better. His spirits were high, and although he was worried that he might never walk again, he was rarely depressed. He also enjoyed recounting to me the story of his recent battle with Yehudi Menuhin that had been publicly waged in the London Times. It was something to do with a conflict at the time between UNICEF and Israel: Arthur was fiercely pro-Israel and Menuhin was attempting to be a peacemaker. Apparently, the language became quite strong between them and then suddenly, in the middle of all the written rhetoric, Annabelle and Arthur had run into Menuhin in the middle of Madrid airport. Typically, gentle Menuhin greeted Arthur warmly, giving him a hug. When Arthur told this story, exasperated by all this goodness and turn-the-other-cheek-ness, he said to me: "Look at those names: Yehudi, Hephzibah, Yaltah – such good Jewish names – so why the hell is he so damned Christian?" Then he threw his head back and roared with laughter.

In the spring of 1982, during a visit to my cousins Christopher and Elaine, I fell in love with a little house down the road from them in Connecticut and decided to buy it. I wrote to Arthur who, ever protective, called his lawyers and asked them about the area and the price I was paying to see that I wasn't being bamboozled.

By now I had crawled out from the noxious dark tunnel I had been languishing in for nearly three years and had finally shed all the horrors of depression, including all the medications. I had discovered that there was nothing I would rather do than play the piano, make music, and pursue my career, so I threw myself into this life with renewed passion and vigour. Just before closing on the sale of my house, I embarked on a series of recitals in Europe, starting with a visit to London, where I was to play for Sir Georg Solti.

The concert in Lucerne where Solti had conducted so magnificently four years previously had added fresh fuel to the fires of my admiration for him and my early hopes of one day finally working with him. To this end, I'd had first to play a successful London debut recital, then a series of recitals in Chicago's Orchestra Hall (where Solti was music director), garnering excellent reviews. With these successes in my "resumé", somehow it was finally arranged that I would have a 15-minute audition with Solti at his London home.

For this meeting with Solti, I was a different person from the poor wretch who had shaken his hand in Lucerne: I was well and happy, I was on the verge of leaving Manhattan to move into my lovely Connecticut house, and my career seemed solid and on an upward swing. Consequently, I was not particularly nervous when I rang the doorbell of his home in the St. John's Wood district of London; rather, I was excited and even a little breathless with anticipation. The door was opened by Solti's personal assistant, Charles Kay. Tall, soft-spoken, and immensely polite, he whisked me down to the basement studio and told me that I could practise while I waited. There was a hand-written letter from Thomas Mann framed on the wall by the piano, several busts and framed photos of Solti (including one of himself being greeted by Pope John Paul II), a large photo of Covent Garden, a bust of Wagner, and a score of Prokofiev's 3rd piano concerto on his gigantic desk, which faced the glass doors leading out to the garden.

Charles Kay had told me to practise. Of course, I was feeling far too distracted and those old sensations of being an annoyance that I had had as a child, practising in hotel restaurants, returned with a vengeance. Still, I started to play through Liszt's "Chasse Neige," trying to imbue it with tons of fire and virtuosity just in case "he" was listening from somewhere nearby, but also only at half volume just in case "he" didn't want to be listening from somewhere nearby. Then, when I had started on Beethoven Opus 111, I heard a noise behind me; Solti came through the glass doors from the garden, dressed in an old, brown-checked shirt and some disreputable old brown corduroy trousers, a little hunched over from the terrible neck problems he'd suffered from over the years, but looking extremely powerful. In his raspy, hoarse voice with the signature Hungarian accent, he proceeded to tell me that he'd heard me practising and had come down to shut the door. After this he barked out a "How do you do?" and told me that I was to go on practising. He then left and I watched him join Lady Solti on the terrace. He sat down and started to read the newspaper while drinking a cup of tea. It was a lovely English spring day and he seemed to be enjoying it so much that I started again to feel guilty for disturbing his quiet afternoon at home. The longer I waited the more nervous I became, my hands getting colder and colder and soon shaking like leaves in the wind. To calm myself, I started to quietly play Chopin Mazurkas, still terrified I was displeasing Solti. Finally, about an hour after I had arrived, he returned, and the first words he blurted out were: "You are Polish!" I then had to explain my Polish background, my Canadian mother, and my home in the United States. He seemed pleased that I lived in New York, obviously a happy place for him, as it was the scene of some of his greatest concerts and resulting ovations. He abruptly (everything he did was rather abrupt – in my admiring eyes his strange rough manners and lack of gentility were all part of the savage charm and, in all fairness, I never felt that he was being rude or unkind – in fact, quite apart from my admiration, I liked him instantly and for lack of a better word, I found him to be very "straight" with me; I instinctively trusted him, something I was not wont to do under normal circumstances) turned his back on me, walked to the opposite end of the room, collapsed into an old armchair, closed his eyes and wearily asked what I was going to play. I replied that I had prepared the Opus 111 of Beethoven, "Chasse Neige" of Liszt and the first Ballade of Chopin.

"Oh! What a lot!" he exclaimed in horror, and my heart sank. Then he gestured for me to begin.

I played the first movement of the Beethoven with as much energy and intensity and rhythmic control as I could muster, although I'm sure I must have rushed in the excitement of the moment. There was a long silence at the end, and I didn't dare start the second movement unless invited to do so.

Suddenly he hurled out a question: "Where did you study?" I explained about Gorodnitzki and Juilliard, and my more recent close association with Rubinstein. At that his face positively lit up. "I knew it!" he said, "I could hear the influence – what a wonderful man – what vitality! No one like him – what an artist!" The phrases were uttered in staccato bursts like machine-gun fire.

Mention of Arthur made the audition less terrifying, and I settled back and began to enjoy our conversation. We were still chatting companionably when Charles Kay appeared and politely inquired if the telephone man could come in to repair the buzzer on the phone.

"Yes, yes, by all means – this noise gives me heart-attacks every time the phone rings!"

So, in came a friendly repairman with a strong Cockney accent, wearing blue overalls and a large belt from which hung all of his clanging tools. As he tinkered with the phone the three of us continued our conversation and Solti asked when I had played in Chicago. Charles Kay reminded him of the details. Of course, I could have mentioned our meeting in Lucerne years before, but I was far too shy. The telephone repair man hadn't a clue who Solti was and was entertaining with his remarks, telling me I should keep on practising so that one day I could be part of an act at the "Olympia." He also asked if this gentleman was any good at the piano, or did he just sit and allow others to do all the work? After he and Charles Kay finally left, Solti sat on the sofa next to the piano and asked me to play the Liszt for him. Since I was by now relaxed and confident, and since this was a piece I had played for many years, it went quite well.

"Obviously you are very talented," he said when I finished. "What do you want me to do for you?" I was, as my father would put it, completely "tongue-struck." But the question was rhetorical, because Solti continued talking, commenting that he was all booked up for the next year but the year after I would play with him in Chicago.

Fireworks and bells of rejoicing rang and flashed across my brain. He asked what my concerto repertoire was and what I would like to play with him. Overcome by this wonderful turn of events, I managed with difficulty to form the words "Beethoven four."

"Oh!" he said, "I would have thought the 'Emperor' because your playing is so big and grand." But I stuck determinedly to Beethoven four because I knew how much better it suited me.

I then brought up the two Liszt concertos and, because I had seen it on his desk, the Prokofiev 3rd. At that he jumped up, knocking a cushion onto the floor, and nearly knocking over a lamp. "Mein Gott!" he said "If only I had known a few days earlier. We had a cancellation and we were looking frantically for a replacement – so we could have played together right away in two weeks!"

He asked me about my career and listened intently as I explained the important role that Rubinstein had played while he was still performing, but how things had slowed down when, in 1976, Arthur had retired, but now I was doing well again. Looking me in the eye he said he wanted to do whatever he could to help, so we decided on Beethoven or Liszt and suddenly, as abruptly as it had started, the audition ended. He was about to leave when, somehow, I mustered the courage to thank him and explain how much that "Rheingold" and all the other Chicago Symphony concerts at Carnegie Hall had meant to me as I had sat there year after year in the fourth row.

He smiled quite marvellously but averted his eyes quickly, slightly embarrassed, and as he reached over to collect my jacket and bag for me, he burst out with: "Well," (pronounced "vell") "that was quite close, but now we are closer, and we will be much closer when we will do concertos. Good-bye." And he left.

Charles Kay ushered me out and then I was walking on air, overwhelmed by the whole experience. I felt like screaming with happiness as I skipped along the street in the gorgeous sunny afternoon with no idea where I was, looking for a telephone booth to phone David Sigall. I recounted the whole story to him in every detail, becoming even more thrilled when David, who also represented Solti and knew him well, told me that Solti always kept his word and that if he said he would work with me he absolutely would. I loved David dearly at that moment – why, I loved anyone who passed me on the street – I loved the whole world, and I remember saying to him that I was completely lost somewhere in London, but I couldn't care less, and heard him chuckle at the other end of the line.

Two days later I played a recital at London's Queen Elizabeth Hall. This recital was a far cry from the pale, grey affair of two years before when I had been feeling so ill. It was a strong program of Bach, Debussy, Chopin, and the Prokofiev 6th Sonata that I had learned especially for Arthur, who had given me the score and who particularly loved the slow movement. The day of the recital was beautiful and sunny, and many of my cousins and friends were there (including Dana, all the way from Paris). The Canadian High Commissioner at that time, Jean Casselman Wadds, was a grand lady who made one proud to be a Canadian. She threw me a huge party and allowed me to invite everyone, including my adorable little cousins, Jemma and Milo Clouston.

The next morning, I had to get up at the crack of dawn to catch an early flight to Geneva. I was desperate to see if my recital had been reviewed but arrived at Heathrow too late to buy a newspaper. While in the air, I struggled to read over the shoulders of the businessmen surrounding me but to no avail. Ignoring the magnificent view of the snow-covered Alps surrounding the city and waiting until the other passengers had left, I was finally able to pick up discarded newspapers and was delighted to find an excellent review in the *Times* by Hilary Finch and another equally good review in the *Daily Telegraph* by Bryce Morrison.

I had arrived at my hotel in Geneva earlier than planned, so I took myself off for a walk and for a raid on the local patisserie – after all, it was Switzerland, and I do love sweets. So, I bought myself three glorious pastries: a Montblanc, which is a heavenly concoction of meringue, cream and chestnut purée, a gooey chocolate mousse-like creation, and a lovely strawberry tart. Thus fortified, I was ready for anything. Annabelle met me at the door of the apartment. We hadn't seen each other in over a year, and she looked wonderful. But, although I had prepared myself to be shocked, it still was an emotional jolt to see Arthur. He was extremely thin, his skin white and parchment-like, and he was lying in a chaise longue wrapped in blankets. Unusually for him, he seemed hardly to respond when I gently kissed him on the cheek. However, once we started talking, I realised he was the same old Arthur; the familiar charm and wit and quick mind inside a body that was failing him. I told him right away about my successful audition with Solti and, without batting an eyelid, he turned to Annabelle and asked: "Solti? Solti? Do we know a conductor called Solti? Wasn't he the one we once heard conduct the Hungarian national anthem?"

I then told him about my recital, and Annabelle read him my reviews. We had so much to tell each other and so much gossip to catch up on. He told me how he had become friends with Georges Simenon (the novelist of "Maigret" fame); he had also seen quite a lot of Martha Argerich (who lived in Geneva), and François Duchable had made a special trip from Paris to visit him. At lunch I was curious to see how his appetite was, as he appeared quite emaciated. But he drank all his soup, which Annabelle fed him, ate a little "steak-au-poivre" and all his pommes-frites and poire Belle Hélène. Because I was there, Annabelle took the opportunity to run out to do some errands. I gave Arthur his coffee, lit his cigar for him (still the great, huge, stinking "Monte Christos No. 3") and fed him some halvah which a devoted Turkish fan sent him, fresh, every week. Then the phone rang, and it was David Sigall, looking for me. Yefim Bronfman had cancelled in Edinburgh, and could I replace him the following evening? I was a little stunned and asked if I could consult Arthur first. Arthur immediately said, with some of the old fire in his eyes, that as a true professional I should do it, and he added that Edinburgh had always been an important city in the music world and reminded me of his first performance there: the Tchaikovsky concerto with his late father-in-law Emil Mlnarski conducting. So I accepted the engagement.

Annabelle returned soon after – luckily, as Arthur was getting impatient and kept asking, with a little of the fretfulness of a long-term invalid, if she was back yet- and I played for the two of them as they sat side by side content and happy with each other. First, the second partita of Bach, then the 6th sonata of Prokofiev, which he loved and from which he made me repeat many of his favourite passages three or four times, "Images" Book 2 of Debussy (which, he cheerfully informed me at the end, had given him a wonderful opportunity for a nice nap), and finally Chopin's 1st Ballade, which he criticized heartily, giving me a fantastic long lesson, especially on the first theme: "keep it as simple as possible; don't break it up rhythmically and don't use big unnecessary rubatos and accents." He felt my tempo changes were a bit extreme and he thought I was too fussy in the coda.

"And don't be a nincompoop and miss the boat at the end by taking too long over the quiet chords between the scales," he admonished with mock severity. Overall, though, it seemed I had done well because he was clearly very pleased, saying I had developed musically over the last two years and grown immeasurably in authority at the keyboard. His praise filled me with happiness. But he then wanted me to play for him the Chopin F sharp-minor Polonaise that had also been on my London program. I refused, and he laughed because we both remembered how hard he had been on me when I was learning the A flat-Polonaise so many years before. Presently, Annabelle brought us more food – home-made waffles with the maple syrup I supplied on a regular basis, because he loved it so much. We watched a few old videos of himself out in California rehearsing with Heifetz and Piatigorsky sometime in the '40s. I was interested to note that he hated the way he played: "I was young once, too, and rushed just like you do!" I pointed out that he must have been at least 60 years old in the film and he laughed until the tears rolled down his cheeks. He later surprised me by saying he hoped I would find a nice husband one day. Ever since I had met him, he had urged me forcefully to stay single, encouraging me to play the field, as he felt a husband would interfere with my music and career. But during this last wonderful visit, it was as if he suddenly saw Janina, the person, exactly for who I was, not just the musician he already knew intimately. He prophetically stated that my career would always be a struggle and that this was perfectly alright, as in the end I'd be the stronger for it. He had no doubts of my eventual success but, with regards to a husband, he wasn't sure he trusted me to find a good one by myself.

"Tell you what," he said, his eyes twinkling mischievously, "I'll find one for you, put him in a large box, bring it to the post-office and have them send it to you. Your Uncle Arthur will take care of you!" And he turned to his Annabelle, who agreed and said that she would help him carry the box.

The conversation continued in a lively fashion; we chatted about all the music that he had recently listened to, with Annabelle explaining how his new earphones allowed him to hear beautifully. And then he turned to Annabelle and with a big smile said: "It's good to have our Nina back with us again!" Presently he decided that he wanted to give me a present and, as his new earphones were on his mind, he dispatched Gregorio (the chauffeur) to go and buy me a new Sony Walkman. And then more food appeared; for supper we had mounds of delicious beluga caviar, then soup, Tripes à la Polonaise, Pommes dauphinoise, and apple tart. By then I had been there over ten hours and Arthur was becoming tired. Melancholy invaded his mood and he kept repeating: "I would have been a real egoist if I had stopped you from going to Edinburgh, but I wish we could have had tomorrow together." It was very emotional and very sad. I promised to come back and visit him as soon as I could and, standing at the front door, I felt a pang of tremendous sorrow when I looked back and saw the frail old man, so great-hearted, with such a powerful spirit, lying in his special chair with tears rolling down his cheeks. I knew that I would never see him again. My heart was heavy, and it was with a sense of lassitude and emptiness that I boarded the plane for London.

A few months later I was up at my parents' home in Canada for the Christmas holidays watching the evening news on the television. A photo of Arthur appeared on the screen and then the newscaster announced that Arthur had died peacefully in his home in Geneva. Annabelle telephoned me the following morning; they had been listening to Rossini's *Barber of Seville* the day before he died.

CHAPTER 9

Concerto in the Italian style ("Concerto nach italiänischen Gusto") by J.S. Bach

"What a glamourous life you must lead!"

I've heard this remark often during the course of my career. It can be, I won't deny it, but only for a small fraction of the time. Mostly it consists of waiting; in smelly airports or draughty train stations, in hotel rooms of varying levels of comfort and cleanliness during the afternoon before concerts, backstage in often primitive dressing rooms under stress, and so on. Laundry is often a problem, dealing with new people in different languages can be difficult, poor or non-existent practising conditions are prevalent, and there is always a battle raging against sheer exhaustion. To survive is a question of a tolerant attitude, which I adopted early on: accept the inconveniences as inevitable, avoid getting upset over small details, and try to concentrate just on the performance. A good book is a great help. There are limits, of course, to one's endurance, particularly if one can't find any humour in the awkward situations. No such problem in Italy.

As the sleek, modern train glided silently into Bologna on a lovely April day in the late eighties, I caught my first glimpse of Michele Cerone as he stood anxiously twitching on the station platform. This was the man who was to be my guide and constant companion for the next ten days, overseeing my first recital tour of Italy. For the past 15 minutes I had been wrestling with my luggage, positioning myself in the corridor for a quick exit. Nervous that I might be getting off at the wrong station, I strained to hear the announcement over the loudspeaker – a futile endeavour considering the global conspiracy of railway people to confuse passengers with unintelligible speech. I was already suffering from all the normal feelings that accompany a first concert tour in a country I barely knew: excited anticipation, a myriad of expectations, and a hefty dose of *angst*. My career was still in its infancy, and it was important for me to make a good impression wherever I went (this being the number one axiom of every young struggling concert pianist, as being invited back is the key to success).

Overburdened with luggage – packing light is not my forte – I more or less tumbled onto the platform, happy to have arrived safely at the right station, body intact and nerves frayed, but under control.

Michele Cerone was looking past me very worried. Aware that I don't fit some peoples' image of a concert pianist, I let him gaze up and down the platform until reluctantly he decided that perhaps the artist was me or, preferably, that I was some kind of messenger from the real thing.

"Signora Fialkowska?" he inquired in an anguished whisper. It was then that I noticed the worry lines deeply etched on his forehead, the rivulets of sweat pouring down his temples and the big wet marks seeping through under the arms and down the back of his crumpled brown jacket.

"Yes, that's me, how do you do?"

"Come Signora, there are problems – *andiamo subito!*"

He took my bags from me, staggering a bit under the weight, and silently we headed for the parking lot. I was bursting with questions but decided that forbearance would be advisable, at least for the moment, as I didn't want to appear too demanding right off the bat.

His car was a tiny blue Fiat Panda that had seen better days and at this point was chock-full of baby paraphernalia. I wedged myself in between a box of disposable diapers, a large purple elephant and various bits of Mr. Potato-head.

Michele was not a good driver; he drove fast with complete *insouciance*, and the noise he made changing gears was deafening. He also preferred to ignore the road completely while conversing with me and would turn his whole body around so he could fully appreciate my facial reactions.

"We are having a 'grande' convention in Bologna this week for the antique booksellers – all the hotels are full – I could not find you a room."

"Oh really?" I replied, white-knuckled, clutching the purple elephant as my driver nonchalantly drove over the corner of the sidewalk.

"*Si*, no place at all." He changed gears again and the car shrieked. I wistfully thought of automatic transmission. "Bologna is a very beautiful city; you must visit her tomorrow – she is "*la dotta*" – *molta molta bella!*"

Not that I could see anything of this; it seemed we were headed away from the town centre and all I could see were numerous beautiful McDonalds, Pizza Huts, Novotels, Ikeas and gas stations – my first impression of the ancient city spiralling rapidly down a farcical drain.

"Si – and we have much troubled times with the money ..."

Ah! Here it comes, I thought with resignation.

" ... to find for the recital to sponsor – but is okay – I have found a donor among the members of our great Italian aristocracy. La Principessa –" (something or other – the name was long and unretainable) "– has very graciously helped me ..." here he crossed himself, "and is okay now."

There was a sudden wild honking of horns as he had casually driven the wrong way up a one-way street. I closed my eyes and prayed. After more noisy gear-changing, we were breezing along a main highway heading for Rome. Hadn't I just come from Rome?

He continued talking about money problems, scheduling problems, audience problems, program problems and in the middle of all this he proudly told me that he was an atheist and a communist, which is when I noticed the Soviet flag swinging wildly around the neck of the little statue of the Virgin Mary on his dashboard. I suddenly felt as though I had been parachuted into the middle of a very bad American film about Italy, filled with grotesquely exaggerated stereotypes. However, this was very much real life, and after about 20 minutes we drew up with a great flourish and screeching of brakes to a rather modern building.

"Here is where you stay!" Only then did I notice the sign "Harry Hopman's Tennis Camp."

Of course, I thought to myself, how silly of me – so natural to stay in an Australian tennis camp for my first recital in Italy. My room was spartan but, happily, the shower worked well and the food was excellent. I had dinner with an African American tennis pro from New Jersey. It wasn't how I normally prepared myself psychologically for a performance, but why not? Cheerfully I changed into my evening clothes and was driven to the concert venue.

Michele was perspiring again and the worry lines in his brow had deepened. The hall was a depressing dark brown without character, and the piano was a rather sad, neglected Grotian Steinweg – a venerable instrument dating back to the nineteenth century, and the predecessor of the modern Steinway, my instrument of choice. Well maintained, it could have produced a lovely sound and the performance could have at least been interesting, but, as often the case on tour, the local technician simply wasn't qualified to take care of such an antique treasure. Concert grands, old and new, are like thoroughbreds; they need constant care and understanding. This piano had had seemingly neither, so the recital became a challenging adventure as I set out to resurrect the remnants of the old piano's soul. I started the recital with a Bach-Liszt transcription whose sole purpose, it transpired, was to act as background music for people arriving, shaking out their umbrellas and greeting one another enthusiastically. They settled down for the Mozart sonata but were clearly uninterested and I could hear a lot of sighing and rustling. Things picked up in the second half, partly because I mentally kicked myself and raised my energy level up a notch, and partly because the repertoire of Fauré, Scriabin, Chopin, and Tausig was more to their liking. By the end, I was playing encore after encore, and everyone seemed wildly enthusiastic.

After "Wilde Jagd" of Liszt, I decided enough was enough and waved good-bye. This was taken as a signal for the entire audience to come backstage. One lady, who spoke French, became the spokesperson and interpreter, and once the autograph signing was over and the endless, hearty, but quite painful handshakes were done, the questions began.

"How old are you?"

"Ah! She seems much younger."

"Where are you from?"

"Ah, Canada." (Wise nodding of heads and a lot of personal information revealed about various relatives who lived in Mississauga or Calgary, or "perhaps you know my cousin Giancarlo, who lives in Winnipeg?")

Then came the two inevitable questions that were to dog my days throughout the trip: "Do you have any bambini?" and "Are you married?" When she had translated my negative replies to her rapt audience, there were great sighs and shaking of heads, even the moistening of a few eyes. "La povera," was heard spoken softly, and I was kissed by one and all with great sympathy, the successful performance all but forgotten, completely overshadowed by the tragedy of my lonely, single predicament. Sadly, they bade me farewell and wished me luck, although clearly, at my age (I was thirty-four at the time), they didn't hold out much hope for any future happiness.

Michele appeared impatiently saying "*Andiamo subito*," which I soon learned only meant that we would be leaving after another ten minutes (minimum) of chatting and farewells. But, finally, he collected my things from backstage and took me, with a bunch of his more colourful friends, to a charming pizzeria. The restaurant owner, on being told who I was, refused point blank to charge us for the meal – delicious tagliatelle with a delicate wild mushroom sauce, a mouth-watering Trotta a la griglia and a macedonia, the fresh fruit liberally doused in Amaretto tasting of golden sunshine and the warmth of a spring day, all accompanied by the house wine flowing from seemingly bottomless carafes.

Finally, dropping with fatigue and three or four more "*Andiamo subitos*" later, Michele drove me back to the Tennis Camp. For a change, he seemed happy and, as we said "Good night," he suddenly clutched my hand and thanked me for being so "*simpatico*." Frankly, although I had wanted to be sympathetic, he had really never given me the chance to get a word in edgewise, so I guess he was thanking me for listening.

I slept well in my tennis camp and awoke the next morning refreshed and ready for anything. Everything looked bright, sparkling, and clean after the previous night's downpour, including Signor Cerone, who turned up resplendent in his weekend garb – a rather garish Hawaiian shirt and khaki shorts. He had also brought along his little daughter Camilla for me to admire. Despite the fact that we had a long drive ahead of us and a recital was to be played that evening, there was a decided lack of interest in actually leaving. In fact, Michele suddenly thought, "What a good idea it would be if we all had another breakfast."

So we piled into the Panda, along with a rather beautiful young girl named Daniela, whose relationship to all of us remained somewhat obscure, and off we drove to the Cerone apartment. I was hoping that on the way I would get to see some of the old City, but instead we drove through endless kilometres of modern suburbs.

In their tiny apartment, smelling of olive oil, garlic, cheap cigarettes and ripe tomatoes, I was welcomed enthusiastically by Michele's wife Maria, who rushed out to the market to get more food. An aunt dropped by, and already present was a grandfather with the most amazing gold teeth. Camilla was certainly cute, but definitely a Monster Child in the making, with the adult population of her adoring circle eager to respond to her every whim. Luckily, since she always got everything she wanted, she tended to be quite delightful.

Breakfast expanded into lunch. After a couple of hours or so, I had given up ostentatiously looking at my watch, exercising my fingers in the air and mentioning how I liked to try out pianos before recitals, when suddenly Michele jumped up, cried *"Andiamo subito"* and in a frenzied panic (my mouth was still half full of bruschetta) rushed me reproachfully down to the car.

"Signora, you have a long drive, so this is not the time to make social talks with people – is very late, you must go – perhaps when you come back you could stay longer."

I tried to protest that it was I who had wanted to leave hours earlier, but he completely overrode anything I said and then, without warning, he left, and I was alone in the minuscule car with Daniela. This is when it dawned on me that Michele was not coming with us but that Daniela, who I now realised was his assistant, was to drive me and oversee the smooth operation of the tour. This was an interesting turn of events, but potentially not a bad one, as the chaos Michele carried around with him was unnerving.

Daniela was quite beautiful, with a perfect figure, dark brown hair, wonderfully tanned skin, and enormous, vulnerable, blue eyes with lashes one could weep for. She spoke a little English and with my broken Italian I was sure we would get along fine. The trouble started about half a mile from the Cerone flat: Daniela did not know where to go. Fair enough, I suppose, although perhaps she might have thought of asking for directions before leaving. I pulled out the map and started plotting our course. Daniela started to cry – first just a few tears and then a veritable deluge. "Now what?" I thought, endeavouring to remain calm and patient. I gently patted her on the shoulder and told her that everything would be fine.

"My boyfriend in Milan, he did not want me to go on this trip!" – or at least that is what I gathered between sobs – "And my papa was angry as well – Signor Cerone should not have made me do this – it is wrong."

"Daniela," I tried to reason with her, "this is just a short trip and a few recitals – nothing terrible."

But clearly this was the wrong thing to say as it opened another floodgate of tears. "I've never been away from home before," she wailed.

"Er, perhaps we should go back to Signor Cerone's, and maybe I could take the train?"

"No, it is not possible."

"Um, would you like me to drive?"

"*O si*, this would be *perfetto, grazie!*"

So we exchanged seats and, after checking the map, headed north. Now more cheerful, she spent the rest of the journey talking to me about her Carlo, who repaired roofs but wanted to be a professional soccer player. I also heard about her family in excruciating detail, and as it was an extended one, the monologue filled the hours nicely – especially as I was only half listening, spending most of the time intent on looking for road signs since Daniela had no idea how to read a map. It was hard to enjoy the lovely scenery, but I did manage to take note of the endless orchards of the Po valley still in bloom and the sudden breath-taking moment when the Alps appeared on the horizon.

We arrived at our destination, surprisingly with enough time to eat, shower and try out the instrument. A lovely 14th-century fishing village, Lazise, on the Lago di Garda, had once been an important port of the Venetian Empire. Now it was a holiday town of picture postcard perfection; very quiet, with only the sounds of the lake water lapping on the beach and children's voices playing soccer in the distance.

Daniela decided at this moment to have another panic attack, as she had never stayed in a hotel alone before. I checked us in, carried her suitcase up to her room and arranged for a small meal to be served early in the hotel's restaurant.

The local organizers of the recital turned up, and we all had spaghetti vongole together. One of the organizers was the brother of the owner/chef of the hotel, who also joined us. It turned into quite a party, and I felt like the proverbial wet blanket, disappointing everyone when I said I couldn't eat much as I had to play the recital, and could I please go and try out the piano?

Daniela, having had a little wine, which seemed to give her courage, actually volunteered to go with me and we walked over to the hall, which was situated within the walls of an atmospheric monastery from the Middle Ages. The piano, a newish Yamaha, was in good shape. Happily, I warmed up and corrected some of the passages that had gone awry the night before. The sun was setting over the lake and the view through the large windows was distractingly exquisite.

As it was getting late, I just had time to rush back to the hotel and change into my evening clothes. Then, slightly flushed and out of breath (because it was already close to 9 o'clock), I ran back in my full evening regalia to the "hall," carrying my silver shoes. The place was empty. For a moment I thought perhaps my watch was fast, but Daniela checked hers as well. It was now five past nine. The piano was there, well tuned, the chairs were placed nicely for the public, but there was not a soul to be seen.

Daniela, by now a relative tower of strength, said she would find the organizers to see what had happened. She was gone a few minutes, so I got up from where I had been sitting backstage and, for lack of anything better to do, went outside to look at the lake and the mountains in the twilight. For a while I was completely caught up in the magic of the place; my body trembled in the chill of the evening, and I experienced that sweet, slightly melancholic feeling one can encounter when confronted with almost mystical beauty, but without anyone to share the strange, gloriously disturbing feeling of enchantment.

The spell was gradually broken by the sound of raised voices, and I walked around to the front entrance, where I found Daniela talking to the organizers. There was a huge amount of gesticulating and shoulder-shrugging going on and eventually I was made to understand that, by some unbelievable oversight, they had forgotten to advertise the recital and that furthermore not a single ticket had been sold. I had to bite the inside of my cheek so as not to burst out laughing as they were all being so incredibly dramatic! As the conversation continued, accusations and recriminations were now surfacing as well as guilt and desperation. I started to change my shoes for the walk back to the hotel.

"Grüss Gott," someone said, and I turned around to see eight middle-aged German hikers trudging along, flushed and beaming after a long day's excursion in the mountains.

With a flash of divine inspiration, I asked them in my halting German: "Would you like to hear a concert?"

"O ja, wunderbar!" and they trooped into the hall, set down their packs, loosened the laces of their boots and removed their hats.

They got a really good performance that night – I was thoroughly enjoying myself, as it had been such a riotous day, with so many colours and facets to it, like a glorious Carnival. The festive, "anything goes" atmosphere infected my playing.

Daniela was suddenly grown-up and had become a figure of authority looking after me well, seeing that I had drinks and sweets backstage and basically acting as my "duenna" and personal manager. I think she had gained in confidence not only from seeing the mess the locals had made of the evening, but also from the deferential and apologetic manner in which they behaved towards her, the manager from the Big City.

I was beginning to find out that, more often than not, every crisis in Italy somehow miraculously resolves itself. In this case the evening had turned out happy for me, for Daniela (with her newfound authority and aplomb) and, I think, for the German hikers. Of course, someone had lost a lot of money, but luckily I hadn't, and somehow we all (performer, presenter and public) ended up together in the local restaurant eating pizza and gelati until well past midnight, singing German and Italian songs. At least *they* did: I just smiled and thought how lucky I was to be there amongst these people who were so full of joie de vivre and so universally kind to me. I still felt as though I was a character in a ghastly B-movie about Italy, but I had learned to settle back and just enjoy the show.

The next few days of the tour passed by in quasi relative calm. There were no major disasters and chaos was held at bay –

that is, until the last day, when Michele was to rejoin our little party in Lazise and Daniela was to return home.

Daniela and I were now fast friends. She was revelling in her unaccustomed role and as a result of this newfound feeling of independence, I gathered she now had a worried, thoroughly insecure boyfriend in Milano.

We got up early and had a gorgeous walk along the shoreline. Our friends at the hotel kept telling us how much nicer it would be the following week when all the tourists arrived (their idea of heaven being a big, noisy happy crowd). But for me, the morning stillness, with a thin mist gathered around the edges of the lake, mirror-smooth and reflecting the silent ring of the mountains, the distant song of a solitary cuckoo, and only an occasional intrusion into this idyllic scene when a Vespa would roar by at full throttle, usually a local boy as the rider, carrying a yard of fresh bread home from the local bakery, was as close to perfection as one could get. Sadly, the magic spell had to be broken, as Michele was due at the hotel by nine.

Five hours later we were still waiting in the courtyard on our little white, slightly rusty metal chairs. Daniela was doing her nails for the third or fourth time that day and I, having finished writing my postcards (and in the process using up the entire stock sold by the hotel), was half-heartedly reading *Mansfield Park* with one eye on the road leading into town from the south.

He arrived at three in a lather of perspiration, with a pronounced twitch in his right eye, his voice several octaves higher than usual and speaking at a furious rate. "*Distrutto!*" seemed to be the "*mot du jour.*" The night before he had put on a big production of *Rigoletto* in Bologna and was obviously extremely overtired, (especially from the celebrating afterwards, I thought to myself).

"*Andiamo subito,*" but first, he needed a little coffee to sustain himself, and a little chat with the owner of the hotel, and a little glance at the local newspaper, and finally a little siesta. We left at four.

At the railroad station in Verona, I had to say goodbye to Daniela, who was catching the train back to Bologna. I was sorry to see her go, as we had become good buddies and she was a lovely girl with great potential. I wished her well, and have often wondered what became of her. But it happens so often in an itinerant musician's life that strong bonds are forged with the local contacts for a few days, especially during the more unusual tours like this one, and then one rarely ever sees or hears from these people again. It's a little sad, really.

We roared through Verona. "Such a *bellissima* city! Look on your left, is the '*teatro*' and over there '*l'arena*' and '*Piazza Bra*' – you must see all these places – it is all '*meraviglioso*'." Michele's sentence was barely finished, and we were already in the outskirts of the town. The glimpses I caught of Verona were tantalising enough to infuriate me, knowing that had he been on time I could have had a good stroll around the town. But to complain was pointless, so I seethed inwardly for a few seconds and then let go, mainly because I was suddenly faced with a nice new problem: Michele was falling asleep at the wheel, and we were heading for some rather treacherous mountain roads. Our destination was Castelnuovo nei Monti, high in the Apennines of Reggio Emiglia. As the roads twisted back and forth, it was becoming increasingly disturbing, since Michele was either having anxiety attacks, or getting cramps in this stomach, or was suffering from not one but two twitchy eyes, or was truly about to drop off. I offered to drive but foolishly hadn't reckoned with Italian male pride; my suggestion was received with offence and wounded dignity. On the other hand, it did wake him up a bit and we eventually arrived intact, if somewhat the worse for wear.

I insisted on being taken immediately to the hall to try the piano, which was a rather pathetic Kawai. But the main problem was the stage, which was at such a steep angle that I had a hard time keeping my balance and the piano had to be tied down with rope so as not to roll into the front row of seats. Clearly I would have an unusually easy time with any arpeggio or scale heading for the treble of the piano.

After playing a few chords, and after much laughter from the locals, who found my balance predicament extremely amusing, we all headed back to the hotel, which was modern and a delight. I hadn't realised this was a ski resort. It had a very holiday-ish, sporty feel. *La padrona*, upon hearing that I was hungry but had limited time to eat, whipped me up the most memorable gnocchi I have ever tasted. They melted in my mouth, and with a delicate fresh tomato sauce and the local parmesan sprinkled all over them became little parcels of gastronomic heaven.

I rushed up to my room to change and then was taken back to the hall. Backstage we walked into a violent altercation. It was so heated and was being carried on at such a vertiginous speed that I really couldn't understand a word so, in resignation, I retired to my dressing room. After a while Michele came to find me with a half-smile on his face. The smile reassured me that the drama was more amusing than tragic, and I settled back to hear all about it.

It seemed the father of the little girl who was to present me with flowers after my performance had not realised that the recital would not end till around eleven o' clock. This was far too late for his little girl, so a discussion had begun with the organisers, escalating into a hysterical argument but, typically, ending in smiles and friendship. How was the problem solved? Very simply: his daughter would present me with the flowers on stage before the concert began; and so she did.

I have no idea why my concert in this town was somehow associated with the local ski-rescue team and first-aid volunteers, but at intermission there were lengthy speeches and then I was presented with a medal. As I write this, I am staring at it – a big heavy silver thing with strange symbols on it. I have no idea what they mean, or why I have it. Still, it is always nice to be given medals, I suppose. After the second half, the entire audience came on stage, and we all had our picture taken together. It was a typical, cheerful crowd who, with customary warmth, welcomed me into their richly colourful lives.

After the photo session, about fifteen of us trooped down to a restaurant for a massive dinner. Most of my new friends were professional skiers, and as their English was non-existent and my Italian was progressing, but was still mainly French with some flowery endings, they decided that instead of talking they would sing to me. As water to a wilted flower, the wine brought Michele back to life and, determined not to be outdone by local mountaineers, he decided to sing arias from *Rigoletto*.

By the time dessert came around, a marvellously gooey cake oozing vanilla cream and liqueur, I was singing Polish songs from the Tatras that I had learned as a child. And as I have an appalling voice, particularly in comparison to the rather lovely voices around me, the fact that they all cheered me on and smiled and hugged me was a testament to the power of good will and plenty of wine. Somehow, we were able to communicate enough at this point for them to start peppering me with questions about myself and my travels. We talked into the wee hours and staggered back to the hotel just as dawn was breaking.

At breakfast *La padrona*, whose gnocchi had brought tears of joy to my eyes the night before, spoiled me further by offering me three different kinds of cake. Not one's ordinary idea of breakfast, but they were quite scrumptious. Michele looked like death warmed over and could only manage some espresso.

"*Andiamo subito*," he said, albeit rather weakly, and left to do some business with the local organizer.

Two of my skiing friends from the night before happened by and, seeing me alone, whisked me off in their car to visit the Hermitage of Castelnovo ne' Monti, a fifteenth-century church which stood at the foot of a peculiarly shaped mountain known as "The Altar of the Gods." It was quite awe-inspiring and, although we really couldn't understand each other much, we got along marvellously, and they insisted on buying me all sorts of rather awful souvenirs.

We joined up with Michele and there was yet another hour of conversation and coffee. In the end, as we left, I was cheered and applauded by my group of new friends, and I waved back, stifling the impulse to do my Queen Elizabeth imitation. But just when I thought we were finally on our way, Michele stopped at the theatre and there was another half an hour of coffee and discussion, including the presentation of more souvenirs, one being an extraordinary postcard of the Virgin Mary that, when tipped at an angle, would give the impression her eyes were closing and then opening again when restored to the initial position (I struggled to keep a straight face and kept reminding myself that I had seen worse – in my own province of Québec at Sainte Anne de Beaupré: a postcard of Christ with brilliant red and sparkly drops of blood coming out of his heart ...).

Michele drove me to the station and after a final, animated monologue on the virtues of atheism, he asked me to pray for him. Then we hugged and said farewell. As the train pulled out of the station, I watched him wave; a solitary figure in a crumpled brown suit, his face already setting itself into a worried expression, anticipating the next drama. Despite everything, I had grown quite fond of him.

For the last part of the journey to Rome, I travelled on one of those fabulously futuristic, rapid trains. It was lunch time and, in spite of my three-cake breakfast, I was, as usual, starving, so I shyly ventured into the dining car and sat down at one of the tables. Presently I was joined first by a jovial young business-man, head-to-toe in Armani and smelling strongly of Fahrenheit Cologne, then a middle-aged social worker in her neatly tailored suit, and finally a wild looking man in his mid-thirties, his appearance a convincing imitation of Che Guevara, complete with straggly beard, old beret, army fatigues, and a sinister-looking knapsack.

It turned out he was from Nicaragua and that his politics made Mao seem like Ronald Reagan. We were treated to a lengthy diatribe against not only America but just about everything and everyone. The jovial businessman would try to interject a witty comment or two, but was soundly ignored and overruled and his efforts were reduced to only an occasional amused wink in my direction. The social worker, after five minutes of disapproving glares towards our rebel friend, concentrated fiercely on her meal, but then thawed out completely when, noticing the scores in my shoulder bag, she discovered that I was a musician and played Chopin, her favourite composer.

The meal was quite simply divine – a richly varied "antipasti," then a "risotto frutti di mare," then osso bucco and finally a fruit salad – and the whole compartment was served by one very large, very jolly, ageing waiter wearing a uniform that was a testament to past meals served; he also sported a smile that could light up the City of Rome. He was sweating buckets and had the charming habit of wiping his brow and then our newly washed plates with the same towel. He raced back and forth in a seemingly chaotic fashion but, somehow, we were all served.

After the meal I reached for my wallet and started counting out millions of lire. Michele had paid me in cash, so I had wads of money flying about. The old waiter was quite shocked and explained to me that I should never keep all my cash in one place, but should put some in my pockets, some in my handbag and some in the suitcase. Then he proceeded to do this for me while everyone commented and looked on approvingly. He also refused to accept the tip I offered him.

Upon our arrival in Rome the social worker gave me her card and invited me to call on her anytime during my stay. The Armani man carried my cases to the taxi stand and our Nicaraguan friend muttered something like "Power to the revolution" and disappeared into the crowd.

As a treat, for my last day in Italy, I had booked myself into the legendary Hassler Villa Medici situated at the top of the famed Spanish steps, basically blowing all my earnings from the tour but not giving a damn.

I know I looked out of place as I walked into the luxurious lobby. I was thoroughly dishevelled, my hair was going every which way, and I'm sure my face betrayed my exhaustion. The concierge was, quite frankly, the most gorgeous specimen of mankind I had ever encountered; he could easily have graced the cover of any top fashion magazine, and he knew it. He addressed me with professional courtesy infused with a strong dose of superciliousness and tended to look beyond me when he spoke.

As I filled out the hotel questionnaire, I felt suddenly lonely and despondent; it had been a long and difficult tour, albeit a successful one, and now I was worn out and being dismissed as a nobody. When he politely inquired where I had come from that day, I ventured to tell him a bit about the past few weeks. One should never underestimate the gallantry of the Italian male when confronted with an unhappy female, even if her distress is on the lower levels of the operatic scale. His cold, dignified facade melted, and he suddenly radiated sympathy and friendliness as we laughed together over some of the mishaps of my tour. Eventually, I reached for my key. He promptly snatched it away from me and, with a beautifully manicured finger, reached up for another key which he pressed into my hand, wishing me a good stay and assuring me that I would not be charged extra.

He had given me the most beautiful suite imaginable; the bathroom alone was poetry in marble, and when I drew back the curtains of my bedroom window, the entire city of Rome lay at my feet. It was breath-taking.

I spent hours soaking in luxurious bath oils and presently headed for the dining room. The evening sky was pink, and the sounds of Rome were a distant murmur. It was 7.30, far too early for the normal Roman to be eating, and I was alone in the dining room. With my newfound spend-and-be-damned attitude, I decided to have a meal to remember, complete with appropriate wines for each course.

I ordered with great care after consulting with the helpful waiters; and I was well into my second course of a delicious risotto topped with delicately shaved fresh white truffles when the maitre d'hôtel ushered in an attractive elderly couple and seated them at the table next to mine. As there was no one else about and, thankfully, no music being piped in, I was able to follow their conversation quite easily – in fact, it was difficult not to do so. They were instantly recognizable as wealthy American, luckily of the civilised, elegant, low-key variety. Beautifully turned out, the lady was asking her husband about his day, and it soon became apparent that he owned a company that imported leather goods to the States from Italy.

After hearing me struggle in Italian with the waiter and then hearing him reply in English, they struck up a conversation with me. Within a few minutes they had invited me to join them at their table, where I soon discovered they were from Minneapolis and great supporters of the arts. In fact, they had actually heard me perform with the Minnesota Orchestra a few years previously. As dinner progressed, I heard all about their lives and I, in turn, told them about my recent travels. It was a very jolly evening, and although I had had every intention of paying my own astronomical bill, my protests were overruled. All I could do was promise them complimentary tickets to all my future concerts in Minneapolis.

And they did come, turning up backstage quite regularly, but they never took me up on my offer of complimentary tickets, preferring to spend their own money to support the Minnesota Orchestra. Such chance encounters during my travels often led to life-long friendships; one of the nicer aspects of my turbulent profession.

To holiday in Italy is invariably a source of pleasure. To work as a foreigner in Italy is obviously somewhat of a challenge. So why do I return to perform, year after year, voluntarily and with pleasant anticipation? Is my memory so selective or so feeble that I can forget all the catastrophes? ... The page turner who dramatically stopped turning my pages and left the stage (for no clear reason) in the middle of my performance in Milan of the Brahms Liebeslieder Waltzes with my friend Jeff at the second piano and with the famed choir of the La Scala opera house? Or the hotel in Rome which was plunged into total darkness when I switched on the hairdryer in my room, provoking accusatory and noisy hysterics from the large, sweaty concierge, or the presenter in Arezzo who forgot to organise a dressing-room and so, for no fathomable reason and a lot of shouting, arranged for me to change into my concert outfit in the chief of police's office where (ostensibly very private) reports were strewn all over his desk, providing quite interesting reading material during the normally interminable intermission time?

Clearly survival as a touring artist in Italy is simply a question of attitude: one can either go mad, or one can laugh. This is a country where the simple act of going to the store to buy eggs can develop into potentially high drama. If things go even slightly wrong, no one suffers in silence; people act out loudly and with grand gestures; there is no such thing as keeping emotions bottled up inside. For a Northerner it can be exasperating or terribly funny – I find a dose of Italy every so often strongly therapeutic and utterly irresistible.

CHAPTER 10

Dances of the companions of David ("Davidsbündler Tänze") by Robert Schumann

In 1982, the year Arthur died, I moved to Weston, Connecticut, where I had bought a little house surrounded by woods. I was about to embark on a new phase of my life with a more serene and tranquil outlook. It was also a time when I first discovered great happiness away from the music world, and for this I credit my distant cousin, close neighbour (our houses were a few minutes' walk apart) and close friend, Christopher Plummer, and his wife, Elaine. With Christopher, I shared common ground, professionally and personally, including a strong Canadian heritage. Christopher was also a connoisseur of pianists and the piano repertory, being himself a remarkable amateur pianist who could play just about anything he heard, in his own complex arrangements. There was a certain competitive spirit between us – actor versus musician – and Christopher enjoyed teasing me, but we were comfortable in each other's company and my respect and admiration for his talent was boundless.

With Elaine it was love at first sight, and for the next seventeen years I spent virtually every spare Connecticut moment in her company. Together we shopped, cooked, scrubbed floors, walked dogs, watched figure skating, and shared British mystery novels. I introduced Elaine to ice hockey (we became fanatic Mario Lemieux fans) and in return she tried, heroically, to improve my stage appearance and wardrobe. We even took holidays together, and I would visit them on various locations where Christopher was filming. One time he was making a film with the reptilian Klaus Kinski in Venice, and I flew over for a week's vacation. Elaine and I spent the days being the ultimate tourists, admiring every church and palazzo, every pebble and every window, and having a marvellous time dressed in T-shirts, jeans and sneakers. At night we would change into our posh clothes and meet Christopher for a grand dinner. Our mood was festive and relaxed, and there was something uniquely special about sitting in Saint Mark's Square at midnight with Christopher, Elaine and Sir John Gielgud (with whom we had just had dinner), sipping Tizianos at Florian's in the moonlight, watching the world go by, memories of Arthur floating in the air.

I helped Christopher choose a magnificent Steinway for his Connecticut home and then spent hours practising on it and wearing it down. He and Elaine and I shared three loving dogs who were equally at home in my house or theirs: a beautiful collie-mix from the Humane Society, a soppy golden retriever who had strayed onto our properties and enjoyed himself so much he stayed until he died fifteen years later, and their adorable *belle-laide* offspring. When I was away on tour

I would dream of my first morning back home, when Elaine and I would take the dogs for a long walk. Often, when the autumn foliage was at its peak, or during the spring months when the dogwoods and forsythia were in full bloom or even when the snow covered the landscape, little crystals of ice on the branches glistening like tiny sequins in the early morning sun, we'd remind ourselves, as the dogs dashed about joyfully, never to forget these perfect moments. Then I would practise with the three dogs by me, the retriever resting his head on my right pedal foot so he could get a constant massage while I played.

This was my new family. We had not been thrown together at birth but had chosen to spend our time together and, although Christopher and Elaine were impressed with my talent, it played only a small part in our relationship; equally Christopher's achievements in the world of theatre and film had a minimal influence on my feelings for him. In fact, when I did go to see him perform, I had a hard time reconciling the genius on stage playing Henry V, Iago, Macbeth, or Lear with the fellow who, upon occasion, washed my car, spent hours watering plants in the garden, and tirelessly planned extravagant improvements to my house. Although the Plummers at home were almost as reclusive as myself, I did over the years meet many of their friends, who accepted me as part of the extended family.

Christopher and Elaine not only knew my parents but liked them tremendously, enjoying their visits to see me in Connecticut and entertaining them royally. The feeling was mutual; Biddy hugely enjoyed Christopher's company, and George was enchanted by Elaine's beauty, wit, charm, and upbeat nature. This lifted a significant burden off my shoulders, as so often Biddy and George had turned up between demanding concerts and performances and unintentionally created stress. With Christopher and Elaine's help, my parents' visits to Connecticut became more relaxed, and I could actually enjoy being with them.

My career was also in a more comfortable state. At ICM, I had a series of excellent managers, the most important being John Anderson, who not only had arranged the Solti audition but also started me off on relationships with the Minnesota Orchestra (my most memorable Schumann concerto to this day was in Minneapolis with Klaus Tennstedt), Pittsburgh and Cincinnati. After John Anderson moved on, Jim Griggs took over. He believed very strongly in me, and it was he who presided over the biggest "coup" of my career, that of giving the world premiere of the newly discovered Liszt concerto, No. 3 Opus posthumous with the Chicago Symphony in May 1990. After Jim, who tragically died of AIDS, Patricia Winter took over and provided me with wonderful seasons of concerts all over North America.

I didn't just play in the cities, but returned repeatedly to some of the smaller venues, building up lifelong relationships and friendships in disparate locations ranging from Madison, Wisconsin, to Amarillo, Texas; from Fort Wayne, Indiana to Pensacola, Florida; from Lexington, Kentucky, to Grand Junction, Colorado, and so on.

Over the years I got to know the U.S. very well and have enjoyed every second of my American travels, other than some of the long waits in airports and a few extremely dicey flights, including an actual crash in Flagstaff, Arizona, where my plane took off in the fog and slammed into another one landing, ripping off one wing and scaring the bejesus out of me; amazingly, no one was badly hurt.

But what could be more fun than having a delicious wine-tasting experience following a performance in the heart of California wine country? Or being taken for a ride on a private plane, startling mountain goats as we banked along the side of Mount Alyeska after an adventurous Brahms B-flat concerto with the Anchorage Symphony orchestra? Flying a simulator of a Boeing 777 after my concerts in Seattle was quite an eye-opener; I managed to miss the runway entirely when I tried to land at Charles de Gaulle airport.

I have eaten breakfast with scientists in Los Alamos discussing late Beethoven sonatas, dined at the Waldorf Astoria with twelve Nobel Prize winners discussing Arthur Rubinstein, and I was fêted in San Antonio, Texas, by descendants of the first Polish community in America.

It was a great time, filled with demanding schedules, cross-country travel, and stressful performances, yes, but knowing I had a secure and joyful life back in Connecticut gave me the strength I needed. And, in spite of the new geographical challenges, my friendship with my New York colleague Jeffrey Swann and his wife Melody remained as close as ever. We even holidayed together in Italy, and twice attended the Bayreuth Festival in Germany together. One of my happiest memories occurred after a splendid performance of "Siegfried;" elation and invincibility were bursting out of us as we strode up the hill behind the Festspielhaus after the performance that warm summer evening to the "Bürgerreuth" restaurant, where we ate a fabulous Italian meal with our hearts and minds completely absorbed in the glorious music, light years away from everyday pressures.

A final reason for my happiness was the advent of Carmel. In the mid-eighties I was invited to the Carmel Bach Festival in California by the elderly and charming music director Sandor Salgo, with whom I had previously worked in Modesto and Marin County. Sandor was a fount of knowledge, not only on musical matters but on such varying topics as female British mystery writers and Thomas Jefferson; he was also a profoundly spiritual musician, and we got along well. After my first Carmel festival I was invited back so often it almost became a habit. It was the cushiest job in the universe, and I adored it. I was given a house for three weeks, minutes from one of the most spectacular coastlines in the world, and I was paid to play a Mozart concerto of my choice and a one-hour program having something to do with Bach (however tenuous the link) with an occasional extra concert of chamber music thrown in. I repeated these concerts twice, and the rest of the three weeks I spent enjoying myself. There was only one piano soloist, so I was delightfully spoiled by many kind music lovers.

The Carmel Bach Festival provided me with not only eight summers of fun, but also a new set of life-long friends, beginning with the Wades. Naturally, I had to practice somewhere because, despite the holiday mode, this actually was a job, so I put in the hours slogging away on Betty Wade's lovely old Mason & Hamlin. Betty was one of those powerful philanthropic figures who not only bought tickets and attended concerts, but financially supported goodness knows how many musical institutions, even to the point of opening her own house to touring musicians such as myself. Her kindness wasis boundless and her husband Jep, a highly cultivated man, had irresistible charm.

Lucy Faridany also entered my life during the Carmel summers. Her mother was the Artistic Administrator of the Festival, and when I first met Lucy, she was a painfully shy 13-year-old who was unusually gifted as a musician. Early on she became my loyal sidekick and I loved having her around for her wonderfully irreverent, wicked sense of humour coupled with her delicate and sensitive nature. The friendship grew and grew, and we have kept in close touch through the years. The sweet, shy little girl has become a shining personality radiating beauty and talent, and the Monterey Bay area is lucky to have such an accomplished musician in their midst.

And finally, the Festival gave me the opportunity to build a friendship with Elizabeth and Arthur Pasquinelli (witnesses at my future wedding). On my free days at the Festival, we three started to take hikes along the Pacific Coast in Pebble Beach, up Mount Devon, along the Garrapata trail, and into Molera State Park down at Big Sur.

After our initial summer together Elizabeth, Arthur and I started taking hiking holidays together, first in Yorkshire, then in the Tetons and Yellowstone and finally along the old pilgrimage trail of Compostela, starting from Le Puy in France. We three were great Francophiles, and I spent some of the most soul-satisfying days of my life walking along the centuries-old path across the French countryside, the smell of honey from a million spring flowers and of damp rich earth freshly ploughed filling the air, fields of wild narcissus swaying in the breeze. In the distance, the sound of church bells ringing with an occasional bark of a dog from one of the farms and the gentle, hypnotic song of a solitary cuckoo would cheer us on our way. After a few hours of tramping, we would enjoy picnics of crusty French bread with cheese and fruit by rushing rivers or on hilltops with magnificent views, the sun beaming benevolently down. At night, we'd arrive tired but with a tremendous sense of fulfilment – and serious appetites – at a country *auberge* where we would be served six-course meals of Epicurean delights, all washed down by the *vin ordinaire*, which seemed anything but ordinary to us – more like nectar of the Gods after our wonderful days spent in the sun and fresh country air. We'd collapse into our cots at a ridiculously early hour and sleep the untroubled sleep of those at peace with themselves and with the world.

Back in Carmel, I eventually became such an established fig-ure that when it came time for Maestro Salgo to retire, Nana, the Artistic Administrator, telephoned me (in the middle of the night, as she had forgotten about the time difference) to ask me for suggestions for his successor. She wondered aloud if I hap-pened to know of any German conductors who might be inter-ested. Half-asleep, I went over to my files where I kept a list of conductors with whom I had worked. The name Bruno Weil caught my eye. He was a young German conductor with whom I had recently performed in Glasgow. The second concert we did together had gone particularly well; it was the Brahms D-minor concerto, and it had been my personal best performance of the piece, with a lot of credit going to Bruno and to the orchestra. David Sigall, our mutual manager, had travelled up to hear us and had been tremendously impressed by our collaboration. More importantly, he took us out to a first-rate Italian restau-rant afterwards which cheered Bruno and I up to no end, hav-ing suffered all week with the rather ghastly Scottish cuisine of our hotel. Bruno struck me as a very serious and thought-ful musician, but with a great sense of humour and an enor-mous talent and enthusiasm for his work. I recommended him to Nana wholeheartedly, and within weeks he got the job.

During his first year as music director in Carmel, Bruno brought over with him his private secretary Harry Oesterle, whom I met briefly – mostly when he would come backstage to congratulate me. I thought Harry was absolutely lovely and was sorry when, in subsequent years, he was busy in Germany running the Irsee Festival (which he had created for Bruno and the Tafelmusik orchestra, and which took place shortly after the Carmel Bach Festival).

We were to meet again, Harry and I, but before I start jumping ahead, it's time to bring the Solti saga to its rightful conclusion.

In April 1985, almost exactly three years after my audi-tion in London, I arrived in Chicago for the big event. Solti had kept his word, although the concerto was neither Liszt nor Beethoven but Mozart K.491, which suited me just fine, since I can't think of a greater work in the piano repertoire. I had not played this concerto before that year but was able to try it out a few months before, first in New Mexico, and then on Mozart's birthday (January 27th) in San Francisco.

To say that I was prepared for the Chicago concerts is an understatement. By now I could play the concerto backwards, forwards, blindfolded, and with my hands tied behind my back. But I was also ridiculously overexcited, and my nerves felt as taut as piano-wire. Luckily, the hall and the piano were very familiar to me, but as I waited on the empty stage for the great man to appear for our piano rehearsal, I had to force myself to breathe normally and to think rationally of all the concerts I had played – without actually dying – over the years. This was, I told myself, just another concert. Of course, my strategy failed, but it kept me occupied for a few minutes.

Solti appeared suddenly and sat next to the piano, telling me without preamble how tired he was (this, I learned, was a habitual refrain of his). We started to rehearse. Frankly, he was a bit of a bully that day, so I was grateful to find that my tempi and interpretation weren't too far away from his; otherwise, I would have been in trouble. He whistled and sang in falsetto and grunted and conducted and suggested and prodded and guided me through the piece. I felt very young and inexperienced, even at the age of 34, and, eager to please, I fell in, albeit protesting a little inside, with whatever he decided. My nerves tightened another notch.

The rehearsals with orchestra were far more amusing, because having already been dealt with myself, I was now able to almost happily observe him whistle and sing and grunt and make the strangest sounds to describe exactly what he wished them to do. Like most orchestras, they were all very friendly towards me and, as with most orchestras, I could feel that secret bond being formed between us; the typical soloist-orchestra alliance against the conductor.

And then came the fateful day. Having read somewhere that it had been a habit of Solti's, back in his Covent Garden days before Lady Solti appeared on the scene, to give his girl-friends white ermine coats, Christopher and Elaine sent me a package, Federal Express, filled with white rabbits' feet and a rude message! My Chicago friends (spearheaded by Dolores Fredrickson, an amazing piano teacher in whose house I used to stay and practise many times over the years, and who was as avid a Solti fan as I was), came out in full force for the first concert. Dolores had once taken me on a bicycle ride around her Highland Park neighbourhood with the express purpose of showing me the Solti home when he still lived there. She came now with a phalanx of her students, who had all heard me play many a time in her home and who were all pre-conditioned to cheer loudly.

I hadn't slept a wink the night before, and I'd spent the day throwing up. A huge Cadillac limousine picked me up at 7 o'clock and brought me to the backstage door. My head was spinning, I was cold as ice and having a hard time pulling my panic-stricken brain together. The Haydn Symphony began. I walked back and forth, back and forth along the corridor and around my dressing room, wearing my big black woollen gloves. I couldn't practise because, if I did, I knew I would miss something every four or five notes and terrify myself, if possible, even more. Finally, I heard the applause and a head popped into my dressing room to announce that I had five minutes. Solti was sitting just offstage sipping something (tea, I believe) from a thermos. He saw how traumatised I was, however hard I pretended to be cool and collected and, trying to be comforting and friendly, came out with the following: "My dear, don't 'vorry', it will be fine. I have played the piano part of this piece and I know it EEEnntimately."

Far from reassuring me, this traumatized me further, but then I found we were being ushered on stage. I smiled bravely, bowed, and took my seat. The long orchestral introduction of about three seemingly endless minutes began while I sat motionless. What were my first notes? I could remember the first bar, but then I went completely blank. On-stage panic set in

for the first time in my life. Not only could I remember nothing, but I could only see black, and my ears had started to ring.
Dragging together my last vestiges of sanity, I tried speaking
sharply to myself: "Look where you are! This is something you
have dreamed of for years – look up there on the podium – for
God's sake, it is Sir Georg Solti – get a grip on yourself!" The
introduction was approaching its conclusion. "All right, if you
can't handle this, then don't embarrass yourself, but just pretend that you are sick and fake a fainting spell!" And just as I
had this brilliant thought, it was time for me to play.

The performance went perfectly well, but it was far from
the extraordinary experience that I had imagined for so many
years, simply because I was too nervous and was playing basically on auto-pilot. Sometimes under these circumstances one
can play beyond one's normal capabilities and truly shine, but
this particular performance was only marginally better than
adequate, and I was tremendously glad when it was all over.
One thing that did calm me down somewhat was that after
one of my little cadenzas, in the slow movement, Solti tried
to bring in the orchestra in completely the wrong place. They
wisely paid him no heed and came in correctly. Somehow, I felt
comforted not only by the orchestra's support but also by my
hero's fallibility.

Naturally, with so many friends and supporters in the audience I got a huge ovation, and I was greatly relieved when both
the *Chicago Tribune* and the *Sun Times* gave me rave reviews. I
always feel a sense of relief when the review is good, though
I don't believe a word of it unless it corresponds with what I
thought myself. But if the review is bad, I am always terribly
hurt and not only believe, but also take to heart all the nasty
things that are written and brood over them for years.

After the first performance I started eating again, practising normally, socialising, and sleeping like a baby. As I was
warming up my fingers in the dressing room before the second concert, the door was suddenly flung open, and Solti came
striding in: "Please you must play for me your cadenzas again –

I missed them in the last concert and must hear them again otherwise ... DISASTER!"

I played the cadenzas for him not once, but about three times each and he said: "Thank you," and left as abruptly as he'd entered. This next performance went well, and Solti commented as I shook his hand on stage: "Very beautiful – this one was much better." I started to feel pleased with myself and by the final performance was quite cocky, even making jokes backstage and not at all disturbed by the fact that Biddy, George, and Peter were all in the audience – something that would normally have added considerable tension. I sailed through the concerto, enjoying myself to the limit and playing the best I could.

After the concert, Solti invited me to spend a few weeks with his family in their home in Italy the following summer, and we parted extremely amicably. The Italian summer never materialised, but I did see him again a few times, and it was still under his music directorship of the Chicago Symphony that I was invited a few years later to perform the world premiere of the newly discovered Liszt piano concerto No. 3, opus posthumous, with my friend, the gifted Kenneth Jean, conducting.

I met with Solti a few months prior to the Liszt premiere, when I was in Chicago to pick up the precious score, which had been locked in a safe – so frightened was everyone that it would be stolen and that somehow our performance would no longer be a premiere. He asked me what I thought of the piece, and we discussed its strong points: two lovely melodies, interesting orchestration, and fascinating, experimental piano writing – and its weak points; shaky structure, rough connecting passages between sections and a general feeling of being an unfinished, youthful work in progress.

Solti will always be, for me, a symbol of a passionately exciting time in my youth. I not only admired Sir Georg Solti, I liked him a lot. He was, as Arthur described him "a good fellow." And he was the conductor of some of the most thrilling Wagner performances I have ever experienced.

And so, the early 1990s found me secure and successful, and seemingly in control of my destiny. I was a candidate for contentment, but with my restless nature it didn't take long for me to become unsettled and ready for a new challenge. Little did I know that I was about to embark on the greatest, most quixotic adventure of my professional life. What I did know was this:

For some years it had been apparent that the North American classical music world was ailing. A number of symphony orchestras were filing for bankruptcy, and the piano recital had all but vanished from the North American scene; also, those little chamber-recital series were fast dying out. I remembered Arthur's silver tray, which rested on a side table in his living room in Paris, a gift from the great American impresario Sol Hurok. On the tray were engraved the names of all the cities in North America where he had performed live. I remember being quite stunned by the number of (even Canadian!) cities (such as Rimouski or Moose Jaw) where he had played, and I hadn't. In those days, a touring artist such as a Rubinstein or a Rachmaninov or a Paderewski would get on the train and, at just about every stop, would give a recital in the local church, hall or even hockey arena. But in North America air travel completely changed the dynamics of concert touring. There was absolutely no chance of any major pianist playing in Rimouski or Moose Jaw. The planes go only to the bigger cities and airfares are generally expensive – small music societies in far-flung communities haven't a hope in hell of attracting top talent. Certain artists like Arthur had also made it a personal policy to never ask for a fee that would exceed the box office intake, but by the 1980s a great many of my colleagues (and their managers) had already started demanding exorbitant fees, completely unaffordable in smaller communities.

On the other side of the footlights, audiences were diminishing, mainly because classical music was vanishing from school curricula. And clearly classical music piano recitals are not for everyone: they require firm concentration, open-mindedness, a degree of sensitivity enhanced by knowledge and the courage to be led into an uncharted world of emotion. Visually, piano recitals are, and should be, absolutely uninteresting after the first five minutes or so, and for maximum enjoyment one needs to sit still for two hours and do a certain amount of mental work. To experience something special in a piano recital, one has to make an effort, and not everyone is willing to do this.

I was also hearing from all sides that audiences were becoming more elderly. I actually dismissed this idea as false; since the beginning, my audiences have consisted mostly of people who have raised their children, paid off the mortgages and gone into retirement. These are the people who have the time and the money to attend piano recitals. The vast majority, it seems to me, attend because sometime in their youth a relative or an older friend or a teacher introduced them to this great art form. Now, in their later years, they feel a longing for something spiritual, beautiful, and out of this world – and music fills this need to perfection.

If children are never exposed to classical music, are never given an instrument to play, have never been part of a band or orchestra or choir, or have never heard a live concert, the magical chain will be broken and audiences will inevitably dwindle to nothing, for once these music-deprived children reach the financial security and relative leisure of middle age, they will have no musical memories to inspire them or re-engage them. This was happening before my own eyes, and my feelings of helplessness kept growing. Not only were whole generations being deprived of hearing live classical music, but I, too, was liable to be deprived of doing what I loved best.

A recording is definitely no substitute for a live concert. It is a marvellous tool for education in schools, for instance, to familiarise students with a work they will shortly be experiencing in concert, or to give children some exposure to the great composers. The CD is a Godsend for elderly music-lovers who are housebound, or for those like me who hear a great performance in concert and rush out to buy a recording of the same artist playing the same work, as a nice reminder of a precious moment. But without fail, however marvellous the recording might be, there is always the lingering feeling that it is missing that extra-dimension of tingling emotion and excitement one had or would have felt in the concert hall. And, of course, the CD encapsulates one single performance that happened on one specific day. It never changes and so becomes static, the antithesis of what music is all about.

Music, the most abstract of all of the arts, is by this same token the most transitory. It would be a contradiction in terms to speak of the "Fialkowska Chopin B-minor Sonata" on the basis of my CD version. A CD is like a snapshot and, nowadays, because of the technology, a heavily touched-up digital snapshot – a glimpse of an event or a place, frozen in time. It is not the event or the place itself, for these are not only alive, vibrant and real, but changeable from moment to moment. Music never stays the same – it comes seemingly from nowhere, has no inherent obvious meaning and has no direct or obvious connection to our daily lives. It cannot be brought down to the level of an everyday occurrence or thought.

Great literature is open to many personal interpretations, but it always has a recognizable starting-point in the form of words and sentences that we can all basically understand. And the visual arts are right there to be seen and interpreted; emotionally accessible (and naturally provocative), because scenes and people and colours and shapes are all drawn from facets of our world that we know and can identify.

Poetry is the one art form that, for me, comes closest to the concept of music; a procession of beautiful words put in the most beautiful sequences – beautiful sounds and rhythms that touch the soul. But where does a Chopin Nocturne or a Mozart concerto or a late Beethoven sonata come from? It is nothing that is recognizably human or from this earth. And even when it is harnessed and put on paper, the sparse indications given to the performers are barely enough to get us through to the end. What do they mean by *piano* or *forte*? What type of *piano*, what intensity, what emphasis, what volume? And an indication such as *Largo* – is it very slow? Or can it be more like an *Andante* depending on the weather, or the instrument, or one's mood? And the eternal question: what does the composer mean? It is the job of every performer to take what they individually perceive to be the composer's ideas and present them to the world in deference and humility, but also with their own interpretation. And so it is that no two performers can ever see any one piece in the same light, and no two performances of any one piece, even by the same performer, are identical. We have to find and re-create our own version of the meaning of every work we play, each time we play it. Our own talent and imagination, but also our humility, completely preclude the possibility of arrogantly deciding that we have found the one and only "true" version, from which we will never budge.

Athletic performances of high speed, extreme contrasts and pinpoint accuracy can produce a sense of admiration and excitement in an audience, much as a gymnast's performance at the Olympics can be thrilling, but a piano recital can offer so much more if the performer also has innate musicianship and is in the midst of a long and intensive relationship with the composers, their styles, complexities, feelings and ideas.

The final prerequisite is an ability to act as a conduit and be able to share – like a fine red wine, a good piano recital needs to have developed and matured for many years before it is presented to the world.

The tragic irony at the time was that dedicated concert pianists were still abundant, but the concert possibilities and audiences were vanishing. I felt I had to do something. One night at a dinner after a concert I gave at Festival Hall in London, I sat next to a strikingly beautiful young woman who worked as a surgeon in a children's hospital. I found her a sympathetic and interested listener. But when I remarked that I felt humbled sitting next to someone who was devoting her life to really worthwhile and important work in the world, she snapped, almost angrily, back at me: "And why do you think I work so hard to save these children? So they can go and hear concerts like the one you've just played. I offer them their lives but you, with your music, you offer them quality in their lives – your work is vital."

I chose to believe her and to believe in the importance she ascribed to my work and to classical music. From that moment on I began a crusade to try and see that as many people as possible should be exposed to the music that I was privileged to know and love so deeply. The profound reverence I feel for the great composers who have been my closest companions for all my life has led to a tremendous sense of duty and responsibility towards them. To me it would be a sin against humanity and a betrayal if I wasn't to devote my life to the propagation of their work.

One day during the summer of 1993 I was lying down in the guest bedroom of the home of Hans and Cathy Braul in the attractive town of Kincardine, Ontario, resting before an evening recital. Playing for the Brauls on their series had become an annual event. The concerts were held in the dining room of a retirement home, the dining-room tables hastily removed after an early dinner and chairs set up for an audience of about 80 people; the piano was an excellent new Steinway.

In lieu of a fee I would request a dinner made by Cathy, a great natural cook. I would also use Kincardine to try out new programs, so the benefits were mutual.

Lying on the bed that afternoon, I reflected on a conversation I had just had with the Brauls. Even with all the energy and enthusiasm in the world (and they possessed plenty of both), their series was having serious financial problems, especially after cuts in government budgets. Would this be another chamber series to succumb to the financial pressures of the 1990s? And then, the answer came to me in a flash: it was time we artists took a stand and did something to help save our profession. I believed that a lot of the older people in the smaller towns missed live classical concerts very much, and lots of younger people had, quite simply, never heard a classical concert live and never would unless something changed. I knew that I – and probably all my Canadian colleagues – wanted to play in smaller communities. If we did, we would be appreciated.

Canada is a country that has an inordinate number of famous and successful concert pianists; in fact, very few countries, even those with much larger populations, can boast of so many. But somehow the connection between talented Canadian artists and the general music-loving public (even if they don't realise they are music-loving) had been lost. If I could find and persuade a group of my colleagues to join me in a purely altruistic endeavour and to agree that we each devote ten days every year for ten years to touring in some of the regions in Canada where classical music was a rarity, non-existent, or in dire straits, not only playing evening recitals, but also going into the schools for school concerts and giving workshops and master classes for the local music teachers and pupils – doing all of this for a purely nominal fee – then we might just succeed in reversing a dangerous trend and bring classical music back to its former revered status in Canada.

The ten-year commitment was something I felt strongly about, because I hoped we could build a project with continuity. If one of us went to a town the first year, another would follow the next year, and so on until it would become a regular annual event in the community's calendar and perhaps a series could be built around us, or we could help attract people if there already was a series in place, especially if it was struggling. The tickets to our concerts had to be affordable for all.

This was my big idea and I jumped up and rushed out to tell Hans and Cathy. They were enthusiastic but cautious, not believing it could actually happen. We went to the Malcolm Place retirement residence, where I changed and waited in the library. Normally I would pull out Tolstoy's *War and Peace* from the bookshelf and read a few chapters while waiting for the start of the concert, marking the page where I stopped with a bookmark. Since no one else ever seemed to read the book, I would pick it up every year and continue where I had left off. By now, as a testament to the number of trips I have made to Kincardine, I am two-thirds of the way through. But on this day, I couldn't read for excitement. For the recital itself, I concentrated on the program, as it was new and I wanted to give it a good send-off, but once it was over, my idea and its ramifications began to consume my time.

First of all, I needed someone to help me with administration. A Canadian manager was necessary, and I didn't have to look far, since the following week I was back in Carmel performing Schubert's *Winterreise* with the celebrated Canadian baritone Daniel Lichti. Daniel's wife at that time was a very successful manager and, sensing immediately that this could be a major and fascinating undertaking with many positive outcomes, she came on board enthusiastically.

Thus encouraged, I sat down and wrote a fourteen-page letter to my friend and colleague Jon ("Jackie") Kimura Parker, outlining my plan. I had become acquainted with Jackie the year before, when we had sat on an international jury together. There had been some excellent pianists in the competition, but there were also a dozen or so who had no business being there and whose performances were either painful to suffer through or worthy but downright dull. The problem was that in this particular competition everyone was given an hour to perform, starting in the second round, and as one knew perfectly well after a maximum of ten minutes what calibre of pianist one was hearing (nerves notwithstanding), there were many fifty-minute periods of agony or acute boredom. To fill the time, when our professional consciences were clear and it was truly obvious the candidate would not make it to the next round, we would write each other long notes, and in this way got to know each other. Jackie is not only a wonderful pianist; he also has that extra dimension of star quality, in the best sense of the word. He is also a terrific and generous person, enchanting both on and off stage. In his notes, he revealed to me how much he missed playing in the small towns of Canada where he had started his career. I now reminded him of this.

His answer came back to me the minute he'd ploughed through my overexcited letter. He rang me up and was so enthusiastic that he gave me the courage I needed for the initial huge effort to get the project up and running. Overnight I became a fanatic to the cause. By the next day, I was hard at work writing personal letters to Angela Hewitt, Angela Cheng, Marc-André Hamelin and André Laplante. I had met Angela Hewitt only once, when she had come to hear me play a Chopin concerto as a young girl at the National Arts Centre in Ottawa. There had been a party afterwards and we had chatted amiably. I had also heard her play on the radio and on television, and I thought she was brilliant. Angela had not yet received the recognition she so richly deserved and which I knew would sooner or later propel her into the stratosphere of the music world, so I hoped she would have time in her schedule for a bit of altruism.

Angela Cheng, with her golden sound, whom I had known at Juilliard as Mr. Gorodnitzki's star pupil, already had a major concert career as a result of her many richly deserved first prizes in international competitions. She was also married and had just started a family. I desperately wanted her to join the group but was worried that she too would not have the time.

Marc-André Hamelin I had met when we had played in a multi-piano gala event in Quebec City the previous year. At that time, his career was in its infancy, but I had been tremendously impressed by his playing and had liked him personally very much, especially appreciating his vast repertoire of Monty Python skits, which he could rattle off by heart with great flair. I knew Marc-André, with his unique mastery of, or, more to the point, wizardry at the keyboard, was destined for greatness, but again, I hoped to grab him when he still had a little time to spare.

And André Laplante? Well, André was my oldest friend of the group, and we shared a lot of history. I had started admiring his music-making when I was 11 years old, and I continued to do so over the years, believing that he is one of the greats. To have him among us would be a real coup.

Angela Hewitt was the first to answer. She accepted without reservation and offered a list of helpful suggestions. The next day a letter came from Angela Chen; she is an angel, and she didn't disappoint. With the boys it took longer, as it was impossible to track them down at first. But once I did find them, they too joined our merry band without a second's hesitation. There were many other successful pianists I could have approached, but these five were not tied down to overly demanding teaching schedules. So, the six of us now formed a dedicated group, hence the name Piano Six, which just happened to also be a good bilingual name – mandatory in Canada.

Now that everyone was on board, the planning could begin. Publicity was fairly easy to arrange. Over the years I had developed numerous friendships with music journalists as well as all of my friends at Radio Canada and the CBC. Christopher put me in touch with an excellent PR person in Toronto, Betty Michalyshyn, who arranged for me to have interviews in publications not exclusively devoted to the music world and to appear on myriad television and radio talk shows. We began putting together tours, and then suddenly another idea came to me. I decided that we needed to inaugurate the whole project with two big galas, one in Toronto and one in Quebec City, where all six of us would appear together on stage. For someone who preferred peace and quiet and a solitary life, this sudden foray into the world of salesmanship, marketing, and dealing with a lot of people went against my nature. For quite a while though, I raced about Canada, doing everything I could to sell the idea, loathing the process and trying not to bore myself with my own rhetoric, but deep in my soul feeling compelled to follow through to the end.

It was an idealistic project and my five colleagues, and the extraordinary volunteers and Board Members, deserve great gratitude for their selfless behaviour. For myself, I did not feel I had a choice; it wasn't a question of volunteering, or of being a good sport or doing a good deed. It was just something I had to do. God had given me a modest talent which I had spent my life developing, initially in relative ease with my family's backing, and I'd always felt I should work doubly hard to somehow compensate for my good fortune.

I had a full schedule ahead at the start of 1995, including the two Piano Six Galas scheduled for early February. There was also Biddy, now a widow, who had become quite deaf and lonely, increasingly missing George in spite of the numerous devoted friends dancing in attendance. My beloved father had died in December 1993 while I was in London rehearsing for a performance of the Szymanowski Symphonie Concertante with the BBC Symphony Orchestra. I actually went ahead and played the concert the following day, convinced in my mind that George would have been extremely annoyed if I hadn't. I only told three people (David, Linn and Imogen) that he had died, afraid that too much sympathy might weaken my resolve. With the support of my three friends, the performance somehow went off without a hitch and I returned home the next day.

For Biddy, life without George was very empty, and I tried to invite her down to Connecticut or fit in visits to Montreal as often as I could. Whenever possible, I took her on short holidays to warmer climates during the long Canadian winters.

Not being superwoman, my nerves started to fray, especially when the time came for the two gala concerts.

For one thing, although I knew all of the pianists, some had never met each other, and I was in a panic that perhaps temperaments would clash musically or even personally. Jackie and Angela Hewitt had both worked tirelessly at arranging the transcriptions for twelve hands and we all met for the first time at the Royal Toronto Conservatory, where the Dean, Rennie Regehr, was an old friend and had made it possible for us to practise, providing four pianos and two electric keyboards in a large room. After the introductions and some pleasantries, we sat down to work, and I held my breath. We had to prepare two separate programs as both concerts were to be broadcast – the first in Toronto by the CBC and the second in Quebec City by Radio-Canada – and the networks had requested different repertoire.

We worked hard and long and with the most extraordinary lack of any ego or one-upmanship. We laughed ourselves silly during breaks and rarely have I enjoyed myself so much in the company of other musicians. The sheer quality of their playing was awe-inspiring. We shared a common desire for perfection, the serious work ethic of the concert pianist – so often lacking in collaborative efforts with string players! – and a strong commitment to the idea of performing in small communities across the country.

Twelve hands thundered through the *1812* and *Meistersinger* overtures with great drama and power – Marc doing a stellar job on the chimes for the *1812*. We also prepared the more subtle and delicate *Oberon* and *Magic Flute* overtures, with great precision, nuances, and amazing fingerwork. There was the fun of an eight-handed Percy Grainger transcription of a Bach organ toccata (which we adapted for our twelve hands) and Milhaud's Scaramouche, full of sunshine and South American rhythms, was helped along by Angela Hewitt's masterly performance on the maracas. We paired off for a series of duets by Dvorák and Brahms, and the two Angelas prepared a scintillating performance of Ravel's *La Valse*. We re-wrote for six pianos part of

Rachmaninov's second suite for two pianos, and lastly, we each prepared some very short solo works.

We practised non-stop for two days in Toronto – very little time, considering we were learning the programs from scratch. I was still fitting in a lot of publicity work and interviews, and after forty-eight hours I had a twitchy eye, was breaking out in occasional cold sweats, and found it quite hard to just relax and fully enjoy this rare event.

The concert in Toronto was held at the Glenn Gould Studio. It had sold out practically the day it was announced, and the happy feeling of excitement and anticipation in the hall was infectious. Backstage, Angela H. was calmly eating a huge meal. Never have I met another pianist who can eat huge meals right before they play – and remain as slim as a model ... so irritating! She looked wonderful as well and was in a marvellous mood, laughing along with the rest of us at André's relentless jokes. Angela C. was pacing the floor looking nervous, warming up her fingers every two seconds on the upright piano in the Green Room – worrying unnecessarily since she was, as usual, utterly and beautifully prepared. The boys sat together telling outrageous stories and comparing bowties, all extremely relaxed and cheerful.

There was a momentary blip when we realised that Marc had left his music back at the hotel, but it was retrieved in time by a kind volunteer and my panic subsided to a more manageable level. I really was a bit of a wreck, unable to eat and feeling tremendously responsible, desperately hoping that my friends were having a good time and that the concert would give the project the boost it needed. I was already worrying about the early flight to Quebec the next morning, and whether all would be nicely set up there for us to go to work immediately on the second program. There was the weather factor as well, since it was February in Canada.

The Glenn Gould stage was actually too small for six pianos, so we only had four and doubled up on two; but we arranged the music accordingly and this worked just fine. The concert was a magical event, starting with a long and extremely heart-warming ovation before we even began the program. The six of us had a marvellous time and the camaraderie between us crossed over from the stage into the audience, making them feel an integral part of the merriment and music-making.

As an encore we played Jackie's twelve-hand version of the themes from *Star Trek* and, being a devout Trekkie, Jackie donned his Captain Kirk uniform. He also, as we accompanied pianissimo, gave the opening narration of the legendary television series with a few amendments and substitutions to tie it in with Piano Six: "Canada – the final frontier ... These are the voyages of Piano Six ... To boldly go where no pianist has gone before." Then he joined us at the pianos in a roaring rendition of the score.

The ovations were deafening, the Toronto audience definitely not behaving in its usual staid, reserved manner. I threw a party afterwards with the help of our capable PR lady, taking over the Opus restaurant and inviting lots of friends and people who could be helpful to the project. Christopher and Elaine joined us at the party, adding an extra touch of glamour, since, coincidentally, he was in Toronto rehearsing for a performance of Sir William Walton's Henry V. The champagne flowed, desserts were eaten, and although I was still too strung-out to truly enjoy myself, part of me did realise that this was an exceptional landmark evening and the start of something big.

The following day we all met at Toronto airport for an extremely early flight to Quebec. The boys had partied late into the night and looked rather ragged around the edges and bleary-eyed. Angela C. looked a little tired, but her lovely smile acted like a tonic on all of us. Angela H. looked fresh as a daisy and, as our plane was a little delayed, sat down and consumed a huge breakfast while the rest of us looked on aghast, unable to conceive how one could eat so early in the morning, especially after our late night. At best, we managed to down half a muffin each. When we finally we boarded the plane, I fell asleep, exhausted.

Nothing could have prepared us for the royal treatment we received throughout our time in Quebec. The phrase "your wish is my command" took on a whole new meaning. Delightfully helpful volunteers, chauffeurs, and piano tuners were on call 24 hours a day. Fruit baskets and wine bottles were in our hotel rooms. Boxes filled with presents – souvenirs from Quebec, goodies to eat – were in each dressing room. When we were hard at work rehearsing, meals were brought in for us from some of Quebec's finest restaurants, so we could eat quickly backstage. Press conferences, interviews and photo shoots were scheduled when we felt we could fit them in; the choice of time and place was ours. Everything was organised for our optimum comfort, and the behind-the-scenes organisation operated smoothly, silently, and efficiently. In the evenings we were wined and dined, and we even found time to go for short walks to stretch our cramped limbs. We all agreed with Jackie when, in a fit of exuberance and sheer joy, he ran down the backstage corridor the evening of the concert, shouting: "If Quebec ever separates from Canada, I want to go with Quebec!"

We performed in the Grand Théâtre de Québec, whose administrators co-produced the event with the venerable Club Musical de Québec. The prime organiser behind it all was an old friend of mine from my Vincent d'Indy days – Louise Samson, a magnificent pianist in her own right who had her finger in just about every major musical pie in the province. For the three days we were in Quebec, she seemed to be everywhere, her eyes on everything. For the first time in over two months, I was able to relax.

When we walked on the stage of the Grand Théâtre that cold February evening, the ovation nearly blew the roof off. The excitement in the sold-out hall was palpable, but when we sat down and waited for Angela's down-beat to begin the Overture to Mozart's Magic Flute, there was a complete, breathless, and expectant silence in the hall.

The piano holds a special place in the hearts of Quebeckers. There was a long tradition of piano-playing in the home and of piano lessons with the nuns as teachers. That is why, even now, although there are very few nuns left, their pupils continue the tradition; indeed, I discovered on my many subsequent Piano Six tours of the province that even in faraway places, such as Chicoutimi, Rimouski, or Gaspé, one could still find first-rate young talents receiving excellent training. This is indeed why I had insisted on the second gala taking place in Quebec City. I knew how appreciated we would be, although I couldn't have imagined the magnitude of this appreciation.

After Marc and André had assured Jackie that French Canadians did indeed follow the *Star Trek* series, and after Marc taught him the French narration, we reprised our hilarious encore for the Quebec audience, before moving on to a reception and a fabulous dinner. It was another magical evening, and we all felt extremely good about what we had done. For me, these five days with my extraordinary five colleagues were uplifting, inspirational and well worth all the hard work and angst of the past year of preparation. The repercussions from the two concerts were phenomenal. We were bombarded with rave reviews in the press, not only for our performances but also for our project. Many more interviews followed for all of us. People started calling in to the office to ask how their tiny communities – places like Campbellton, Wainwright, North Bay, Mission or Chicoutimi – could be included. Piano Six eventually visited all of them up to six or seven times over the following years. Word of our project spread like wildfire.

In Quebec our gala raised enough money for the Grand Théâtre to purchase a brand-new Hamburg Steinway piano, which has been used ever since for chamber and orchestral concerts. But there were other more unexpected repercussions, especially in terms of friendships between the six of us. For example, Angela H. And I started corresponding, first by fax and then by e-mail, sometimes two or three times a week, always supportive of each other. It developed into a very warm friendship. Then, a few years later, Angela C. and I were asked to perform the Mozart double and Bach double concertos in Ottawa at the National Arts Centre. We both worked ridiculously hard, separately and together, and the final product was one of my most successful concerts there. Similarly, Jackie and I had a wonderful time playing the Mozart double concerto with the Manitoba Chamber Orchestra to commemorate their twentieth anniversary.

Finally, Marc-André was inspired to write a transcription of Scott Joplin's *Maple Leaf Rag* for the six of us, which we performed as an encore on the next three occasions when we were all together again. For there were indeed three more gala concerts, one of which was in Winnipeg as a benefit for the Winnipeg Symphony Orchestra. The other two were to celebrate our own fifth anniversary – one in Lanaudière, in that magnificent outdoor amphitheatre, and the other in Ottawa at the National Arts Centre, co-produced with Julian Armour and his Ottawa Chamber Music Festival.

All the galas were memorable, but after Ottawa, by mutual consent, we decided that we had done enough of them. They were great fun and marvellous spectacles, but it was becoming virtually impossible to find a mere couple of days, even three years in advance, when all six of us could be free at the same time. Besides, our main work lay in the smaller communities, where we knew we were needed.

Our sponsorship came first through private channels; the McConnell family providing us with the bulk of our initial support. As soon as they allowed themselves to believe that musicians could actually be altruistic, the (initially a little reluctant) Canada Council for the Arts came on board and progressively showed us increasing generosity, becoming one of our staunchest supporters. Other provincial Arts Councils and Foundations followed suit. Most heart-warming of all was the generosity of individual Canadians, impressed by or grateful for our project.

The first tour went out in September of 1994, when Jackie Parker visited some of the smaller Maritime Communities in Nova Scotia. My first tour followed a few months later, starting in Portage la Prairie, and then visiting some of the Mennonite communities of Southern Manitoba. Ten years later, the project had won awards, been written up in countless articles not just in Canada, but in the US and the UK, and been the subject of television specials. Most importantly we had visited over a hundred communities multiple times, as well as reached tens of thousands of youngsters in whose schools we performed.

Piano Six came to a close in its tenth year, during the time I was incapacitated with cancer in my arm. Unable to practise the piano much during those eighteen months, I was able to spearhead (with Judy Lesage and Mary Ingraham, my dear friends and dedicated board members who had supported the project fanatically from its inception and were now ready to retire) a new and expanded project based along the same lines, but with a new and dedicated administration headed up by Debra Chandler, and an excellent Board, headed up by an old colleague and friend, Kathy Elder. The new project consisted not only of pianists but also of world-class Canadian singers and string and wind players, and maintained the standard of excellence set early on by my Piano Six. This new project was known as Piano Plus.

One last note from the Piano Six gala in Quebec. In the audience that night sat my cousin Alison. She had taken piano lessons as a little girl and had loathed them. Out of family loyalty she had come to Quebec, bringing along her young son, and was totally transformed by the music she heard. Alison began following the careers of the Six, going to each of our concerts when we passed through Montreal. Her interest developed by leaps and bounds and she started listening to other pianists and collecting CDs. She is now a regular concertgoer and one of the more informed members of the public. Music has added a new dimension to her life, bringing her great joy. She is definitely a Piano Six success story, perhaps one of our very first. I believe that there have been hundreds, maybe even thousands of such success stories because of Piano Six since that night back in 1995. Indeed, as long as I live, Piano Six and its successor Piano Plus will remain my most important professional achievements. And my own experience on tour for Piano Six seems to me to deserve a chapter in its own right.

CHAPTER 11

"Everything Waits for the Lilacs"
by John Burge

To present a piano recital every year, in every corner of every Canadian province or territory, was a lofty but unrealistic ambition, Canada being the second largest country in the world. But burning idealism provides a powerful incentive, and certainly during the ten years of the Piano Six project we travelled thousands and thousands of miles. I personally survived ten tours between 1994 and 2002, unpacking my suitcases in no less than nine of the ten provinces, and the list of communities we reached – often repeatedly – is impressive.

With each year, I found myself becoming increasingly attached to my native land, not only to its great variety of landscapes and peoples, but to the glorious, limitless space and freedom it offers. It also became evident to me that, although Toronto, Montreal and Vancouver are great multicultural cities, much of the soul of the country lies in places such as Timmins and Jonquière, Lillooet and Campbellton, Nanaimo and Steinbach, where people are invariably generous, appreciative, enthusiastic and seem to possess in abundance an innate curiosity and a passion for education. Characters here seem to be stronger and more colourful. Original thinkers and eccentrics flourish, and the children of rural areas are less blasé and consequently far more receptive to new ideas. Here too are the roots of Canada's unique relationship with the arts, not to mention its unique brand of humour.

Canadians are shy, polite people; they do not wave flags much and are hopeless at self-promotion. To the rest of the world, Canada was still at that time, if the world cared to think about it at all, a mystery; a big clean place with lots of snow, lots of hockey, and one pianist named Glenn Gould. Yet if someone made a list of the achievements of Canadians over the past hundred years or so, both in the artistic and scientific worlds, it would astound the world, not to mention most Canadians. The wildness and richness of our land, the harshness of our winters, the beauty of our springs and the almost violent clash of the fall colours all combine with an outrageously disparate society to produce unusually fertile conditions for the growth of original minds. Piano Six provided me with the opportunity to appreciate and marvel at this great country, so little known and so little understood, even by its own people.

As I recall my Piano Six tours, I see a kaleidoscope of images, unforgettable faces and places, and a myriad of unique experiences. I see myself in the Mennonite Church of Altona, Manitoba, trying to explain to a very serious young girl, dressed in the conservative attire of the Old Order Mennonites (long, simple dress and bonnet), the function of a Polonaise, with its noble rhythm, in a grand 19th-century ball. I paint a picture of soldiers in colourful uniforms stamping their feet and ladies in flamboyant hooped dresses gracefully dancing at their sides; of glittering chandeliers, gold-rimmed glasses filled with sparkling champagne; of grand staircases and marble balustrades. The face that stares back at me is respectful, but the eyes are blank and uncomprehending, and the girl's playing continues to be competent, bland, and metronomic – Chopin is shuddering in his grave. In desperation I take the hand of the pastor's wife, Marilyn Hamm, a vivacious lady and very fine pianist, and ask my poor, befuddled pupil to start playing. After showing Marilyn the basic steps of the dance (which I had learned from the Rubinsteins), she and I set off down the aisle of the church. Marilyn dances the Polonaise impeccably, and as we wind our way around the back and up one of the side aisles, the playing suddenly metamorphoses as I'd hoped; my little pupil, curious and full of repressed talent, has been watching us out of the corner of her eye and has begun to pick up on the flavour of the dance. By the end of the Polonaise, she is beaming with pride, confident and free, and we are all laughing with the joy of it all. It was a beautiful moment, and I wished that Chopin himself could have been there to share in the fun – but then, perhaps he was.

My first ever Piano Six recital was in Portage-la-Prairie. "You will find your hotel next to the huge Coke can," was the intriguing sentence written on my itinerary sheet. In fact, there actually was a giant, Andy Warhol–like Coke can that was visible for miles around, standing between a factory and my hotel. It turned out to be right behind my bedroom, so that at night, lying on my bed, I could admire it all lit up. My room, which was donated by the hotel to support the project, was a bit grim, and I found myself hoping that not all the hotel rooms on Piano Six tours would turn out to be like this one (some were worse, many infinitely better!). It resembled something out of a cheap porno, with an orange shag carpet, a bedspread full of cigarette burns, peeling beige paint on the walls, large holes in the ceiling, a bedside light that refused to work and, incongruously, a framed piece of old-fashioned needlework depicting pansies around the words: "He that believeth in the Son hath everlasting life."

The hotel had a restaurant that was simple but surprisingly good. The waitress was friendly, and the room overlooked an indoor curling rink, allowing me to ponder the mystery of curling's appeal while I munched on my chicken sandwich.

My local contact was Sandra Gartshore, who drove me to the performance venue, the United Trinity Church, and helped coordinate my stay impeccably. Sandra was the first of a long line of extraordinary people without whom Piano Six would never have stood a chance. She saw a chance for herself and for her community, and grabbed it, moving heaven and earth to make the event happen. Piano Six asked for very little money, but when there is no money to begin with, someone has to go out and raise it. Sandra even resorted to door-to-door soliciting.

The pastor of the church, a jolly fellow with a ponytail who was a magician on the side, gave me a hearty welcome. The piano had been brought out from Winnipeg and was a well-tuned seven-foot Yamaha. My program was uncompromising – a program I would have played for a New York, Toronto, or Paris audience. I saw no need to "play down" to people just because of their geographical location. What I did do, though, and encouraged my colleagues to do as well, was to talk between the pieces, giving short explanations and points of reference. Even after Judy Lesage had started writing her top-quality program notes when she joined us as a volunteer a few months later, I still felt this verbal contact was an important part of the evening.

At least a quarter of my audience in Portage was under the age of 16, and they were incredibly responsive. I played Scarlatti sonatas, a Beethoven sonata, some Chopin and Szymanowski, and ended with the massive Schumann "Fantasy." During the last movement of the "Fantasy" the attention was so intense, the silence so absolute, that I couldn't have asked for better performing conditions. At the end there was a standing ovation, a lovely bouquet, encores, and then a pleasant, low-key reception at a piano teacher's home.

The next morning, I taught a master class at the church, after swapping the latest "priest-minister-rabbi" jokes with the pastor. The children who played for me were well-prepared and talented, so the morning passed by like a pleasant breeze. Back home in Connecticut, I received a letter from Sandra in which she wrote: " ... on a personal note, your concert and master class reminded me of what piano playing was all about, and also made me realise how important playing the piano was to me. I have been so busy the last few years juggling family, teaching, husband plus sorting out various personal difficulties, that I had lost sight of what it was that had first drawn me to the piano."

Knowing I had been able to help, in a small way, even one person, fuelled my determination to make this project. If Sandra had not been the inspiration to me that she was, I'm convinced we would never have been so successful.

Toward the north end of Lake Huron lies the mystical island of Manitoulin. Sacred to the First Nations peoples, it contains the only bit of North America that has been under continuous native ownership. An ancient legend of the Odawa people recounts that the Great Spirit Manitou wished for an Island retreat, so he created Manitoulin. It is here that all the great Indian dead were brought to be buried – the greatest of Chiefs, wisest of Medicine Men and Women, the bravest warriors and leaders. In the early 1860s, much of Manitoulin was taken by the government for non-Native settlers. The Wikwemikong Peninsula remained under Native jurisdiction, probably due to a small miracle, but also due to the tenacity and resolve of the Natives living there and the heroism and cleverness of the Jesuit priests who lived among them and assisted them in their struggle against the English Governor and his cohort in Upper Canada. The Wikwemikong Unceded Indian Reserve, as it is now called, is located on the eastern side of the Island, covering 105,300 acres. It is the home of the Odawa, Ojibwa and the Pottowatomi tribes, known as the People of the Three Fires: the Ojibwa are the Faith Keepers; the Odawa are the Traders; and the Pottowatomi are the Fire Keepers.

With its rugged landscape, pristine lakes, sugar maple groves, evergreen forests, stone-fenced meadows, gentle beaches, and wilderness trails, it is truly an enchanted island. When I arrived there in April 2000, spring was just about to burst forth, and little pink Spring Beauties, bright yellow dogtooth violets, crocuses and deep purple grape hyacinths were already in bloom.

Holly Scott, a local resident, pianist and teacher, was the woman behind our first tour on the Island, and she poured her heart and soul into the project, co-ordinating a four-day tour consisting of three recitals, six school concerts, several receptions, and all of our meals. She also had to reckon with the Aboriginal concept of time, which is somewhat different from ours, and would lie awake at night worrying that I might arrive at a Native School to be greeted by an empty hall! (Not yet having met me, she didn't know that, most likely, I would laugh, find a bench and take a nap until they were ready for me.) Holly had to also work out all the logistics, as Manitoulin is big and she didn't want to tire me out with long drives – and my party consisted of six people in all – piano technician, cameraman, driver, etc.

After my second Piano Six tour, I realised that driving hundreds of miles in the day, to keep the budget low, and then playing a recital at night and two school concerts the next morning was too much for me. Angela H. and Marc had, right from the start, used drivers, and except for Jackie (who preferred to drive alone, as he felt it relaxed him after performances), all the rest of us now followed their example. And so it was that I met Nancy Ripley, who became my driver and companion for Manitoulan and all my subsequent Piano Six tours. She is the best road manager imaginable. Quite apart from her total competence to deal calmly with any situation, she is one of those amazing people who always sees the bright side of things. She understands musicians and our insecurities and is brilliant at teasing us into good moods and making us laugh. I am not the only Piano Six artist who insisted on Nancy's presence for every tour. And the nice part is that, somewhere along the line, Nancy and I became not just Piano Six friends, but real friends.

As always, the tour was sandwiched between other engagements, and I had already been to Europe twice that year, so I was my usual tired self, and Nancy had to do a lot of jollying–me–along to get me up and active every morning.

Holly turned up at the Wedgewood Inn, where we were staying, to greet us, and all the pent-up emotion, nerves and excitement of the pre-tour preparations suddenly became too much for her and she burst into tears – though mostly tears of relief and joy that we had actually turned up and that from now on nothing dreadful would happen that couldn't be dealt with relatively easily. Soon we were all sitting around the dining-room table, eating cake. Holly, now fully recovered, told me that my first recital had sold out within hours of its announcement. That is when she'd asked if I could play a repeat recital the next evening. This one sold out in two days. So, a third recital was planned, to be held in Holly's home for the last night; another immediate sell-out. She told me that I had already changed people's lives, even before I'd played a single note. An elderly widow, who had lost her husband the previous year and basically given up the will to live, shutting herself up in her home, had suddenly reappeared and bought a ticket for the recital. There was another lady who was desperate to attend, but her house had recently burned down, and she literally had no extra money to spend. Holly had struck a deal with her – she would get a free ticket if she helped to sell CDs during the intermission and after the concert.

The next morning, we started with the school concerts. As usual, I was far more nervous for these performances than for the evening recitals, as children are potentially a ruthless audience, and I feel a tremendous responsibility for making this early (sometimes first) encounter with classical music a happy one. As was invariably the case in the rural or smaller, isolated communities, the children were well behaved. At my request, Nancy had made some posters for me: the Parthenon in Athens, Mozart as a child, Beethoven, a Monet painting and a

Picasso painting. I wanted to be informative, but also amusing. I talked about the evolution of keyboard instruments and how it affected various composers, in this way managing to incorporate a brief overview of the different eras of piano composition. I pointed out significant passages, rhythms, harmonies, and chords for them to recognise and identify in each piece, so that even if they weren't particularly receptive to the music, they would have something to do, and (I hoped) not be bored.

I began with a movement of a Mozart sonata and talked about the Classical period and its harmonious, beautiful classical lines (like the Parthenon) and its clear orderly progressions. But I stressed that, although the impression was always one of logic, straight uncomplicated lines, and exactitude, with a great composer like Mozart it was his ability to manipulate the system and risk daringly wonderful innovations that made his music unique – and the same was true of the Parthenon, which at first glance, looks like an ordinary rectangle, though in fact its splendour and beauty come from the imagination and unique vision of its architects. After explaining the kind of instrument Mozart would have been using, I played my sonata, then moved on to Beethoven (the rebel), Chopin and Romanticism, Debussy and the Impressionists, and finished with a flashy Lutoslawski etude.

Then came the question period, which lasted nearly an hour. Most questions were predictable:

"How old were you when you started to play?"

"How many hours do you practise a day?"

"Do your fingers hurt when you play loud?"

"Are you married?"

"Why not?"

"Don't you even have a boyfriend?"

"Is that your piano?"

"Did you bring it with you?"

"Why do you make faces when you play?"

"How much money do you make?"

"What is your favourite song?"

"Where is the farthest place you have played in?"

"What was your favourite place?" (Manitoulin, obviously!)

But there were also some more serious questions, which surprised and pleased me. I was asked if playing Chopin was an emotional and therefore tiring experience; if it was hard travelling so much, and did I travel alone? And (by a little girl) if it was an especially hard job for a woman. It was a challenge to keep the answers interesting enough for all of the children, who ranged in age from about six to seventeen.

The next morning at a school in Manitowaning, a First Nations boy of about six raised his hand and very confidentially and clearly informed me that the previous day he had been sucker fishing.

"Was it fun?" I asked.

"Yes, but I didn't catch anything."

"Oh! That's too bad."

"Oh, it was okay." He drew a deep breath and then added: "You can come with me next time!" I was properly grateful but, not to be outdone, the little girl next to him, all blue eyes and blonde curly hair, quickly told me that she had been bowling the previous day and would love me to come with her the next time. At this point, I felt we were on dangerous ground as the invitations started pouring in from all sides. So, trying to change direction but not break the mood, I suggested they all come up to the piano to see how it worked. Instantly a single file formed, and the instrument was closely scrutinised. The ultimate compliment came later, when one child asked me to play some more, and the others applauded enthusiastically. Even after my short, descriptive encore – Mendelssohn's "Spinning Song" or Prokofiev's "Suggestion diabolique" or Grieg's "March of the Trolls" – the encounter didn't end, as everyone requested autographs and continued to ask questions. By now there was a good chance these children would not develop the prevailing attitude that classical music was boring.

The particularly lovely part of my school concerts was the handful of children for whom something in my performance really sparked their imagination. They never seemed to get enough of the music and of my explanations, and would hang around bombarding me with questions until they were led away by their teachers. Most of them were the obvious leaders of their classes – bright-eyed, energetic, curious, and quick-witted. But there were also the class eccentrics with their spiky colourful hairstyles and multiple body piercings, who would stay behind, wanting more information. Very often the class clown would be hooked. And there would always be some little boy or girl, silent and shy, not outwardly very bright, who had obviously been touched by the music and could only stare at me in wonder. Whenever these children actually found the courage to say something to me – usually just a simple "Thank you," and a quick, heartfelt hug – I found myself filled with emotion, tears brimming in my eyes.

In every school where I performed on Piano Six tours, the children who were hooked and stayed behind following the concert made up between ten and twenty per cent of the school audience. Translated into the general Canadian population, ten to twenty per cent makes for an awful lot of classical music lovers and supporters.

Much had been made on Manitoulin of my Cree ancestry, and the night of the first recital at the Ojibway Cultural Foundation, Chief Glen Hare, wearing his full-feathered headgear, made a wonderful speech, welcoming me back into the First Nations family and presenting me with an exquisite pair of hand-made moccasins. Good feeling abounded and both Chief Hare and Holly, who also spoke, mentioned how my presence had provoked a rare "rapprochement" between the Native population and the White population (as they tended mostly to go their separate ways on the Island, the relationship was not always especially friendly).

In the cultural centre where I played, a shop sold Native crafts and jewellery, all extremely tempting. There was a porcupine-quill box which I admired greatly as I browsed in the shop that evening, but it was priced at over 400 dollars and

246

I never even considered buying it. First Nation generosity is quite unbelievable; wherever I went on this tour, I was showered with presents: good luck charms, beaded purses, native jewellery, wampum bags. But I was truly overwhelmed when, after the second recital, Chief Hare, who had returned to listen to the same program, gave me without fuss or fanfare the little porcupine-quill box. He had noticed that it had captured my fancy the night before.

It was during the second afternoon that I lived an almost frighteningly intense experience. I was to give a school concert at the Pontiac Public School right on the Wikwemikong Reserve. My audience was 100 percent Native, and it was assumed that none of the children had heard much (or even any) classical music or ever been to a piano recital. Holly was fretting about how they would behave, but she needn't have: the children were already in their seats waiting for me, and among them were many of their parents as well: an audience of well over five hundred people.

I was welcomed with a powerful Drum Chant expertly performed by a small group of Braves – middle-aged men, but a few younger adults as well. I became apprehensive about my program: would the audience be receptive to the refined delicacy of a Mozart sonata after the sheer volume and raw energy, not to mention emotion, of their own music? However, I should have trusted my material, because right from the start they were hooked, and the Braves, instead of leaving after their presentation, stayed on and even participated in the question-and-answer session. Certainly, the noise in the audience was louder here than elsewhere while I was playing, but it wasn't intrusive or distracting, and Nancy, who was watching closely, told me that they were commenting on and discussing the music, captivated.

I was surprised at the end when an Elder, after a little speech, told me that as a gift, they would perform for me an Honour Chant – apparently a very great and uncommon compliment, and especially unusual as I am a woman. I was made to stand

247

in the centre with the Braves and their drums all around me. At first, I was enjoying myself and this rare experience, and also thinking what a good story it would be to take back home. But then the eerie sounds linking our present 21st-century minds to the psyches of peoples living thousands of years ago started to affect me adversely. The chanting was fascinating, but relentless and filled with tension, and I could sense its mind-altering potential, could see how its hypnotic quality could be used (and probably once was) to incite to battle; empowering the participant but also making him vulnerable. Group experiences such as this I find frightening, for the whole idea of relinquishing control of one's individual identity and subjugating one's mind to other powers is anathema to me. The time-honoured, ritual chants were well-executed and quite unearthly, but the frenzy they inspired played on my trained artist's overly sensitive nature and appeared to me dangerously close to potential mass hysteria. My fatigue from the performance and from the previous days was also beginning to take its toll, so there was nothing left in me to resist this onslaught. I began to perspire, my vision blurred, and my mind started to wander out of control. I was losing my sense of balance and started to sway. Nancy, in the audience, began to worry but then, like a tap suddenly turned off, the chanting stopped abruptly, and I was able to somehow collect my wits.

They weren't finished with me yet, however. The Elder now took my arm and together, accompanied by the Braves and the entire audience, we danced the Indian two-step. This was fun, and the exercise restored my shattered nerves. A party-like atmosphere developed, and no one had any intention of stopping the event to go back to classes. I was given many gifts and chatted with literally hundreds of people, all asking questions or commenting on the concert. The youngest member of the Drum group, named Cheyenne, 19, with long, dark braided hair and flashing dark eyes – too cute and attractive for his own good – asked me for my autograph and suggested that I also write down my phone number and put "with love" as a dedication.

Perhaps I would like his phone number as well? He flirted outrageously, but had great charm and presence and was one hell of a drummer – given the chance, I was sure he would go far.

It took us a while to extract ourselves. I had another performance that evening, but time pressure was blissfully ignored, and a brief tour of the reserve was still to come. Particularly interesting was the new health clinic, where the chief doctor was a Native woman. Half the clinic was an up-to-date, modern healthcare facility, while the other was a traditional healing-chamber, the domain of the Medicine Men with their stores of bones, healing herbs and grasses.

At the Ninkee Gallery I acquired my prize Native artefact: a giant healing-drum, decorated with designs and figures from Native legends and beliefs. Beautifully and colourfully painted, it now hangs on the wall of my home in Germany, along with my growing collection of First Nations Art.

The Manitoulin population of European descent was equally hospitable and generous. Every day we would have lunch and dinner with a different family, in lovely homes with beautiful views and charming gardens. Very occasionally, there would be time to escape and walk along a beach, or lie on a rock by the water, soaking up the warm spring sun, but such moments were all too few. On the final day, I gave a master class and then the recital in Holly's home. By this time, the level of my admiration for gentle but determined Holly was sky-high. There were forty people there and most of them had already heard my program at least once. I played my heart out, especially during the four Chopin Ballades in the second half. Holly gave a lovely speech at the end, and I was given some Island maple syrup, and a jar of Island honey.

The recital in Holly's sitting room was not the first time I had played a concert in someone's home. For years, I had been giving sold-out recitals in Jan Narveson's living room for a hundred people or so, all tightly squeezed in, and by now (after a 25-year relationship) I probably know most of them, and this makes for a very warm and intimate atmosphere. Jan is an internationally respected and admired professor of philosophy at the University of Waterloo, Ontario. His passion for music prompted him to create a chamber music series in his own home where, over the years, he has presented literally hundreds of top-quality concerts. An eccentric of the best kind, Jan never drives a car less than twenty miles per hour over the speed limit, sports at all times (other than in his own home) the most disreputable felt hat imaginable, which drives concertgoers absolutely potty if he happens to sit in front of them because he tends to bounce up and down in time to the music with joyful abandon. Also, as far as I know, he has never worn a tie (except for the day he received his richly deserved Order of Canada), and from about mid-February to mid-December he happily wanders around barefoot. One of the best things about Jan is his wife, Jean, a complete darling with a wonderful, subtle sense of humour. The Piano Six project proved to be a windfall for Jan, as he could finally get to hear, in his own home, some of my colleagues who had never previously passed through his doors and, at this point in their careers, without Piano Six, were unlikely to do so. As it was, every year since its inception someone from Piano Six played on his series, and all concerned benefited from the experience.

Similarly, on the other side of the country, many thousands of miles away, a Dutch couple named Eikelboom, who immigrated to Canada over 30 years ago, missed the house-concerts they had held in their home back in Holland, and started up a recital series in their large house in Maple Ridge, British Columbia. Their property lies in the spectacular Fraser Valley with snow-capped mountains looming on either side. Located not too far from Vancouver, Josine would persuade artists appearing in the city to make a small detour to Maple Ridge before their Vancouver appearances and use her series as a warm-up. I was coming to their house, giving master classes and recitals, and staying with them, years before Piano Six began. I had grown very fond of Josine and her dear husband Adriaan, not least because of Josine's delicious homemade breads, jams, soups, and cheeses. Once again, it gave me intense satisfaction to be instrumental in helping this good couple's series with the possibilities offered by the Piano Six project.

Piano Six didn't always run so smoothly. But whenever my prevailing emotions were a mixture of irritation and disbelief, I would eventually realise that the situation was uncomfortable but hilarious, and that I should try to enjoy myself and definitely take mental notes!

There was a memorable day, for instance, when I was trying to travel from Wolfville, Nova Scotia, to Chicoutimi, Québec – no easy task at the best of times. Wolfville (and Acadia University therein), is a habitual stop for Piano Six. John Hansen, the head of the piano department, and his wife Barbara are great supporters of the project, and every year the department produced outstanding young pianists for our master classes. The hall is an old hockey arena that has been transformed into a jewel of a theatre, and Wolfville itself is a delightful town with wonderful old Victorian-style inns, first-rate eateries and a location on the Bay of Fundy, with its red beaches and powerful tides. It lies in the middle of the fertile Annapolis Valley, where orchards abound and in the springtime the entire area seems to be one large bouquet of blossoms.

But the weather was far from spring-like during my second visit there and after two days of performing and giving master classes, I woke up on a late November day to a giant snowstorm. Being Canadian, I like snowstorms, but as a precaution, I decided to leave half an hour early on my drive to Moncton airport, some 230 miles away. A group of friendly students had come to see me off and wish me a "bon voyage," and as I circled the rental car around the drive to the main road, I rolled down my window to wave a fond farewell. Trouble was, the window wouldn't roll back up again. Having tried and tried to no avail, and since time was short, I gave up and pressed on. The wind and snow never let up, creating white-out conditions, and although I had the heat on as high as it would go and had put on every article of clothing I could find, by the time I arrived in

Moncton, four hours later, a sheet of ice had formed all down my left side, including my left cheek, which was purple and burning with a mini-case of frostbite. A true pianist, I had a least saved my left hand, which had remained tucked under my left leg for the entire trip. The motherly lady at the rental car office in Moncton was horrified by my appearance and made a grand fuss over me, which cheered me up. Even better, Piano Six wasn't charged for the car, and I had enough time to find my way to the airport coffee shop, drink a bowl of hot soup, and start to thaw out.

When I climbed onto the tiny plane that was to fly me to Bagotville airport, I found it seated twelve and I was right in the front, practically in the pilot's lap. The events of the day had worn me out, so I promptly fell asleep. At one point, I was awakened briefly and, glancing out of my window, saw that we had landed in what appeared to be a parking lot, with a shed and a gas station. There were 16-foot-high snow banks on either side and the snow was still lightly falling. Where were we? One passenger got off, and I watched him as he put on a pair of cross-country skies and left hurriedly. When I next woke up, we were landing in Bagotville. I picked up my bags and looked around for the person who was to drive me to Chicoutimi. No one came. I tried the various phone numbers on my itinerary sheet, but no one answered.

I could have wept with frustration, but I also began to wonder how far the airport was from the town. Did I actually have enough cash for a taxi if it was a long distance? As I sat on a bench, a heap of misery, counting my dollar bills, the lights in the airport started turning off. A friendly airport official, along with a security officer (the only two people left in the building) came around and told me they were closing down for the night. I explained my predicament and they kindly telephoned for a taxi and postponed closing until it arrived. This was a blessing, as I wasn't relishing the thought of waiting outside, where it was a cheerful 20 degrees below. The mystery of the no-show driver turned out to be the result of a miscommunication. Someone had been out to meet me much earlier because they had been given the wrong flight number. There had been general consternation among their ranks as well, but all turned out fine. After a good night's sleep, I felt fit and ready for anything.

Chicoutimi is a marvellous little town and is filled with old friends of mine from my Vincent d'Indy days, part of an artistic community that is thriving. Chicoutimi also boasts many fine restaurants and its location, along the fjord-like Saguenay River, is breathtakingly beautiful. The people speak a French-Canadian dialect quite unlike anywhere else in the province and are exceptionally warm-hearted and generous, so all in all, I was well rewarded for my arduous journey.

During another tour, on Quadra Island, my trials were every bit as serious but had a far more humorous aspect. The island, idyllically situated on the Strait of Georgia between Vancouver Island and mainland British Columbia and accessible only by ferry, is home to retired professionals in search of beauty, tranquillity and peace; a generation of die-hard hippies who moved there in the 60s and have never left, becoming an integral part of the island's slightly quirky atmosphere, with their health food stores, restaurants and craft shops; and to some of the finest West Coast Native wood sculptors. Quadra itself is lovely, but the sunsets are what make it unique. With the snow-covered high peaks of the Coastal Range in the distance, the evening colours reflecting on the bay and the granite slopes are almost painfully beautiful to behold.

I was with Nancy on this trip, so I was already in a jolly, ready-for-anything mood. That evening, in front of a sell-out crowd of 260 people, I began my program. The Bach Partita was new and a little shaky, but this was a perfect try-out venue, and I was pleased when I got through the piece without any major disasters. Feeling quite happy, I began my Mozart Sonata K.310. I mentally sat back and listened carefully to what I was doing with this familiar piece, making adjustments here and there and attempting to offer a strong, convincing performance. Halfway through, the hall suddenly went pitch-black. I finished the movement without too much difficulty and got a big hand for my efforts, but we were soon informed that the power would not come on again for a long time, as the cable from the mainland had somehow been severed. Ever resourceful, the organizers, Nancy and most of the audience searched around the building and came up with four candles, a box of matches and a flashlight. We managed to somehow stick the candles onto the piano and for the contemporary Canadian work (a lovely piece John Burge had written for me), a man stood behind me shining a flashlight so that I could read the score. The concert continued in fine form with Schumann's "Faschingsschwank aus Wien" and a brilliant transcription of Mendelssohn's "Wedding March" by Liszt. We had a candlelit reception afterwards and, if anything, the soft, flickering light enhanced the evening and brought me closer to my audience, creating an authentic 19th-century atmosphere.

It was during the same tour that I received an urgent message to call David Sigall in London. Apparently, the legendary pianist Martha Argerich had cancelled her engagements with the venerable Concertgebouw. The concerto was to be the Chopin E-minor (which I can play in my sleep), and they were asking specifically for me to replace her. The rehearsal was to be the next day and, being only a few hours from Vancouver airport I could, conceivably, make it to Amsterdam in good time. My God, I was tempted! Such a wonderful orchestra, and the Chopin E-minor is one of my favourite pieces. But I couldn't accept. There is nothing more reprehensible than treating one organisation and one audience differently from another just because of size and geography; at least that is what I kept telling myself – and besides, what kind of example was I going to set if I suddenly started cancelling Piano Six concerts because something "better" had turned up, quite apart from displeasing the Canada Council on whom we depended so greatly for our funding. So, I refused the magnificent offer and moved to my next stop – Squamish.

Squamish is a special place among the Piano Six venues. When I first performed there in 1997, they hadn't had a piano recital in over twenty years. Joanna Schwarz, local heroine, worked like a beaver to bring us to Squamish, and that first year, a piano was brought in from Vancouver for the concert. Joanna had persuaded the local Rotary Club to help sponsor the concert then hold an auction afterwards, the proceeds of which would go towards buying the piano. The recital was a gala affair, and there was quite a feeling of excitement; the wives were in evening gowns with wonderfully brilliant colours and lots of spangles. Many of the Rotarians, who worked in the lumber business, had never been to a recital before, and were a little worried about when to clap, and whether they were going to be bored sitting for so long. But I think I soon put them at ease, with my chats between the pieces, and I believe the program itself was varied and accessible enough to keep them entertained. Joanna had managed everything perfectly, right down to the hot meal served backstage immediately after I played and before I made an appearance at the auction.

To cut a long story short, they bought the piano, a regular series was started, and all my Piano Six colleagues have appeared in Squamish. Many new artistic organisations have emerged, and while one cannot say that this cultural resurgence is solely due to Piano Six, Joanna is adamant that it played an enormous role as a catalyst. This is another reason why, on this return visit years later, I decided I couldn't cancel; besides, Joanna is a friend, and I couldn't let her down. However, feeling that I deserved some sort of compensation for my lost concerts in Amsterdam, I stopped on the road just before Squamish and spent a great deal of money at a Native crafts store, buying more West Coast carvings for my collection. I then put Amsterdam, once and for all, out of my mind and drove into Squamish.

My first event was an afternoon school concert. Joanna introduced me to the assembled classes, making a great fuss over how lucky they were to have such a "famous artist" come to their school and take the trouble to perform for them, etc. etc. I fell into my routine, giving an energetic presentation of about 45 minutes. Then came the question-and-answer period. During all of these Piano Six years, the children I had met had been absolutely well-behaved, charming, curious and fun. The Squamish children were no different and started in with their questions – no different that is, except for one horrible little boy of about twelve who raised his hand and asked the following question: "Why do you think you are so great? Where is your entourage? No real star would ever play in Squamish, so what are you doing here?" A vision of Amsterdam and the glorious Concertgebouw Hall flashed across my mind, and I reflected a little on those silly laws that make murdering children illegal in Canada.

Oftentimes there would be long periods on tour when Nancy and I would begin to despair over our diets, which seemed to consist entirely of sandwiches and French fries, with an occasional side salad of iceberg lettuce browning at the edges and tomatoes, pale in colour as well as in flavour. But there were also culinary surprises of all kinds, in the strangest of places. For instance, on the road from Portage-la-Prairie to Neepawa, a big sign for a restaurant read: Café de Paris: Italian Specialities and a Chinese Smorgasbord. The chef either couldn't make up his mind, had a strange sense of humour, or was just overly ambitious. An *embarras de choix*, but in fact, the food was quite palatable.

In Deep River, along the Ottawa Valley, our hotel had a restaurant, Pure and Simple Edibles, which served the most wonderful pierogis, imaginative salads and the best raspberry pie ever – so good, in fact, that on the last day of the tour, Nancy and I got up at five in the morning in Timmins so that we could be in Deep River (which was on our way to the airport in Ottawa) in time for lunch and specifically for more pie. It was worth the effort.

One of the more surreal culinary experiences came in North Bay, Ontario. Our stop there was due to the heroic efforts of Lynda Kennedy, a pianist who had studied in Paris and longed for the day when she could return for a visit. North Bay is definitely more sports- than arts-oriented and Lynda's work – keeping music alive in the community – is arduous. Her husband was, at that time, the head of the Music department at a high school. They have three wonderful children who had no opportunity to hear world-class concerts. Her success against the Philistine element in her town is evident when one visits her Brava Music Studios, where I gave my master classes. The studio had a faculty of ten and the students were beautifully trained and a joy to teach.

Lynda, with virtually no support, had moved mountains of lethargy, ignorance and resistance to bring Piano Six to North Bay. When our short stay came to an end, she told Nancy that she was going home to cry because her Piano Six experience was now over, at least for a year. Needless to say, I made a huge effort with my master class, school concert and recital because I was so impressed with Lynda's dedication and selflessness.

What Lynda never knew was that after my recital and a reception, Nancy and I had suddenly become hungry, so we drove around town at about 11 at night, looking for some place that was still open, other than bars with loud music. Sure enough, down a little side road we found a Chinese take-out. The wind was whipping across Lake Nippissing; it must have been minus forty degrees outside. We ran from the car into the little restaurant and, quite frankly, should have walked right out again. The place was rundown and filthy – truly disgusting. The owner, who wore a grimy cap, a brown stained shirt and disintegrating bedroom slippers, took our order and shuffled back to the kitchen. We looked for chairs to sit on while we waited, but most were either broken or covered with squashed bits of food and our boots kept sticking to the floor that clearly hadn't been cleaned since the day it was installed.

As our meal was being cooked and a pervasive smell of rancid, hundred-year-old grease overpowered our nostrils, a huge man roared up on his motorcycle and came inside. Wearing denim, black leather and chains, this Hell's Angel had masses of grey hair flying out from under his cap, some of it tied back in a bushy ponytail. Ignoring us, he went behind the counter and started making phone calls. As we were the only people there, we could obviously hear everything that he was saying. But what was slightly unnerving was that he wasn't speaking in English or in French or indeed any recognisable First Nations tongue. First he spoke Russian, and then he had a conversation in Chinese and, finally, in some language that I guessed was Romanian. Without ever acknowledging the "chef" in the kitchen or, indeed Nancy and me, he finished his phone calls and then roared off. It was all rather bizarre. Back at the hotel, we tried to eat some of the food before deciding that a few more years in this world was a desirable ambition, and a few more mouthfuls of this revolting mess might jeopardize that.

In Lillooet, a small community in the middle of British Columbia's driest, desert-like region, with huge canyons and arid mountains, we found a delectable German Bäckerei with the most wonderful poppyseed rolls. The recital in Lillooet was held in the Freemason Hall, and in my dressing room was a tiny closet filled with fascinating Freemason Vestments and paraphernalia. Incongruously there was also, hanging on the door of the closet, an old pair of red and white checked flannel pyjamas! It was also in Lillooet, right in the middle of the 17th of the 24 Chopin Preludes that I was performing to a really very attentive enlightened audience, who had all brought their children along with them, that a kitten suddenly appeared from nowhere and walked across to the piano, over my feet and the pedals, and then disappeared off into the audience. General merriment ensued, and I added this event to my growing list of "animals-crossing-stage" occurrences: the barking Corgi in Warsaw, a mouse in Cincinnati, a parrot in Santa Barbara, and now a kitten in Lillooet.

The next morning, after we had wheeled out the old upright piano, which had been stashed in a cupboard with basketballs and lacrosse gear, I gave a children's concert in the gym of the Cayoosh School. I was not the first Piano Sixer to play there as Jackie and Angela H. had both made appearances in previous years. The concert was going really well as the children, familiar with the Piano Six routine, certainly were not shy or overawed and kept asking for more and more music, enthusiastically applauding and making me feel obnoxiously pleased with myself. I was just beginning to think that surely, Jackie and Ange couldn't possibly have had such a success, when a young lad of about eight raised his hand (after I had played pieces by Scarlatti, Mozart, Grieg, Mendelssohn and Chopin) to say, slightly exasperated: "This was all very nice, but couldn't you play us some Bach or some Beethoven?" The other children applauded enthusiastically and, although I felt somewhat humbled, I was also filled with pride for my project. These children not only remembered the giant artistic personalities of Jackie and Ange, but they also, a year and two years later, remembered and loved the music. Being only human, I secretly hoped my Chopin would make an equally strong impression on them!

That particular tour provided Nancy and me with two rather unusual sleeping arrangements. In Oliver, we were surprised to find ourselves bunking in the room over the offices of a KOA campground; the owners of the campground were Piano Six supporters and had kindly donated the use of this room. There was only one bed and Nancy, very nobly, slept on the floor. It was also in Oliver that we stumbled across a fantastic East Indian restaurant that graciously stayed open for us (they usually closed at 9) when Nancy explained to the owner that our concert ended at 10, and we would be starving. And so, during my encores, Nancy rushed down the hill to the restaurant, where the owner-chef and his wife had packed up a magnificent feast, which cost us next to nothing, and then rushed back to the hall to collect me. We then took our food back to the campground and our funny little room, where we enjoyed the fragrant curries, crisp pappadums, homemade chutneys and delicate saffron rice, sitting on the floor.

The next day we drove to Nelson, British Columbia, where we stayed at the charming 'Inn the Garden.' There, we were offered the run of the place as there were no other guests. We had the entire top floor, two bedrooms and a sitting room and the choice of five bathrooms! We were in Nelson for a few days, but saw the owner of the Inn only twice – when we checked in and when we checked out. The only other person we saw was an employee who came in for a few hours in the morning to serve us breakfast and to clean our rooms; the rest of the time we were completely alone. But after a short while in the house, we started hearing doors opening and closing. It was a little unnerving. When we went out, we deliberately set the doors at a certain angle only to return and find them closed shut or wide open, and yet no one was in the Inn other than us. And it wasn't only the doors, because one evening, while we were sitting quietly upstairs reading, the CD player downstairs suddenly started playing music. When I mentioned these strange happenings to our presenters, they replied: "Oh yes, it is haunted, like most of the old buildings around here."

It was also in Nelson, while I was sitting alone in the dressing-room during the intermission of my recital, that two youngsters of ten or so raced by excitedly in the corridor outside, shouting to each other: "Did you see how fast her fingers moved?" "Yeah, totally awesome! She is really cool!" I grinned in my solitude, savouring the delightful sensation of being considered "cool"!

The second Ballade of Chopin is a piece that I had recently started using during Piano Six school concerts. It is not only a masterpiece, but is also very evocative, not too long, full of exciting contrasts, and more or less follows the story of a lovely poem by Mickiewicz, which Chopin used as his inspiration. "Switez," or "The Lake of the Willis," tells of a lake in Poland with a mirror-like surface that reflects the moonlight and is surrounded by mysterious flowers. A long time ago, some Polish girls were enjoying bathing in its waters, when a horde of wicked Cossacks appeared over the hill intent on doing them harm. The girls prayed to heaven to save them, and God heard their prayers. They magically disappeared into the earth and reappeared as mysterious flowers. The poem ends with the warning: "Beware, anyone who touches them!"

For the children, I would update the story a bit and embellish here and there. And I would always get a huge kick out of their reactions when, after the simple, gentle, opening pages of the music, which lull the listener into a semi-coma of tranquillity, Chopin suddenly writes a crashing rush of octaves in the left hand and violent, wild arpeggios in the right, evoking dangerous horsemen with evil intentions.

In Thamesford, Ontario, I told the children about the mysterious lake and the story clearly captured their fancy: Nancy, standing at the back, was behind a group of older boys (12-year-olds), who provided a whispered, running commentary while I played: "This must be the girls swimming ... yikes, the bad guys are coming!"

But perhaps one of the best moments of my entire Piano Six adventure came when, at the end of this performance, a group of six-year-old girls walked to the exit holding hands, discussing what they had just experienced. Their leader, a solemn child with glasses and long curly hair, was overheard saying: "You know, I could just *see* those flowers grow!"

CHAPTER 12

"Navarra"
by Isaac Albéniz

To most people the idea of travelling the world playing concerts, receiving flowers and ovations, and meeting fascinating and famous people sounds enviable. But as I've said, it can also be lonely, uncomfortable, tiring and tedious. Oftentimes you arrive in a town late at night and check into a hotel, which can be unpleasant with either insufficient air-conditioning or heating. An uncomfortable bed and unhealthy junk food just add to the misery. Sometimes on the day of the concert you meet the presenters only briefly, practise on a problematic instrument all morning, play the concert at night, miss eating dinner because the restaurants close at 8:30, and then leave the next day having had access to little of the area's charms, which probably do exist. But this scenario is luckily fairly rare. Experience helps. After a while you've been to most places and know what to avoid and where to add on extra days, if possible, to visit friends or enjoy the location. But at the beginning of my career everything was new and unexpected. Stimulating, but also terrifying, my early years on tour were leaps into the unknown. And when I didn't even speak the language of the country other than a few phrases, life could be quite scary for a young girl. Admittedly, most of the time I enjoyed the adventures and positively looked forward to visiting new places and experiencing different cultures; Mexico, which I first visited shortly after my Italian tour, being a case in point.

My subconscious mind detected a change of timbre in the roar of the engines, and I awoke from a light sleep to hear the grinding of the flaps being lowered. The plane was making a wide circle, then it banked sharply. A few thousand feet below,

I spotted the vast ceremonial site of Teotihuacan, the "City of the Gods," with the Pyramid of the Sun dominating the eerily geometrical ground plan. It was my first glimpse of Mexico, and a challenging program lay ahead of me. As we made our final approach, I noted that the sprawling city was wrapped in a dusty-pink haze. Only after deplaning did I realise the lovely pink haze was the worst air pollution I had ever experienced.

Standing on the ramp just outside the door was a young man with my photo in his hand, anxiously staring into the face of everyone who walked by him. I put him out of his misery and, in what seemed like a desperate hurry, he grabbed my handbag from my shoulder and urged me to follow him. We jogged all the way to the immigration booths, arriving there in a lather of perspiration, passing through before anyone else without any problem, and then I started to walk towards the luggage carousel.

"No, no, Señora, this way, por favor," and he gestured towards the street and a waiting car. "Sorry, but I have luggage." His face fell. "My evening clothes and pyjamas," I explained. "I do need them, you know." He sighed heavily. "I mean, you don't expect me to perform in blue jeans, do you?" Stony silence – and naturally, my bags were the last to appear. But Enrique, my young escort, perked up in the car, which was driven by a pretty, young girl named Paulina. They chatted together excitedly in Spanish all the way into town, completely ignoring me. I was dropped off at the Alameda Hotel and curtly told to be ready at 11 the next morning for the rehearsal. Then they roared off in a cloud of dust – I had probably made them late for a party.

The hotel room was large, impersonal, and rather rundown, but comfortable enough. I settled in and ordered room service. The only real inconvenience was that whenever I tried to call the US or Canada, there would be a wait of about ten to fifteen minutes before the connection was made, something I found very peculiar.

The next morning, I woke up with my heart pounding at a furious rate. It was unpleasant, but I had been warned about the altitude (Mexico City is nearly 8,000 feet above sea level), so I lay still and hoped my heart would adjust itself quickly.

Enrique showed up smiling and drove me to the Palacio de Bellas Artes – all marble and 1930s Art Deco. He took me into the orchestra offices and introduced me to the staff. I sat down and waited for something to happen as they carried on a lively conversation among themselves, drinking coffee and eating *churros* (those delectable tube-shaped fritters, dipped in sugar and filled with *cajeta*, or sweet goat's milk custard), ignoring me totally. After a little while, I ventured to ask if I would be rehearsing soon: "Oh no, not for another few hours." And they went back to their conversation.

"Perhaps I could practise while I wait?" This caused a brief hiatus in their chat, and they looked at me, puzzled and vaguely irritated. "Or perhaps I have time to visit the Anthropological Museum or the Diego Rivera Museum?"

"But we have a Rivera mural right here in the building, as well as murals by Orozco and Siquerios!"

"Good – excellent! I'd love to see them ..."

But they went back to chatting, and just as I was starting to feel more than pinpricks of impatience, their conversation was interrupted by the arrival of a rather dashing young man. Immediately there was a sudden, tremendous increase of intense typing and chairs that had been moved to facilitate more comfortable conversation were pushed back to their respective desks. There were also a lot of *"Buenos dias, Maestro's,"* but no one introduced us, so I had no idea what the conductor's name was. He seemed very energetic and friendly and preferred to speak French. I asked if I could practise, and he said this could be arranged but that I was needed for the rehearsal immediately. Now it was my turn to feel puzzled, and I glanced over at the office staff now all diligently working away or speaking officiously on the telephone.

The conductor walked me over to the hall, apologising profusely for the quality of the orchestra; he assured me I would see a marked improvement by the time the performance rolled around, and I was not to be discouraged by the first rehearsal. It was a full-sized orchestra with numerous Eastern Europeans and a few Americans interspersed with the Mexican musicians. Unlike the office staff, they were a very friendly bunch, but utterly undisciplined – chatting, laughing, and walking around ten minutes after the Maestro first tried to get their attention. The rehearsal was ghastly; unlike most second-rate orchestras, they were far from tentative. They played with great gusto and vigour, very loud and with absolutely no rhythm. It was a hot, damp day, and we were all perspiring a great deal. The conductor was gesticulating furiously, and I felt a little sorry for him, as no one was paying the slightest attention and he was clearly embarrassed by his orchestra's performance, hoping that I wasn't too put out by it. He had no need to worry, as I have always, perhaps perversely, enjoyed a challenge and this one was particularly huge, the piece being, after all, the Rachmaninov 3rd piano concerto.

After rehearsal, we went back to the office, ostensibly to set up practice times for me, but with dismay I saw the coffee cups return and the pleasant Maestro slip away from me, lured by the luscious brew and some lively altercations. I sat in a corner waiting less and less patiently. At least my time wasn't totally wasted, as a radio technician wandered by and I managed to glean from him the conductor's name. Since everyone is on instant first-name basis in Mexico, I finally called out to him: "Francisco – please, I've been waiting here doing nothing for half an hour – can someone at least drive me back to the hotel?" He barked out a few parting commands to his staff and rushed over to look after me. Taking me first to the third floor to see the Rivera mural entitled "Man at the Crossing of the Ways," he proved to be very knowledgeable about his country's history and culture and was a most enlightened companion. We then went to a marvellous restaurant, the Fonda Santa Clara, where I first experienced chicken cutlets with a piquant *molé* sauce, made with chocolate. The guacamole appetizer and various salsas were outstanding. Francisco had spent many years in France, so we had a good deal in common and plenty to talk about. He told me that it was the future son-in-law of the president of Mexico who had recommended me to him, which surprised me as I have no idea where the son-in-law could have heard me, but I was tentatively grateful for his recommendation.

Back in the massive marble hall, I practised away all afternoon while Francisco sat and listened, making notes and impressing me with his conscientiousness and desire to make something of the performance.

The next morning, I woke with my heart again beating a lively tattoo. Still waiting for my body to calm down, I walked over to the hall to find out if they were planning some kind of transportation to the airport for me the next day. Much to my surprise, the reaction to my request was extremely agitated. It soon became clear that, unbeknownst to me and certainly unbeknownst to my management back in New York, there was another concert scheduled for two days later in Guanajuato, and I was to be the guest soloist. Fairly amused and not particularly worried, since I was in no hurry to return home, and the extra money from a second concert was welcome, I nevertheless had to change my flight and asked the staff for assistance, regretting it the minute I opened my mouth as it provoked another round of discussion and coffee drinking. Finally, I suggested that I could change the flight myself, which prompted audible sighs of relief and some shoulder shrugging, then I went off to rehearse.

This rehearsal was a slight improvement on the first. I admired Francisco's dogged determination and was secretly delighted to go over passages repeatedly, as it was a piece I had played only a few times before and the routine was reassuring. The afternoon was spent practising in what was a sort of dimly lit closet, as the hall was unavailable.

After the rehearsal, I wandered up and down the Paseo de la Reforma, looking for the Eastern Airlines offices. It began to rain, drizzling at first and then turning into a veritable downpour. Soaking wet, I ran back to the hotel and, braving the telephone system (which I should have done in the first place), managed to call the airline and change the ticket. The rain intensified, flooding the streets, and there was a spectacular display of thunder and lightning.

The car sent to pick me up for the performance arrived 45 minutes late, which turned out to be no big deal as the concert was delayed at least an hour. Even with this delay, the hall looked empty, and during my performance members of the orchestra continued to trickle in and take their places – Haydn's "Farewell Symphony" in reverse. Francisco was beside himself with anxiety and nerves. At heart he was a perfectionist, so his life must have been a constant torment. Somehow, we all ended together, and the small audience made a surprisingly noisy racket in appreciation. A group of piano students stormed backstage and enthusiastically hugged me and bombarded me with questions about technique, practising and teaching. They were adorable and put me in a wonderful mood for the dinner with various notables that followed. Most interesting for me was the presence of the legendary Hungarian pianist Gyorgy Sandor and his son Mike, both of whom, thankfully, had been caught in frightful traffic and had missed the excruciatingly awful performance. I sat next to them at dinner and was vastly entertained by their company.

At eleven o'clock the next morning a big black Chevy Sedan, circa 1965, roared up to the entrance of the hotel. It had no air conditioning but sported coloured bobbles framing every window and a plastic Madonna with a fluorescent halo. I looked sceptically at my suitcases and at the vehicle, already bursting at the seams with people and luggage. However, everything somehow fitted in. Abelino, who resembled every non-Mexican's mental image of Pancho Villa – the notorious revolutionary hero – complete with an amazing moustache, was our driver. Apparently, it had been his birthday the night before and he had been taken out by friends on a drinking binge, so our trip to Guanajuato was punctuated by repeated stops for him to throw up by the side of the road. I sat next to Francisco, who had clearly not recovered from the performance of the previous evening and who spent most of the trip earnestly going over every note, analysing what had gone wrong. The rest of the party consisted of the blessedly tiny accountant, Maximo, and his equally tiny wife, Conchita, and Maria-Luisa and a friend of hers from Chile, whom I found to be quite interesting. She was a communist who had been expelled from Chile and had gone into exile in the Soviet Union, but she and many of her colleagues had become disillusioned there because they were given living quarters far superior to those of the ordinary folk, as well as fancy cars, televisions and other perks that put them in a privileged social position. Since class distinction went against everything she believed in, she had left, and now lived in Mexico and had become a great supporter of the arts.

It was hot as hell in the car, and I was lucky to be next to the window. During the five-hour drive, we stopped only once for drinks and to stretch our legs. By the end we were all exhausted, perspiring and hot, literally sticking together as we drove up to the hotel with dreams of cold showers foremost in our thoughts. Unfortunately for me, the shower was delayed a little, as they had forgotten to book my room and it was the height of the tourist season. We had also arrived in the middle of the Cervantino Festival, so rooms were hard to come by.

Francisco suggested that I share his room, and the ladies looked very shocked, one of them whispering in my ear that he was the lover of the president's wife, and I was to be careful of him. I found their gossip slightly mean-spirited and probably inaccurate, but it did make for a good story. Anyhow, a room was finally found for me, although it lacked a private bathroom and was more of a linen closet than a bedroom, as it had plenty of cupboards but no window. I was too tired to care at this point and headed for the public shower, wondering if Mexicans were always this off-hand and lackadaisical in their treatment of artists or if being a woman pianist made me somehow special.

In the evening, while the rest of my group went to the movies, I wandered the streets and alleyways of Guanajuato for a while. An utterly charming, old Spanish silver-mining town dating to the mid-16th century, beautifully preserved and very clean, it was great fun to explore as one kept finding hidden staircases and pathways and the strangest jumble of balconies, rooftops, and walls, all completely asymmetrical. It was a photographer's delight. The air was light and fresh and a welcome relief from Mexico City.

In the morning, Conchita took me on a more formal tour. We started with the Museo de los Momias. Fully expecting to see something resembling Egyptian mummies, I was absolutely horrified to find myself in a longish corridor where, on the right-hand side, were huge glass display cases and caskets filled with dead bodies in various states of decomposition, which had been exhumed when the local cemetery had become overcrowded. The dryness and the special combination of gases and minerals in the local soil had somehow halted the decomposition process and mummified the remains. Conchita enthusiastically told me that some of the women were nuns who had been walled up alive after having been raped, the unborn babies still visible in their wombs, the women's faces displaying horrendous grimaces. After no more than a glimpse, I refused to go any further, probably hurting Conchita's feelings. She wondered if I'd like to buy a postcard or a souvenir at one of the stands outside the museum where they sold little cadaver dolls. Small children raced in and out of the display area shouting and laughing as their families put out their Sunday lunches on adjacent picnic tables. All I could think was that their stomachs were made of sterner stuff than mine.

We continued our tour, and I bought some exquisite silver earrings and a beautiful little gold cross, which relieved Conchita and assuaged any hurt feelings from my earlier reaction to the much-prized mummies.

Abelino then took me to the Juarez Theatre, where I practised a little. He was still not fully recovered from his drinking binge and fell asleep at the back of the hall, snoring loudly. Eventually we returned to the hotel so that I could change and do my hair. Francisco was swimming in the pool, and everyone in our party was eating *hors d'oeuvres* on the terrace. By 7, I was ready and waiting to go as the concert was, after all, at 7:30. No one else seemed to be in any hurry. Even Francisco was still in his bathing trunks, eating baby shrimp in a spicy sauce by the pool. At that point I gave up and just let events unfold without interfering – it seemed the most logical thing to do and, to be honest, was fun in a perverse sort of way.

We all arrived at the huge open-air stage in one of the city's more impressive plazas about ten minutes late. The concert, a repeat of the program in Mexico City, was very simple: the Rachmaninov 3rd piano concerto and, in the second half, Tchaikovsky's 6th Symphony. As it was the closing concert of the festival, there were to be fireworks after the Tchaikovsky, and already there was a party-like atmosphere in the audience, with small children rushing about and drinking among the adults. It was an extremely hot evening, and, although my hands rarely perspire, I thought it wise to bring a handkerchief on stage. The handkerchief was destined to serve another function, that of hiding several thousands of American dollars that Maximo suddenly insisted on paying me as I stood next to the platform ready to go on. I had only two options: either stuff the crisp new bills down the front of my dress or hide them in the handkerchief. I opted for the second option, since the first would have been decidedly uncomfortable.

There was however a major impediment to the progress of the concert: the piano hadn't turned up. Someone had forgotten to give the order to move it from the theatre to the outdoor stage. So we stood around, poor Francisco embarrassed and worried, and I, since it was all beginning to take on the appearance of a complete farce, becoming less and less nervous. The audience started getting raucous as they waited, singing songs, drinking and doing "the wave." Finally, a loud cheer went up as a big open farm truck rolled up with the piano in the back; the poor instrument was then rather brutally thrown onto the stage, where it was quickly put back together with the pedals and legs haphazardly hammered in.

Without further ado, we climbed onto the platform amidst loud applause and wolf-whistles, and I quickly shoved my handkerchief filled with hundred dollar bills into the piano, praying that a strong gust of wind wouldn't blow the money all over the stage! I sat down only to find that the bench, a wooden one and non-adjustable, was at least a foot too low. I looked up at Francisco, but his face was a picture of stress, so I decided not to make a fuss, but simply imagine I was Glenn Gould and see what it was like to perform with my eyes at keyboard level.

Not that the keyboard was in very good shape; it had obviously been badly jolted during its short journey and the keys were all off-centre, with one or two of them permanently down. The concerto began, and very soon I realised that something was very wrong with the pedals. Almost immediately I heard a large crack and to my dismay the entire pedal mechanism simply broke away from the main body of the piano and lay lifeless on the stage floor. Now if it had been a Mozart concerto, even Mendelssohn or even conceivably Chopin, a total lack of pedal could have somehow been circumvented, but with Rachmaninov, the pedal-less prospect was daunting.

The concertmaster and his assistant, a friendly young woman from Poland, were the only ones aware of my dilemma, as they were sitting right next to me; they shot worried glances at each other, at me and at my feet. Everyone else seemed oblivious, and the audience was clearly using my performance as a nice background for their rather noisy but cheerful party. So I decided to press on: two and a half movements without any help from the pedals! At first, I was quite amused and almost got the giggles, since my contortions to try and hold the lyrical lines together and make them sound vaguely legato were quite spectacular. But then the novelty began to wear thin, and the effort became physically very tiring. Of course, this unaccustomed clarity did have an upside: I became incredibly easy to follow, and our ensemble was really quite good.

Francisco, totally focused on holding everything together, had no idea of the drama being played out behind him. In fact, he looked positively pleased as we ended with a cascade of octaves and crashing chords. The audience was delighted for the opportunity to make a lot of noise after all the waiting, so the ovation was deafening. Meanwhile, on a neighbouring hill, the fellow in charge of the fireworks heard the cheering and applause and looked at his watch: 10 o'clock – end of the concert, slightly later than he had expected but, better late than never – and he set off the string of fireworks: the Tchaikovsky symphony never got played.

Francisco was desperate for about 10 minutes, but soon recovered his good humour, and we all went off to a big party given by the governor of the province. The music, from a mariachi band, heavily mic-ed, blared unpleasantly loud, but the food was extraordinary, a huge buffet of enchiladas and tacos, chiles en nogada and frijoles refritos, roasted chicken and tamales, spring salsas and the wonderfully flavoured Pibil. No one spoke of the concert; actually, no one could speak at all except at the top of their lungs as the music was so loud, but everyone was smiling. The mariachi band was soon followed by a female pop singer who was, if anything, even noisier. In a strange way, it was all rather fun, and I returned to my closet in the hotel with my ears ringing, dead-tired, but not unhappy.

At seven in the morning, just a few hours later, I was up for an interview with the *Excelsior* magazine. Bleary-eyed and with a throbbing headache, I found the interviewer set up by the pool. Her regular photographer had been unable to come, so she had borrowed one from another newspaper. The photographer was clearly from Eastern Europe, although I assumed he was a Mexican citizen. The interview began with all the predictable questions, and at one point I found myself discussing the merits of the Juilliard School in New York and how it was considered a magnet for most of the best young pianists in the world. I rattled off some names to illustrate my point.

The photographer protested, saying that everyone knew that the Moscow Conservatory produced the most prize winners in international competitions. Slightly irked – it was after all my interview and not his – I pointed out that, yes, indeed, the Moscow Conservatory did produce many prize winners, but that after one "victory tour" they were generally never again allowed out of the Soviet Union. I rattled off some more names to illustrate my point. Furious with my reply, he said it was part of the Soviet system to give everyone a chance and to rotate the pianists who travelled to the West. Maintaining my composure, I asked, "A chance for what?" And suggested they weren't allowed out again because the system was afraid that they would acquire a taste for Western freedom and defect.

I was beginning to wonder who the hell this man was. We were starting to draw a crowd. Having caught his breath, he suddenly announced that music in the West was controlled by Jews, and rattled off his own list of names. This outrageous generalization enraged me, and I said that in the U.S. there were many Jewish musicians, but no one could complain about their talent or quality, to which he hit back with the remark that Jews were not musical and that I should give him the name of just one Jewish composer, if I could (he really was extremely ill-informed and stupid!). So I rattled off another long list of names, temporarily shutting him up.

I was happy to see that my Mexican friends (at this point they were all there, listening) as well as my Chilean friend, were most unimpressed by his outbursts and rhetoric. My interview continued as he sat in a corner, seething with political rage and still not having taken a single photo. I was just expanding on the quality of the many outstanding Mexican pianists whom I had met in my life when I was interrupted again by our so-called photographer, at this point seemingly quite deranged, with the challenging remark (a complete non-sequitur) that Russian and Czech hockey players were the best in the world. I just laughed, so he continued his harangue by informing us that the members of the Canadian National team were all professionals and cheats. I sighed and started listing names again.

What made this episode so totally farcical was the fact that neither of us spoke the other's language. The poor Mexican interviewer was kept busy translating – and no doubt, censoring – some of the man's ruder or more inflammatory remarks. When they finally left, I asked my Mexican friends if they happened to know who this fellow actually was.

"Didn't you know? He is a Russian and is one of the official journalists in Mexico for *Pravda*," they informed me. To this day I haven't figured out why he was posing as a cameraman – he didn't take a single photo of me – in Guanajuato at seven o'clock in the morning.

Francisco never turned up for breakfast, and after repeated calls to his room was given up for lost. Abelino didn't turn up either (surprise, surprise!), so the remainder of our party took a taxi, as I had a plane to catch in the early afternoon at the Mexico City airport. It was less squished in the taxi, and it was also air-conditioned, so the return trip was infinitely more pleasant. Halfway we stopped for a drink, and who should drive roaring up, brakes screeching, in a great whirlwind of red dust, but Abelino and Francisco in the black Chevy. Abelino had overslept and Francisco had switched rooms, so they had been telephoning the wrong room to wake him up and he, too, had overslept. They insisted I ride with them, so I transferred my bags to the old Chevy, and they drove me, cheerfully but very hungover, to the airport. I caught my plane with only minutes to spare, Francisco and Abelino having decided to stop for a little coffee and conversation shortly before we reached the city limits.

I have often since returned to work in Mexico, having learned over the years to love and admire its citizens, but without fail every visit has been an adventure – daily disasters are inevitable, and one learns to accept them if not with grace, then with humour. A shifting of mental gears is definitely required before the plane lands in this colourful, complicated, and completely exasperating country.

CHAPTER 13

Variations on "Rule Britannia"
by Ludwig van Beethoven

Since childhood my head was filled with visions of an England harbouring Secret Gardens and "hosts of golden daffodils," bleak Yorkshire moors where phantoms lurk in the heather, strange monster hounds bounding across the Devonshire moors, endless country lanes bordered by giant hedgerows, lambing seasons and hunting seasons, bluebells and cockleshells, kings who invented religions and lopped off their wives' heads, Round Tables and Star Chambers, dynasties named after plants, wars named after flowers, talking rabbits and reckless toads, Thornfield Hall and Saint Mary's Mead, Middlemarch and Misselthwaite Manor, Princes in the Tower and Paupers who would be King, tea and crumpets and bubble and squeak, honest Peggoty and fussy Miss Tiggywinkle, Tintern Abbey and Abbey Road, pubs and sticky puddings, P.D. James and P.G. Wodehouse – I could go on forever! It was no surprise that I was highly predisposed to having a marvellous time touring England, and it was my great good fortune that my very first season there, playing the concerts Arthur had arranged for me in the mid-70s, proved to be enough of a success for me to put down roots which eventually grew into a flourishing British career.

Every subsequent year I would return for at least one London appearance, and then I'd merrily hop on the train and head for the provinces. In those days, British Rail was a delight, and I loved my trips to Huddersfield and Nottingham, Truro and Newcastle, Preston and Manchester, and so many other towns and communities. It gave me endless pleasure to sit by the window and watch the English countryside pass by.

London soon became as familiar to me as Paris or New York, but whereas in those two cities I had maintained only a few good friendships, my social calendar in London was forever full. For one thing, I had cousins in abundance from both sides of the family in England. My father's cousins lived in Acton, and it became a tradition that, however tired or busy I was, I would spend my first London evening in their home. There, my cousin Basia, whom I both loved and admired, would spoil me by preparing pierogis and nut-cakes and many other delicious Polish dishes. Fragile, loving, sweet and idealistic, she had survived the horrors of a labour camp in Siberia during the early years of the Second World War, then a horrific trip south to the Middle East once Russia had been attacked by Germany and the Poles in labour camps were freed (but certainly not assisted in any way). Arriving in Lebanon, she eventually obtained a degree in architecture and finally ended up in London, where she settled. She married Edward, a dear, positive, funny man, also a Polish exile, who counterbalanced her slightly melancholic, earnest nature. Happily, she lived long enough to return to her beloved Poland, following the liberation in 1989. She kept a scrapbook of all my publicity photos, reviews and programs, and was at all my London performances. Being childless, she considered me her daughter and was fanatically partisan about my career. Chopin was her favourite composer, and it pleases me to think that the final time she heard me, I played an all-Chopin recital at Wigmore Hall. My deepest regret is that she never met Harry, because it had been her most ardent wish that I should find happiness in love.

I also had Clouston cousins, to whom I am devoted, who lived for a time in London and then moved to Oxfordshire, where I would visit them on free days. My cousin Vicky is not only one of the kindest people I know, but also a marvellous cook and a kindred spirit with a profound knowledge of French literature. Not having children of my own, I took vicarious joy in watching her lovely children grow up.

And every day that I was in London, I would practise up in Kensal Rise at Jack and Linn Rothstein's home. Non-pianists probably don't realise how difficult it is to find decent pianos (or any pianos at all) on which to practise while on tour. Linn, a fellow Canadian from Victoria, would mother and boss me, and Jack would buoy up my spirits, instilling in me the virtues and advantages of a perpetually positive attitude. Both would listen critically to my programs (Linn being a world-class pianist, and Jack a first-class violinist and conductor), giving excellent advice and encouragement and then feeding me nourishing soups, fish and healthy salads.

Of course, my buddies Annabelle, Imogen and Angela H. all lived in London as well as plenty of other friends, musicians and non-musicians. We would get together on a regular basis, sometimes in their homes or sampling with them the delights of London restaurants, concert halls and theatres.

And finally, there was my long-time manager David Sigall. I was with him for over thirty years and think of him far more as a friend than a manager. David subscribes to the old-fashioned adage that an English Gentleman should never be seen expending energy, because the mere mention of hard work or earning a living is dreadfully common and in extraordinarily bad taste. He makes a big show of indolence and lethargy, but of course I know better, as I have seen him full of energy and excitement after concerts when his artists have performed well. He would pretend to be exasperated by our temperamental shenanigans and ambitions, but beneath the façade we always knew that he cared for us. His support, both personal and professional, remained steadfast throughout most of my long, crisis-ridden career.

After many years Recently, by mutual consent, David and I parted company. Both of us faced major upheavals in our lives some years ago and, at least in my case, I wished to make a fresh start and find a new impetus to my British career. Being a true gentleman, David completely understood and put no obstacles in my way, and I moved on to the young, vibrant and immensely likeable managers at Ikon Artists. David and I have remained good friends.

I consider many of my performances in England to be highlights of my professional life. I think it is because English audiences make me feel relaxed and content, there is a gentle benign-ness in their attitudes towards artists, and an air of pleasant anticipation – without any accompanying critical tension – which makes me so happy to play for them.

My most ambitious project ever was undertaken in London. There was a Karol Szymanowski Festival at the South Bank in 1990, and I had agreed to play the Symphonie Concertante as well as three recitals. Since I had never played a note of his solo works before, and only had a few months in which to learn them, this was a daunting prospect, especially since I was already booked to play a completely different BBC recital at Saint John's Smith Square around the same time. Also, I was scheduled to play Bartók's 3rd piano concerto for the first time with the Royal Philharmonic Orchestra, plus the Brahms d-Minor concerto in Scotland, and in the middle of it all, had to rush to Chicago to play the world premiere of the Liszt 3rd piano concerto as well as *Totentanz*, also a new piece for me. And all this within a few weeks!

In preparation for this marathon, I spent four months barely leaving the piano bench, working eight or nine hours a day, memorising like mad. Szymanowski is one of the most complex of composers, with a unique harmonic language that defies logic and exudes neuroses to the point where a performer can begin to feel ill. I believe I lost the Plummers their cleaning lady because my constant playing of Szymanowski drove her crazy. It is a tribute to the calm enthusiasm of my London public that I ended up enjoying the concerts thoroughly, in spite of the angst and tension in the music.

Perhaps my favourite concerts of all came as a result of two tours that I made in the late 1980's with the Royal Philharmonic Orchestra, tours that were characterised by the somewhat haphazard but strongly democratic, "no coddling the soloist" side of the English music business. The sheer good-natured fun and wonderful music-making that results is a good trade-off!

While I had arrived with a hacking cough and streaming cold, this was not otherwise a stressful trip, as I didn't have much repertoire to maintain. There was the Brahms D-minor concerto for Hong Kong (I was going on there afterwards), a Chopin recital for the BBC, and for the Royal Philharmonic tour I was playing one of my favourite concertos: the Grieg. Well, not my very favourite – I prefer in my heart the Chopin concertos and various Mozart and Beethoven concertos – but the fact is, the Grieg is delightfully uncomplicated to play; it has lovely melodies that are pleasing to the audience, performer and orchestra alike; it is flashy enough to elicit standing ovations at the end (always an ego-booster); it is technically the easiest of the great Romantic concertos and, as I'd performed it since the age of 14, it holds no terrors for me. All it requires from me is some very basic maintenance work and an occasional run-through at half-speed. In fact, I was contemplating using the tour as a rest cure.

The next morning, I did a lightning raid on Boots, the pharmacy, stocking up on Kleenex, Vitamin C, nose-spray and postcards, and then wandered over to Kensington Court, where Ingpen & Williams had their offices. David was already at this desk, looking tanned and rather more cheerful than usual. He had just returned from a skiing holiday, and I was filled with envy. Skiing had become a forbidden delight, as it would be irresponsible to indulge myself right during the high point of the concert season, which happens to coincide with the high point of the ski season. The last time I had been skiing was during a divine week in the early 1980s in Austria, and I missed it sorely.

So, hacking away, I sarcastically remarked that it must have been an exhausting trip for him and perhaps he should take another holiday in which to recover, to which David responded that, yes, he was exhausted from the trip, but two or three weeks at this desk was all the rest he needed to recover completely! Our bantering was interrupted by an assistant who complained that not only had the RPO still not given her my travel schedule, they had said that as everyone in the orchestra was finding their own way, they assumed I would too.

The tour was to start the next day, but I figured they would suddenly wake up to the fact that I was the soloist and they actually needed my presence. Even after several angry phone calls from David's assistant, they still maintained I should find my own way but oh, would I be good enough to attend the receptions given by the sponsors after most of the concerts? It would help them out greatly and oh, by the way, perhaps I should be warned that by the time the receptions were over it was quite possible I would miss the last trains back to London! The situation was developing a comical aspect and, since none of the decision-making was up to me other than my unshakeable refusal to drive myself, I sat back amused and observed the unfolding events.

This was my first tour with an English orchestra, and I still thought that all would be resolved soon. After an hour or so, I reluctantly left the office and found my way up to Linn Rothstein's house, ostensibly to practise but, not having seen her in six months or so, we had hours of gossip to catch up on, though I did manage to fit in a few hours at the piano.

The next morning, I practised hard at Linn's, but there was still had no word from the RPO other than my rehearsal would be that afternoon at 3:30 in Fairfield Hall, Croydon, with the performance at 7:30.

Linn's husband Jack decided to drive me to Croydon himself. So, at 2 o'clock we piled into the car and set off on our journey, fortified by fruit and sandwiches which Linn had packed so we wouldn't starve. It was a long, nightmarish drive, plagued with traffic jams. Soon it was evident that we would be late, and while I hated to inconvenience the conductor, Sir Charles Groves, with whom I had never worked before, I didn't really mind, because I thought the RPO might realise they should have organised official transportation. As it turned out we were only five minutes late, but the orchestra was already on stage and had finished tuning, so I dashed up and apologised for my tardiness, barely taking the time to rid myself of my gloves and jacket.

Sir Charles accompanied beautifully, although I had a hard time figuring out his beat (to be honest, I have a hard time with most conductors' beats!). In the end, I decided I could trust him and just didn't watch him much. We raced through the Grieg, rehearsing only one or two places, and I was hurried off the stage as they had to rehearse a new piece by Howard Blake for cello and orchestra with Stephen Isserlis as soloist.

Linn and I had been to Fairfield Hall together many times before for concerts of mine, and it had become a rather hilarious tradition for us to eat at the cafeteria. I had never quite recovered from my first visit there when I had requested two Cornish pasties and they had been served on a plate with spaghetti, rice, and potatoes as the accompanying vegetables. It was reassuring to see that the food had not improved. Linn and I laughed a lot, and I stocked up on the carbohydrates.

At 6:30 the orchestra left the stage, and I was permitted a few minutes to get to know the piano and warm up. Not that my hands were the slightest bit cold; for some reason, the heat in the hall was on full blast, even though outside it had become very warm, and we were all perspiring and developing heat rashes. This was extremely un-British; most of the concert venues are freezing cold and damp. Another quaint British tradition is that, more often than not, one has to share dressing rooms with other soloists or conductors, differences in sex notwithstanding. After the initial shock over this excessive chumminess, you just get used to it and cope – at least there is always someone close by to zip up evening dresses or manipulate unreachable buttons or clasps.

Stephen, magnificent cellist that he is, was quite nervous. He was younger than I, and at the very start of his career. He was not on the tour, so this was his only RPO concert of the season, and it was important to him. I was still completely relaxed and wandered about, chatting with various members of the orchestra, feeling utterly in control and insufferably smug as the piece held no qualms for me at all.

As they so irritatingly say: "Pride cometh before the fall," and my fall was stunning! Stephen had gone out and performed his piece brilliantly, and then it was my turn. I sat down at the piano only to find that the wretched piano technician, who had been tinkering with the instrument moments before the concert, had lowered the bench to an almost Glenn Gouldian level and, as is invariably the case, I was having the devil of a time operating the mechanism to raise it. Sir Charles had noted my head bobbing up and down with the exertions of trying to elevate myself, and had misinterpreted this as a nod to begin the concerto. I was just about to get up from the bench to see if it was going up or going down when I turned the knobs, when suddenly I heard the opening timpani roll! It was useless to try and figure out which beat Sir Charles was at, so I just didn't play the first all-important chord and came in with the octaves immediately afterwards. I nearly died of mortification and could feel my whole body burning with shame. I knew that Jack and Linn would be killing themselves laughing out in the audience, but somehow this didn't cheer me up much. The rest of the performance went well, although I was on autopilot for most of the time, trying to gather up whatever shreds of dignity were left to me. When I apologised to Sir Charles after the concert at the reception, he hardly knew what I was talking about and probably hadn't noticed, as the orchestra plays a crashingly loud A-minor chord concurrently with my lost opening. There was lots of good food at the reception, but I was still feeling a bit overwrought and not hungry, so instead of eating, I dutifully chatted with the sponsors. My cough was also back with a vengeance, and I felt ill. Linn fed me sandwiches and a banana in the car on the long drive home. This was not the easy first concert and auspicious beginning to the tour that I had expected.

The next day, the first of April, was a free day, and it was absolutely gorgeous. I spent the morning practising Brahms and Chopin, Linn shouting out suggestions as she cooked my lunch, and in the afternoon we went to the Portobello Road Market for a little shopping spree. The sun was shining and London's gardens were in full bloom. I could feel my strength and good health returning and, after a good night's rest, I felt fit and ready for anything.

Richard, the young operations manager of the RPO, telephoned fairly early the next morning. I foolishly thought that perhaps he had finally got his act together and sorted out my travel plans. Not quite ... he was actually calling to find out if I had a car and if he could cadge a ride home with me after that night's concert in Corby. I patiently pointed out that I, so inconsiderately, didn't have a car (my sarcasm was quite lost on him), and that furthermore my promised train tickets had not yet arrived. He seemed perplexed and, apologising madly, rang off to try and solve these frighteningly complex problems. I had a moment of sympathy for him. After all, he was very young.

I had a short practise at Linn's and an even shorter power-walk, then caught the train to Kettering. The ride was blissful, as we passed through some lovely countryside and it was lambing season – little wobbly bundles of wool tottering about, pure white against the fresh new green of the meadows. The leaves on the majestic, gnarled old ash and oak trees were still just a pale film of colour, but the fruit trees and the forsythia were in full, resplendent bloom – deep purples, reds and delicate pinks, brilliant yellows and whites. Everything looked newly washed and as bright and vivid as a child's imagination, and I sat with my nose pressed to the window, drinking it all in, ridiculously happy.

The train ride was only an hour, and then I had to change for another smaller train to Corby. At Kettering station, I ran into Mats, a young Swedish cellist who was on trial for three weeks with the orchestra as he sought the position of principal (which he eventually got). Like me, he had made an embarrassing mistake in the Grieg in Croydon – during his mini-solo in the second movement – so we commiserated together. He had studied at Juilliard when I was still teaching there as Mr G.'s assistant, and we found we had many mutual acquaintances. At Corby, there was, naturally, no one to meet us at the station and, even worse, there were no taxis. Luckily, the weather was still pleasant, because we ended up walking over a mile to the hall, Mats carrying his cello and myself carrying my heavy garment bag.

I listened in while the orchestra rehearsed Delius, the perfect music for such a lovely spring day, and I ate an apple and some chocolate from the care package Linn had prepared for me. Sir Charles seemed relaxed and rested, and we had a pleasant chat before the concert. This time my bench was set correctly, but when I sat down on stage, the orchestra members did their utmost to make me laugh, contorting their faces into panic-stricken grimaces as I put my hands on the keyboard. By watching Sir Charles like a lynx, we started together beautifully, and everyone gave me exaggerated looks of relief. The comedy was re-played in the slow movement, where my Swedish friend redeemed himself as well. I then settled down and enjoyed the performance thoroughly, Sir Charles and the orchestra giving me a warm and sensitive, almost serene, accompaniment. I felt energised and happy afterwards, and was sorry I couldn't phone and tell someone all about it, but those were the pre-cellphone days. I was reduced to amusing myself during the second half by playing with one of the orchestra member's dogs, who, like me, was waiting backstage for the concert to be over.

The party after the concert was given by Northern Telecom. I sat at a table with a very lively bunch of Telecom officials, who promised to come and hear me when the orchestra played in Derby the following week. It amused me thoroughly throughout the tour to see how the head honcho of each sponsoring company would avoid pronouncing my surname in his post-dinner speech. I would be variously referred to as "our delightful soloist" or even in quite American fashion as "our new friend Janina." Not one attempted the name "Fialkowska," which was just as well when I think of how my poor name gets mangled in the States. After the meal, I was approached by Richard, who had actually rented a car himself and triumphantly drove me back to London. He was very adept at apologising for his earlier lack of planning of my travels, so I didn't bother to shower him with reproaches, even when he earnestly explained that he was gaining in experience.

Not enough experience, it seemed, because the next day I was faced once again with a totally disorganised journey. Had the Grieg required a lot of practise and worry, I would have been a nervous wreck. I spent the morning at Linn's, eating a leisurely breakfast, reading the *Times*, doing my laundry and working in a desultory fashion, waiting for a call from Richard. It never materialised, so eventually, after a huge fortifying lunch, Linn drove me to Victoria Station, where I boarded the train for Eastbourne. On arrival I found my way to the hall and tried out the piano, which was surprisingly good. Since it was still hours before the concert, I ended up taking a long walk along the waterfront. The Channel was very wild that day and the wind, whipping across the crests of the waves, carried with it a heart-stopping chill, aggravating my cough, which had lain dormant for the past two days. I beat a hasty retreat, only to find out that my dressing room was bitterly cold and damp, and I was still faced with hours of waiting.

The appeal of Grieg never failing, I received a huge ovation that night from the elderly but enthusiastic public. I was given some lovely flowers and the host of our dinner referred to me as "our gracious soloist from Poland" and complimented me on my English for most of the evening. The company at dinner was pleasant, but they served (in Sir Charles's words) "absolutely disgusting" salmon fillets, cooked dry on the outside and raw on the inside, with potatoes that never stood a chance and "greens" that were boiled into nothingness. I was grateful, once again, for Linn's care package.

It was Sir Charles himself who drove me back to London that night in his big red BMW, accompanied by his charming wife, Hilary. I was surprised and somewhat alarmed that Sir Charles himself was driving, as he seemed extremely tired, the road back to London was just two lanes, and it was also raining. However, they put me in the back seat and told me to go to sleep, which I promptly did. We got to London at two in the morning, and I wondered what on earth I would have done if they hadn't offered me a lift.

The next day was a doddle because it was the London concert in Festival Hall, with little worry about how to get from point A to point B and back again; I also had a dressing room to myself for a change. Everyone, other than Sir Charles, the orchestra members and myself, but including David Sigall, turned up in jeans, saying that as it was Sunday afternoon they were entitled to be casual. Twenty minutes before the concert was to begin, my dressing room was still full of friends and well-wishers – so much for privacy, as Jack helped me into my evening dress, Linn checked my hair and David searched for and found an errant earring that had dropped on the floor. It was as if the concert were a mere *bagatelle* of no consequence with everyone chatting away unconcernedly until finally, five minutes before the Overture, I shoved them all out so as to attempt to build up a little tension and prepare mentally for the performance.

Sir Charles cued me in to my first chord with exaggerated care and I was off, excited to be playing a concerto so unusually well rehearsed with two performances already under my belt. The hall was packed, and I poured on the emotion and exaggerated the dynamics and colouristic effects, searching for the most beautiful sounds in the lyrical passages. I had a really fine instrument, and it was all very gratifying.

Backstage after the concerto, we all decided this was the best performance yet. David showed his customary five minutes of enthusiasm, Basia was beaming with pride, Jack and Linn busied themselves packing up my things, dear Professor Peter Feuchtwanger (an old friend who had once sat on a jury with me) turned up with no less than eight of his students, and all of my Clouston cousins stayed to keep me company backstage during the second half.

Eventually everyone said their good-byes and left, and Jack, Linn and I waited around for someone to take us to the reception. After about twenty minutes, we began to realise that I had been forgotten, which at this point was somehow not surprising. So Jack busied himself with finding out where the bloody event was being held. He found a stage manager who suggested we try a certain reception room upstairs; this we did, to be greeted with exasperating remarks from the orchestra administration, delivered in casual tones, such as "Oh there you are, we were wondering where you had got to."

There were many speeches (today, I was "our remarkable soloist") and some rather good sandwiches, scones, and tepid tea. The party was either for, or given by, the Friends of the RPO (I couldn't figure it all out, having missed the earlier speeches). Obviously, the Friends were a rather eccentric lot, including one lady whom I had already spotted at two of our previous concerts since she always sat in the front row with her teddy bear.

Moreover, the teddy bear's name was Sebastian (I was told), but no one seemed to know her name, as it was Sebastian who was listed as the Friend of the RPO. He also did the applauding at the concerts, while she refrained. I nobly mingled with the strange crowd, trying to do a good job of being the gracious soloist. When it was over, I made Jack and Linn take me out to dinner; as it was Sunday and most places were closed, we went to a grand hotel in Grosvenor Square, which had a great buffet, and I ate to my heart's content.

Late that night, after lengthy phone calls home, I fell asleep secure in the knowledge that after the next concert, which was to be in Cambridge, Sir Charles had promised to drive me home!

The next day I was free and had lunch with Ian Maclay, the extraordinary manager of the RPO, a very clever man, a terrific executive director and a serious flirt. Ian always claimed he had never heard me play but re-invited me every few years because, he said, he liked me and had heard that I was popular with the orchestra! And I liked him, mainly because he made me laugh so much and effectively reduced the stress of being on tour; he was, underneath all the joking, very kind and unusually loyal. In fact, I have now known him for over 30 years, and he has become somewhat of a legendary figure amongst the London orchestra people. I only wish that others in our business could take a leaf out of his book and approach the music world with such efficiency, knowledge, pragmatism and, above all, integrity and humour.

Next, I met Linn and we had our hair done, followed by a raid on a patisserie where we bought decadently rich cakes, oozing with chocolate and vanilla cream, for tea. There was an icy cold, very powerful wind blowing, and my cough was beginning to sound positively tubercular. Linn brought me home and gave me ginger tea, and then she and Jack and I dashed off to the Queen's Theatre, where we saw a marvellous Alan Bennett play *Single Spies*. Prunella Scales' impersonation of Queen Elizabeth was perfect, and we split our sides laughing. It was all extremely therapeutic.

The following morning, as I walked from the station to Linn's house, the wind was so driving and cold, it literally knocked the breath out of me, and my cough was now definitely bronchial. Linn and Jack were out, so I managed a good three hours of solid work on my BBC program and the Brahms D minor concerto for Hong Kong. I also called the RPO offices to see if I needed to put my reception clothes in my garment bag. Unfortunately, it was Richard who answered, and he wasn't sure if there was to be a reception and was even less sure how I was to get back to London. I sighed and counted to ten (and cruelly neglected to inform him that I had made private arrangements with Sir Charles).

This being my first visit to Cambridge, I had intended to catch the 3:35, as I wanted to walk around the town before the performance. Liverpool Street station, where I was to catch my train, was in a state of total chaos; they were remodelling, and the station currently had no roof and, even worse, no waiting-room, so we were completely exposed to the freezing cold wind and sleeting rain. One after another the trains started being cancelled, including mine. Then it was announced over the loudspeaker that all passengers to Cambridge should go to King's Cross Station. I was in a mild panic, not quite sure what to do. I walked all over Liverpool Street station, searching for a phone booth to call the RPO offices, but I never found one. What I did find was a kindly stationmaster who advised me to stay put as there would be one train to Cambridge, which would leave in about twenty minutes. At this point, I was so cold, my hands had turned quite blue, and my cough had disappeared as if it had been temporarily frozen solid.

I found the one train, along with hundreds of other stranded travellers, and we all piled in. Not a seat was to be had, as I had been neither quick nor aggressive enough, so I stood the whole way, slowly thawing out. Apparently, the ice storm and raging winds had knocked power lines and trees onto the tracks but, luckily for us, all had been cleared and we made it to Cambridge shortly after 6 p.m.

My troubles, however, were far from over, as there was an endlessly long queue at the taxi stand, and I stood for another half hour being buffeted by the wind and the precipitation, which was half-snow, half-ice. A man from the local radio station appeared and began to interview the people in the queue about the perils of travelling on British Rail. When I told him that I had a concert in one hour, he was thrilled to bits as it made his reportage far more interesting. I was glad to oblige, in a noble sort of way, as I was at this point soaked to the skin and shaking violently, and talking to him made me forget the horror, temporarily.

Naturally, I saw nothing of Cambridge and, when I finally got a taxi, rushed to the hall, arriving too late to try out the piano. I must have looked a mess, especially since my lovely new hairstyle was sadly bedraggled, and although I pride myself on my un-primadonna-like nature, I really did feel close to tears. I think my friends in the orchestra sensed this and were all frightfully nice, with Sir Charles giving me a big hug and Ian dropping the jokes for a fraction of a second and becoming attentive and sweet. Hilary Groves actually gave him a talking-to, saying that it was appalling that I should have to go through all of this before a performance. I thought she was quite eloquent but, of course, it was all to no avail.

My dressing room was mercifully warm, and I soon dried out, salvaged my hair, and changed. It was also a mercy that I hadn't tried the piano, or I really might have ended up throwing a colossal tantrum as it became evident from the very first chord that this was an instrument which hadn't seen a technician since Boedicea invented blue make-up. The Corn Exchange is a bizarre hall and very resonant, so the out-of-tune-ness of the instrument was, if anything, amplified, and when I played certain notes I could feel the entire orchestra wince. Having survived all the dramas of the day, I wasn't the slightest bit nervous, but I did have a challenging time trying to minimise the horrid effects of the piano. By the last movement, I had worked out that, paradoxically, this was most effectively achieved by

291

pounding the hell out of it, something I found to be great fun. Sir Charles assumed I was doing this because I was angry, which I assured him later was not the case at all – that in fact I was only amusing myself. The audience loved all the big sounds and was wildly enthusiastic. As there was no reception, I was able to catch a train back to London right after intermission, thus avoiding a huge detour for Sir Charles and Hilary if they had had to drive me back to Linn's after the concert was over.

The next day was a free one. In the evening I worked at Linn's, then took the entire family out to a favourite fish restaurant in Golder's Green. They were off to the Canary Islands the next day, leaving me the keys to their house so that I could practise when I wished. I told Linn that I thought she was being completely selfish and heartless leaving me to suffer all alone and rushing off like that in search of the sun and warm beaches!

The next morning, they were off, and I was gloomy. I was also worried about my dwindling cash reserves. Credit cards were not accepted everywhere at that time and all this travelling about (which I had originally assumed would be taken care of by the RPO) was using up my small store of cash. I was quite literally down to counting my pennies. Jack and Linn's house was sad and lifeless without them. The neighbour came over and complained that I was playing too loudly and had woken up her husband, a restaurateur, who had worked late at night and who needed to sleep in the mornings. I moved to the less pleasant piano in the front room – which had no common wall with the irate neighbour – and my sour mood increased. The weather outside was horrible, pissing icy rain, and I was tired and fed up.

I took myself off to the Tate Gallery, but the Turners failed to cheer me up; the reverse, in fact, as I started to find them depressing. A new pair of rather fetching ankle-boots that I bought on Bond Street for the remainder of the tour, which was to take place up North, did a better job restoring my spirits. David finished the job by turning up to spend the evening with me. We decided to go and see the new Tom Stoppard play

The Artist Descending the Staircase, and as it was short and very witty it restored me to my normal good humour. We ended up at the Garrick Club for an excellent dinner of smoked salmon mousse, saddle of lamb and a chocolate bombe. We chatted amiably about all sorts of things (other than my career) until about 11:30, when we started to yawn at each other, so he took me home, where I collapsed into my bed and slept without moving for nine hours.

The next morning, I decided that before heading up to Leeds I needed to see some green, so I went to Regent's Park and found my way to the Queen Mary's Gardens, where I sat on a bench by the pond admiring the masses of tulips and the flowering azaleas and wrote a long letter to my father, who was turning 78 that week.

Back at the hotel I picked up my luggage and struggled to the Underground; I could have taken a taxi to the station, but was strapped for cash and trying to save money. At Leeds station I ran into Ian and his harem of assistants, so we all boarded the train together to Bradford. I shamed Ian into carrying my suitcases, and he complained loudly the entire trip about their weight. Our hotel in Bradford, although quite modern and attractively furnished, had two colossal drawbacks: its noisy location and the amazingly uncomfortable beds, which felt as though one were lying on an *accent circonflexe*.

Upon arrival in Bradford, I raced over to the hall and tried out the shabby and slightly clangourous piano. The performance that night was extremely mellow, and for the first time in my life I was feeling so relaxed that when I looked at the sold-out audience I suddenly realised that all the attention was focused on me, that I was the central figure, and for a moment enjoyed a lovely feeling of power – until this lapse of concentration made me almost lose my place in the concerto. There was a reception, given by Kodak, with lots of good buffet-style food – "and we would especially like to thank our renowned Polish soloist" – and I wondered why they considered Polish citizenship to be so much more glamorous than just acknowledging, as it stated clearly in the program notes, that I was Canadian. Not that I have any objection to be called Polish, as I am extremely proud of my Slavic heritage, but what's wrong with being Canadian?

The next day I drove with Sir Charles and Hilary through Harrogate and Ripon and part of the Yorkshire Dales, which were breathtakingly beautiful, to Newcastle. Sir Charles was in a hurry, so it all went by far too quickly. In Newcastle, I practised on the piano at the Sinfonia Centre, then rushed back to the hotel to watch the running of the Grand National on television – five minutes later, I couldn't even remember who had won, but as everyone else was so caught up in the excitement, I joined in.

The next morning Sir Charles, Hilary and I set off for Sunderland, where the next concert was to be held. It was a glorious spring day, and we made a detour to visit Durham, where a large roast beef lunch with Yorkshire pudding and all the trimmings put all three of us into an excellent mood. Sir Charles wanted to show me the Cathedral, which was indeed impressive, and I was intrigued to find there the tombs of the Venerable Bede and Saint Cuthbert. The magnificent bells started to ring just as we entered the cloisters – it was a great moment.

Unfortunately, we had to move on to Sunderland to try out the hall and the piano and, as usual, we were slightly pressed for time. As we crossed the Cathedral Quad, with its meticulously manicured greens, a gang of young thugs, all chains, pierced noses and navels, shaved heads and clad in black leather, came towards us drinking beer and belching loudly. One of them threw a beer can onto the green. Sir Charles immediately said in an authoritarian tone: "Pick that up right away!" Hilary and I held our breaths, convinced we were about to witness a horrible fight, but to my surprise the lad simply said: "Sorry, sir," and picked up the can and went on his way. My admiration for Sir Charles rose another couple of notches.

Sunderland is not a pretty town, and we had no idea where the hall was and every single person we asked for directions was roaring drunk. After finally locating it, we found that the piano they had brought in for me was a Yamaha Baby Grand. Sir Charles was furious and even the most laid-back members of the orchestra were outraged. I wasn't bothered, myself. Obviously, I would have preferred a Steinway Grand, but I knew that I could manage fine on the Yamaha, and that in doing so would become a heroic figure! In fact, it was a challenge that amused me. But the orchestra was so upset they sent their Chairman to my dressing room to inform me that if I didn't want to play, they would understand completely and would substitute an orchestral work.

Thinking they were all being a little over-dramatic, I reassured everyone that I didn't mind at all playing on the smaller instrument. It was actually a very well-regulated piano, and the performance would have been a complete success had my Swedish friend Mats' cello not slipped from under him in the middle of the third movement! The audience was lethargic and non-responsive, which was a bit of a downer, but after the concert several friends in the orchestra drove me back to Newcastle, where we found a pub and drank gallons of beer and ate pub snacks. I suddenly realised that my cough had finally disappeared and that I felt completely well again.

The last day of the tour was absolutely glorious. First of all, I ate a huge English breakfast of eggs, fried bread, grilled tomato, bacon, bangers, black pudding, grilled mushrooms, toast, marmalade, and tea, and then six of us – four orchestra members, one administrator and me – squeezed into the Audi hatchback belonging to John Bimson, the Principal Horn, with me lying comfortably in the back amidst all the luggage. Everyone was in incredibly good, almost holiday-like spirits; we had a guidebook to the best eating places in Yorkshire and Derbyshire and were determined to try out as many of them as possible.

Our first stop was in the Yorkshire town of Bedale, where a market has been held on its cobbled main street since the 13th century. After a summary look at the glorious old church, we got down to the real business of the day, sampling the quite delicious coffee and cakes at Plummer's restaurant. The local farmers were having a meeting upstairs, and it was fun to see their tweed caps and old jackets hanging side by side on a row of pegs by the door. They all wore Wellington boots, spoke in the broadest of Yorkshire dialects, and the smell of their pipes seeped through the floorboards down to where we were enjoying our repast. It all reminded me of the James Herriot stories set in the Yorkshire Dales.

Our next stop was a pub in Tadcaster called The Angel and the White Horse. It was a lovely old pub, and I once again had a scrumptious roast beef lunch with a mouth-watering lemon meringue pie for dessert. After wiping off the final crumbs of flaky pastry from our lips, we staggered over to the adjacent stables to pet the enormous, beautiful white Shire horses. One of them, Extra Stout, was in the *Guinness Book of Records* as the tallest horse in the world – an astonishing nineteen and a half hands. He was very gentle and sweet and let us stroke him without protest, after which we watched as a blacksmith put new shoes on him.

Then off we went along winding scenic roads through the Derbyshire Dales, our next gourmet destination being Chatsworth, home of the Duke and Duchess of Devonshire. The grounds were magnificent, with a herd of deer quietly grazing in the distance. Since it had been at least two hours since our gargantuan lunch, we headed for the tearoom. The scones were lovely and buttery, and the blackberry jam and clotted cream came from the estate, fresh and full of country flavour. We were all so pleasantly relaxed that we almost forgot the time and had to travel a little more quickly than was legal to reach Derby on time. It had been a wonderful day with a wonderfully congenial group of people, who all had the same idea of fun: visiting old churches, walking in the country, admiring the glorious scenery, eating ourselves silly, laughing most of the time. To make a memorable day perfect, the piano in Derby was a marvellous instrument. What with that, and being surrounded on stage by my well-fed, smiling friends, it turned out to be an especially fine performance. Sir Charles said to me, as we shook hands with genuine affection on stage: "Well – this one takes the biscuit!"

The reception was once again given by British Telecom, and this time the host came out with "our marvellous soloist, Joanna," – quickly adding, to show that he really knew me well (so that no one would think he was committing a faux-pas by using my first name), "who is a great hockey fan!" This non-sequitur puzzled the assembly, but the awkward moment soon passed. After the reception I said goodbye to all my new buddies, feeling tremendously sorry that the tour was over. I was driven back to London by the orchestra Chairman, arriving at the hotel at three in the morning. I had one day to recover before recording my Chopin program for the BBC.

Nearly four years later, Ian did me yet another good turn, putting forth my name to the orchestra committee as a possible soloist for their upcoming Northern tour. I was hired once again and was thrilled.

This tour, however, was quite different from the first, the main reason being the repertoire. It was also a shorter tour with only four concerts: three Schumann concertos and, in the middle, a Liszt Extravaganza in Middlesbrough, where I was to perform two Liszt works – the E-flat concerto and *Totentanz*. If the Grieg concerto requires minimum effort for maximum effect, the Schumann concerto is the total opposite. It is a major work of incomparable beauty, but it is rarely a crowd-pleaser. Whereas the Grieg sounds fantastically difficult and has a huge, booming ending, the Schumann, which actually *is* fantastically difficult, sounds gentle and unassuming and, with such an important role for the orchestra, rather like a piece of exquisite chamber music. An audience will invariably enjoy the Schumann concerto, but will rarely get all excited over it, and often their attention will wander, relegating the performance to the status of pleasant background music.

The challenge for the performer is two-fold: to secure an alliance with the conductor so that a magical interplay and homogenous partnership is formed and, secondly, to create an underlying tension in the performance – even in the playful opening of the second movement – that grabs the audience's attention from the first chord and holds it captive right to the end. In this way one can highlight all the exquisite intricacies of the piece, as well as the more obvious lyrical statements. There is great passion and emotion in the Schumann concerto, and breathtaking beauty; it is the performer's job – not an easy task – to make sure that the audience actively shares in all of these marvels.

The Schumann is also renowned for its memory pitfalls. Almost every pianist who has performed it has, at one time or other, lost his way in the third movement – and as the orchestra has little to do around that danger point, it can be a humiliating disaster. This has not yet happened to me, although once or twice there have been milliseconds (which felt like centuries) of panic, when I got off just slightly, for one or two notes, luckily getting quickly back on track again. The Schumann truly is one of the hardest pieces to perform, and it is interesting that many of the most renowned pianists, past and present, have never tackled it.

In the Liszt compositions I was to play in the middle of the tour, there are specific bars that are extremely tricky, but nothing I felt unable to master even when nervous, and both works are sure-fire crowd-pleasers: short, obvious, well-contrasted, well-crafted and with fantastic build-ups to spectacular climaxes. Still, they do need a certain amount of practice every day, so I never imagined that this tour would take on the "holiday" aspect of the last one.

Having played a recital in Toronto the evening before, I arrived in London, in the middle of February, completely exhausted and with a bad cold that somehow felt familiar. A strenuous recording session had filled my previous week, but had resulted in my first CD with orchestra, performing the relatively unknown but lovely Moszkowski concerto, the Andante spianato, Grande Polonaise of Chopin, and a haunting, powerful contemporary work for piano and orchestra by the Canadian composer Peter Paul Koprowski.

My lodgings in London were in the house in Kensington where the Ingpen & Williams offices were located, owned by the pianist Margaret Kitchen, widow of David's wise and colourful former senior partner Howard Hartog. Margaret had generously invited me to use her guest flat whenever I came to town. Not only was this extremely pleasant, but it now meant that I could go home to America with a sizeable profit in my pocket – something that had become increasingly difficult to achieve, with the costs of London hotels skyrocketing in the 80s.

The only downside to the apartment was the lack of central heating. There were electric bars in the bedroom, but the bathroom had no heat in it at all, which made washing, especially one's hair, somewhat of an ordeal during the winter months. Notwithstanding being chilled to the bone occasionally, I was incredibly grateful to Margaret and enjoyed my little flat very much. There was also a bus right around the corner that took me directly to Linn's, a wonderful Polish restaurant called Wodka two minutes away, delectable Indian restaurants on Gloucester Road a few blocks over, and a Marks and Spencer's close by, where I could buy sandwiches and fruit when I was in a hurry. At night, I could go out for pleasant walks either in the park or around the quiet neighbourhood, often wandering over to Queen's Gate, where Biddy and George had rented their first apartment after they were married in 1945.

Long before this tour, I had started to agitate for a travel plan from the orchestra, including details of my transportation from one city to the next, but it was like trying to draw blood from a stone, and not surprisingly the tour began with nothing remotely resolved – even though what I was asking for was purely practical, and in their interest as well as mine. Perhaps I had been spoilt in America, where each orchestra has a system of volunteers to take care of the artist's transportation. More often than not, the volunteer is a delightful elderly lady who has been working at this job for years and who is incapable of carrying any luggage and tends to forget where she has parked the car, resulting in endless meanderings around airport parking lots. Generally, though, most orchestras in North America try to arrange things so that the artist has only to worry about his or her performance.

My conductor, Gunther Herbig, was very different from Sir Charles. He believed in rehearsing a lot and in great detail, which was refreshing but also exhausting. He is a fine musician, but not a natural accompanist (like so many great conductors, since accompanying piano concertos is quite a separate talent) and far from letting this handicap him in any way, he just made sure that he worked at the concertos hard enough and long enough to ensure that the resulting accompaniment would be perfect. And so it was that after the first rehearsal for the Schumann concerto at Henry Wood Hall I was a little disappointed, feeling that it all sounded rhythmically slack, musically uninteresting and, frankly, just plain dull. But then Gunther showed his true colours and started to impress me. (I had noted, incidentally, that the orchestra liked him, which is always a good sign and rather unusual.)

He asked me if I could stay on after the rehearsal to go over certain passages. In fact, we went through the entire concerto, bar by bar, which was interesting for me and not at all onerous. He then asked me if we could look at *Totentanz* a bit, as he didn't know it well. I was feeling tired by then, but was happy to oblige, as it is rare to find a conductor so willing to work on the piano concerto; a little pedantic for sure, but without a trace of arrogance, and when I'd make a suggestion, even suggestions that had nothing to do with our sections together, he would listen attentively.

The next day the Festival Hall performance took place. The morning rehearsal was again somewhat depressing; I felt it all seemed lifeless and that Gunther's seemingly inflexible conducting was handcuffing me. As usual the orchestra, surely the friendliest in London, if not the world, was supportive and reassuring. But Gunther got full marks for persistence, for once again, there was a knock on my dressing-room door when I was trying to have a nap and there he was, determined to go over the whole piece once again. I appreciated his intentions, but I was suffering from jetlag and a miserable cold, and his requests to repeat passages over and over began to get on my nerves. He left only minutes before the start of the concert, and I had to rush to get my evening clothes on as well as somehow arrange my hair and make-up.

David breezed in, assessed the situation, looked at my face and suddenly said: "Why don't you just have some fun and try to throw him in two or three places?" This notion really appealed to my rebellious streak, and although I didn't deliberately try to throw Gunther (that would have been much too unprofessional) I did manage to shake the shackles that had been clamping down around my interpretation and ended up smiling throughout the performance. But best of all, I got a truly wonderful accompaniment from Gunther, who stuck to me like glue, never losing me once either technically or emotionally. It was a sold-out hall, and I believe the audience enjoyed the light-hearted performance as much as we did. All my friends crowded enthusiastically backstage: Jack and Linn, Basia, the Cloustons, Annabelle, Imogen, Margaret Hartog, my little Lucy from Carmel, and Camilla Panufnik, widow of Sir Andrzej Panufnik, whose marvellous piano concerto I had recently premiered in the United States. I was happy and relieved. There was a reception given by Kodak, "our delightful Polish pianist" was thanked, and then over to a small party at David's home, which was perfect.

The following day, however, was a nightmare. I had hardly slept and felt like death in the morning, unable to eat. I packed, feeling utterly nauseated, my head spinning every time I bent over. My suitcase was heavy and carrying it caused my heart to pound noisily in my ears. Luckily, I didn't have too much trouble finding a taxi to King's Cross, where I caught the train to Darlington. My ticket was in first class and the compartment was empty, so it was easy for me to take a nap, but I awoke feeling even worse. I tried writing postcards, but that nearly finished me off. At Darlington I had to wait on the cold platform with some extremely noisy and smelly youths who had just been on a football outing. The little district train to Middlesbrough was nasty and dirty, and the ride was tantamount to being on a roller coaster as we undulated across the countryside.

From the previous tour I had thought that Sunderland was a pretty awful place, but Middlesbrough was even worse. It appeared to be one large chemical factory, and the air was unpleasantly pungent, stinking of sulphur and God knows what else. The hotel was filthy and unattractive. I forced myself to drink a lot of water and eat a few spoonfuls of soup and some apple sauce. I then staggered over to the hall, where the big RPO truck was already parked. The hall was freezing cold, as they had the side doors wide open to facilitate the unloading process.

I kept my big winter coat on and managed to play through the Liszt concerto, but I felt that my whole body was giving out. Before starting on *Totentanz*, I decided to go to the bathroom and dash some hot water over my hands and face. I was sure that I would at least throw up and thought I might as well get it over and done with before the rehearsal. As I headed across the stage to the bathroom, the local presenter, who had been listening to my practising and overseeing the set-up on stage, worriedly asked if I was feeling all right. I managed to produce the word: "Actually …" and then my knees buckled under me, there was a terrible booming in my ears, and suddenly everything went black.

I woke up to find myself lying on the couch in my dressing room, surrounded by the concerned faces of the RPO technical staff, Peter (the now extremely worried presenter), and Gunther, who, typically, had turned up early to go over the two Liszt pieces with me before the orchestral rehearsal. I tried to reassure everyone, but was quite frightened myself. Presently everyone left but Gunther, and he and I quietly sat and talked through the concerto, as I shivered uncontrollably.

He suddenly stopped and, taking stock of the situation, told me to rest and said he would be back in a minute. When he returned, he told me he had asked Peter if it would be all right to switch from the two Liszt pieces to the Schumann for the performance, and poor Peter, although they had apparently quite recently had the Schumann on their concert series, agreed with alacrity, relieved that at least something would be played! I was harder to persuade, as in my heart, I knew that the Liszts were easier for me, even without rehearsal. But Gunther wouldn't even begin to entertain the idea of a performance without rehearsal, and, in retrospect, I think he was right.

He walked me back to the hotel after cancelling my part of the rehearsal and said he would check on me at seven. I then threw up repeatedly what seemed to be everything that had found its way into my digestive system for the past twenty years, until I felt wretchedly weak, but at least the nausea passed. And so, from sheer exhaustion, I slept until Gunther rang my room to make sure I was well enough to perform. He then came up and walked me over to the hall.

As I suspected, having suffered from similar bouts two or three times in the past, the performance went fine, as I knew the Schumann well, and was too tired to worry about anything other than just getting through it. To say that I felt awful was an understatement. There was a violent ringing in my ears, which didn't help matters at all. As usual, I had to share my dressing room with Gunther, who was quite adorable and solicitous. He told me I had great courage, and I felt this was the nicest compliment I'd received in years; it made me feel very strong inside and very good. At intermission, after my performance, he personally walked me back to the hotel and told me to go to sleep.

There was a wonderful side effect to my ordeal: Anne Mackenzie Young, the current General Manager of the RPO who was replacing Ian for a short while, announced that for the rest of the tour she would be driving Gunther and myself. This was not only good news to me but also to Gunther, who had been having his own, less dramatic, but nevertheless tiresome problems with the logistics of the tour. So, it was with a much greater peace of mind that I awoke the next morning, feeling fragile and unwell but, on the whole, vastly improved from the previous day. I ate a careful breakfast and was the centre of much solicitude and cosseting from the orchestra members and from Annie, whom I was beginning to like tremendously.

We were to leave at 11 o'clock, but Gunther, with his rather endearing Germanic pedantry, said we should have a "travel conference" ten minutes beforehand. We decided that Annie would drive, Gunther would map-read, and I would shut up and sit in the back seat. During the two-hour drive, we got to know one another much better, all of us equally and pleasantly interested in each other's lives and stories. Annie taught us some Cockney rhyming slang, and Gunther told us a little about the grim life he had experienced growing up in East Germany, which made me wonder how such a nice man could emerge from such inhuman conditions. He used his stopwatch to time our journey (the same way he would use a metronome to check tempi at rehearsals), and when he packed his case backstage it was always exactly the same way, with almost military precision. But these funny quirks were tempered by an unassuming, patient, pro-woman, liberal-minded nature, and a fine, knowledgeable musical mind. And once he had mastered the idiosyncrasies of my specific interpretation of the Schumann, he became increasingly flexible, until working with him was pure delight, as he gave me that rare gift: the opportunity to shine.

The restaurant at the (thank heavens!) salubrious hotel in Hull had an ambitious young chef who went in for exotic combinations. The menu offered delicacies such as: Salmon "Teryaki" with "Roesti" Potatoes and Angel Hair "Carbonara." I settled for the Roast Chicken with Gado Gado and the intriguing sounding "House Fires," which turned out to be a misprint on the menu and was actually the more mundane "House fries." I ate only a little and my friends ate heartily.

In the afternoon I practised a bit in the hall. My performance felt strained due to my feeling quite weak; also, my ears were still ringing badly. But I made a big effort and got lots of encouraging smiles from my friends in the orchestra. In the end, it was quite a triumph, as the hall was sold out and the crowd was wildly enthusiastic. I was just pleased I had made it through the Schumann in one piece.

In the same way the last day of the previous tour had been a magical experience, so it was for this tour. The sun was shining, and even though it was still February, there was a hint of spring in the air. The three of us set off at 10:30 in a relaxed mood, Gunther with his stopwatch at the ready, reading in careful English every sign we passed and painstakingly plotting our journey on his map. Soon we were in North Yorkshire, then on to the Dales. Gunther nodded off, but I forced myself to stay awake because the drive was so beautiful; the long vistas of rolling hills, freshly green, with the omnipresent stone walls of Yorkshire and the rushing streams overflowing with the vitality of the season. Everywhere there was an intense feeling of joy and renewal.

After a while, we got out our Best of British Pubs guidebook and presently found ourselves eating delicious roast lamb with mint sauce, roast potatoes and peas at the Royal Oak Pub in Appleby, which was filled with a cheerful Sunday crowd. I had a mug of local cider and suddenly felt better than I had in months.

In Carlisle we eventually found the hotel, which seemed to be deliberately hiding behind one-way and dead-end streets to discourage people from finding it. Even more bizarre was its car park, which was miles away and had to be unlocked and then locked up again by the girl at the front desk every time a car arrived or left. Our hotel had another interesting characteristic: if you wanted any hot water for the shower or washbasin, you had to turn on the tap and let it run for ten minutes before any semblance of heat made an appearance. This information was passed on to me, when I called down to the front desk to complain that I had no hot water and really had to wash my hair before the performance.

I found the hall, which was new and rather uninspiring, and tried to practise my Chopin concerto a bit as I was playing it in Toronto two days later, but I soon found I had only enough energy for the Schumann. The final concert went very well, and

Gunther remarked that, at this point, he was so happy with the Schumann, he thought it was a shame we couldn't tour North America with it.

At 10:30 p.m. I boarded a night train, which I found a pleasant alternative to night driving or night flying. Back in London the next morning, I packed up my things and found my way to Heathrow Airport and Air Canada, where I was mercifully bumped up to First Class.

The very next evening I was in Toronto, where I performed the Chopin E-minor concerto. It was the first concert of a five-city tour with the Kraków Philharmonic and their music director, my old friend Gil Levine. The tour, sponsored by the Polish American Congress, was a sort of goodwill affair, highlighting the strong ties between Poland and North America, and it was also gruelling and high-profile, with performances at both Lincoln Centre in New York and the Kennedy Centre in Washington D.C.

The reviews in the *New York Times* and the *Washington Post* were flattering, the concerts successful; Gil was superb, and at the post-concert receptions (which were also very high-profile, particularly in Washington where the reception was attended by not only the Polish Ambassador, but also by senators, congressmen, cabinet ministers and government advisors, who either had many Polish-Americans in their constituencies or who were of Polish descent themselves, such as Zbigniew Brzezinski and Jan Nowak–Jezioranski) my name was always pronounced impeccably and in full. They even referred to me as the "Polish-Canadian" pianist.

And yet … often, as I sat on a plane jetting between North American mega-cities, an efficient itinerary neatly printed up and safely stowed in my purse, secure in the knowledge that a chauffeur and limousine would be meeting me at the airport, I found myself wistfully harkening back to my tours with the world's friendliest top-flight orchestra and a lovely leisurely lunch with my two friends on a beautiful spring day in a pub in Appleby, Yorkshire.

CHAPTER 14

Mazurka: Our Time ("Notre temps")
by Frédéric Chopin

The atmosphere in Poland that winter was grim. There were food shortages and fuel shortages and the Communist government had clamped down hard on the Solidarity movement, which, as a result, had gone deeper underground and gained more and more support. This was the context for my tour of Poland in 1987.

The evening before I was to fly to Warsaw, I had been invited to the London home of Elaine Plummer's closest friend, Tita. Being of a warm and motherly nature, Tita, who was concerned for my welfare over the next few weeks, had decided to fill me up with good, healthy food and had prepared an enormous, nourishing meal of thick vegetable soup, fish pie, green beans and a sinfully rich chocolate cake covered with huge globs of Devonshire cream. That night I left her home duly fortified and a few kilos heavier.

In the morning I caught the early plane to Warsaw and then immediately transferred to the flight to Wroclaw. We boarded some kind of flying machine that seemed to be held together with scotch tape – I swear I saw holes in the fuselage stuffed with pieces of newspaper and cardboard. Snow was falling quite heavily and, rather than spend the next hour or so in a state of complete terror, I promptly fell asleep.

I was met in Wroclaw by Hanna, who was to be my "guide" during my stay there. Vivacious and an enthusiast for all things forbidden or scarce in her country, she went with me to the hotel to see that I was checked in properly. It was one of those hideously unattractive, modern communist buildings, which inevitably appear shabby and derelict the day after they are built. Hanna was anxiously watching my face, knowing that it was horrible but hoping I might not make too much of a fuss – or perhaps not notice. As a typically hospitable Pole, she felt humiliated, and I certainly wasn't about to rub the humiliation in any deeper. We made plans to meet the next morning, and she rushed off to tuck her little girl into bed. As she was leaving, she pressed into my hands a bag full of apples, which, during the winter in Poland, were worth their weight in gold.

Feeling a little peckish, I went down to the dining room only to find it closed. I went to the front desk to ask what was going on.

"The restaurant is closed for twenty-four hours," I was told – no explanation, just a bald statement. I was tired, overwrought and hungry, my last meal having been a hurried breakfast at Heathrow Airport. I needed bright lights, hot food and a friendly waiter. Besides, my less-than-functional room upstairs was cold, and the carpet was filthy and felt like wet cement. After further inquiry, I was told that all the restaurants in Wroclaw had been closed down for twenty-four hours – still no explanation as to the whys or wherefores. This was a country where informative official explanations were unknown and people still went to prison, or worse, for being inquisitive. Besides, I didn't want to go out – it was sleeting in a sort of hazy fog, and the few fluorescent streetlights that were operating were a sickly yellow-green colour.

The girl at the desk finally unbent a little and gave me a glass of hot water and a tea bag, which I took back upstairs. Feeling downright miserable, I took out an apple and searched in my handbag for my Dorothy Sayers mystery. Rummaging around, my fingers came across an alien form: a big chunk of something wrapped in aluminium foil. "Oh Tita!!!" – that lovely, wonderful woman –" ... may the blessings of heaven shower down upon you and all of yours unto the twentieth generation!" That glorious woman had secretly put in my bag a huge piece of chocolate cake. It really takes so little to change one's mood radically. I spent the rest of the evening comfortably wrapped in my coat (I was convinced the blanket on the bed had "things" moving in it), reading (with the help of my pocket flashlight, as the wattage of the light bulbs must have been around two), and eating apples and cake.

Hanna turned up early the next morning after dropping off her daughter at school. She was shocked to hear there had been no breakfast at the hotel. Leaving me at the hall to warm up before rehearsal, she rushed back home and soon reappeared with a large plate full of sandwiches, which I ate ravenously. The hall was repellently ugly: a smallish, dirty, dark grey concrete block with no attempt, inside or out, to provide any kind of atmosphere other than morose. The orchestra's mood reflected the building, although they were polite, and the conductor was competent but nondescript. I lost myself in the Beethoven 4th piano concerto and felt a great deal happier. Even under the worst conditions, a piece like this never fails to lift one's spirits.

The 24-hour restaurant closures seemed to have come to an end by lunchtime, so I suggested to Hanna that we go to the best restaurant in town and I would buy her lunch. I had been given a large number of zlotys, which I was forbidden to take out of the country, so I intended to spend as many of them as I could. Hanna took me to an attractive old restaurant, and I finally had a meal, albeit a rather stodgy one: herring with potatoes, *barszcz* (clear beet soup) and sausages. Hanna asked me timidly if she could order some orange juice, which was rather expensive. She told me that her parents had somehow got out of Poland and were now living in California. With her husband and child held hostage, she had only once been allowed out to visit them, and she would never forget the fresh oranges. Her heart was absolutely set on one day moving with her entire family to California, where she would drink orange juice morning, noon and night. The stuff one got in Poland came out of a tin from North Vietnam and tasted vile, but she said it was enough to remind her of the sunshine and freedom.

I got to know Hanna quite well over the few days I was in Wroclaw. She had been a professional guide for Orbis – the official, government-run, one and only travel agency in Poland – where she herded busloads of people around places like Bulgaria and Yugoslavia, staying in fourth-rate hotels and eating in cheap restaurants. She had cut back on her job to be near her little daughter. Hanna was a girl of many interests, first and foremost her Catholicism – the Catholic Church at that time not only nourished the soul of the Polish people, but also provided a forum of protest against the government. Hanna was also fascinated with Buddhism, yoga, health food, water cures, physical education, German literature, microbiology – "anything," she confided in me, "that can help me forget the life here."

A superb professional guide, she gave me a comprehensive tour of Wroclaw, of which the "old" part turned out to be an attractive Medieval German town. (Before the Second World War, Wroclaw was, in fact, the German city of Breslau.) Wroclaw had been seventy percent destroyed during the war, but the restoration was an extraordinary achievement. We admired the magnificent town hall dating back to the 15th century, the Muzeum Narodowe, the University and many fascinating churches including the 13th-century church of St. Adalbert in the Dominican monastery.

That night in the hotel restaurant there was food but nothing to drink, and I refused to even consider the tap water. In Poland I usually drank *sok porszeczkowy* or blackcurrant juice, which was unavailable, so I made them boil water for me.

The next morning the air quality was so dreadful, so sulphurous, it was hard to breathe. I had a concert in the late afternoon, and found the audience very strange. On previous trips to Poland, I had been greeted with great enthusiasm. Classical musicians all liked touring in Poland for that very reason: Polish audiences were renowned for their warmth and demonstrative behaviour. But this audience was gloomy, silent, and barely acknowledged my presence as I walked out to the stage. As I played, I felt I wasn't reaching anyone and started putting colossal efforts into trying to cheer up this acutely depressed group of people. When I finished, I felt absolutely worn out. Suddenly, after the first curtain call when I came out for my solo bow, the audience stood up en masse and started cheering wildly. I played a couple of encores and then a pall descended over everyone as they put on their dreary overcoats and went back to their dreary lives.

There was no food at the hotel again that night, so I finished off the last of "Saint Tita's" cake and ate some more apples. The next morning, completely fed up, I walked into the Pewex shop, which I had previously avoided, and started buying. During the communist era Pewex shops sold all sorts of "luxuries" for American dollars. No ordinary Pole could afford to be a customer there. I stocked up on bars and bars of Belgian chocolates for me and also for my friends, who hadn't seen chocolate in their stores for over two years. I bought orange juice for Hanna and a French Cognac for Hanna's father-in-law, as it was his name-day party that night, and I was invited.

The big excitement of the day was that Hanna had been able to get me tickets to see the restored Panorama Raclawicka (Panorama of the Battle of Raclawice), at the time Wroclaw's most famous tourist attraction, a truly enormous circular painting, 120 meters long and 15 meters high, commissioned in 1894 to celebrate the centenary of the defeat of the Russian army by the people's militia of Tadeusz Kościuszko near the village of Raclawice. It had been placed on public view in Lwów, which was then part of Austria – the only one of the partitioning powers that would have tolerated such nationalist propaganda – and it remained there until 1944, when it was substantially damaged by a bomb. After 1944 it was, for obvious reasons, hidden away only to reappear in 1985, fully restored, hundreds of miles to the West in Wroclaw. Polish people had to wait up to two years to get in to see it. It was hugely impressive and made me feel extremely close to my father, who remembered it enthusiastically from the time when, as a boy, he had admired it in Lwów, before the war.

Hanna kept me busy. After the Panorama we met up with her husband Lech, a professor of German at the University and a taxi driver on the side, their daughter Alice and Hanna's sister and her two children. We were all to go to the zoo. What struck me immediately was the white, waxy, almost transparent quality of the children's skin, the blue rings under their eyes and their incredible thinness. They looked like the old photos one would see of tubercular children in a sanatorium. Hanna had told me that the air quality in Wroclaw was so bad that respiratory ailments were rampant among the children, and every year they were all sent to the mountains for a month. The zoo was a muddy, sad affair with the ubiquitous dark concrete and pathetic, sickly looking animals in dirty dark cells. It was thoroughly depressing.

I had another concert at 6. It followed the same pattern as the day before; again, the audience came alive just long enough to squeeze some encores out of me before slipping back into their depressed apathy.

After the Second World War, the Germans living in Breslau (Wroclaw) were forcibly evicted and in their place thousands of Poles from the east (most particularly from my father's hometown Lwów, newly annexed by the Soviet Union) were transplanted hundreds of miles to the west, where they settled. The Poles from Lwów were notorious for their party-loving, café-loving, theatre-loving, music-loving, and all-round fun-loving natures and, unlike the younger generation of Hanna and Lech, they still remembered what having a good time and feeling a sense of freedom were like. They may have been devastated by their loss of freedom, but at least they could remember what life had been like before the communists took over and, inwardly, were not diminished.

Perhaps the only time during the whole trip when I saw adult Poles being genuinely happy occurred after the concert, when I was invited to Lech's father Zbigniew's name-day party. It was great fun and, somehow, I got along wonderfully well as everyone spoke English, French or German as well as Polish. There were singers and lawyers, the director of the Opera, an editor and a lady who captained a training vessel – about twenty people, quite a few of whom had attended my concert. Unlike so many of the Poles of my own generation whose parties I had attended in the past, no one was the slightest bit drunk (although the vodka flowed freely), and there was a great deal of friendly discussion, joking and some remarkably beautiful singing in three- or four-part voices. I left with regret.

Lech drove me to the railroad station and at midnight put me on my train to Warsaw. Somewhat to my surprise I found myself sharing my compartment with two elderly sisters. As they were clearly rather shaky on their pins, I volunteered to take the top bunk, much to their relief. I climbed up and found myself in a coffin-like situation, the ceiling only a few centimetres from my nose and a reading light that didn't work. This was a nightmare since I'm acutely claustrophobic, but I figured I had no other option, so I lay there, wide awake, and suffered for a while. Pretty soon it all became too much for me. I gave up trying to sleep, climbed down and spent the night standing in the corridor – which wasn't very pleasant either.

We pulled into Warsaw station at 6:30 in the morning, and there was no one to meet me. Carrying my massively heavy suitcase, I headed for the taxi stand. With about twenty other people, I waited 45 minutes in the pitch-dark, freezing, cold and damp. Finally, one taxi turned up, and I shared it with a nice man whom I had befriended in the line. It was a good thing, too, as he saw to it that I wasn't cheated by the driver.

The Victoria Hotel was already over ten years old and showing signs of shabbiness, but it was still the best hotel in the country. I was shown immediately to my room, where I spent the next hour washing off the pollution and grime of Wroclaw and the train, putting the clothes I'd worn there in a plastic bag to be burned when I got back to America – or at least washed a great many times.

The food was definitely better in Warsaw, but I still never managed to eat a green vegetable or fresh fruit while I was in Poland, other than Hanna's apples. The meat was still mostly either unidentifiable or some kind of sausage. Fish, other

313

than herring, seemed non-existent. There was plenty of food in the hotel, but my body was unused to the poor quality, and it started to affect me after a while. The Victoria also believed in low-wattage bulbs, and the Do Not Disturb sign did not deter the maids, chatting loudly to each other, from walking right into the room at 8 o'clock sharp in the morning, whether you were fully clothed or stark naked. They also enjoyed sampling my Rochas perfume, but I really couldn't hold this against them!

The sun had come out in Warsaw and the rebuilt "old town," where I had walked that afternoon with my young cousin Konrad, was as attractive as ever. But there was an intense feeling of gloom, dissatisfaction, and depression in the air. There were no bright colours or lights anywhere to buoy one's spirits, no smiles, no laughter. The atmosphere was dark, grey, and heavy, and I felt a universal, deep-rooted tension that was certainly evident among my cousins.

My father had had two older brothers, each of whom had one son who, in turn, also had one son. My first cousin Wladek, gentle, quiet and melancholy, lived in Warsaw and was an architect – what a soul-destroying profession that must have been in that authoritarian country of concrete blocks! My other first cousin, Konrad, a computer scientist, prize-winning science fiction writer, linguist and philosopher, lives in Vienna and works for UNESCO but is also a Professor at Warsaw University and lectures in the States. He had come from Vienna to see me and to visit his dying mother. Konrad's son, also Konrad, is a published poet and, at that time, was writing his final law exams. Wladek's son, Gabriel (or Gabryś), was much younger, only around twelve years old at that time, and I instantly fell for him. He was so full of laughter, jokes and sunshine, although he had already endured a series of tragedies in his young life. Within a few short years he had lost his mother in a car accident and both his grandparents, who had brought him up.

At the restaurant, the adults were full of cynicism and black humour about the hopeless current situation. Although Konrad the elder was living in Vienna, he claimed that he wished to return one day to buy a house in Warsaw. Wladek had clearly given up. (A few years later, he died tragically young.) The poet, young Konrad, was surprisingly clear-minded about what the country and people had become, and spoke intelligently about the impracticality of the artistic world's idealism, of the lethargy and alcoholism of so many young people, and of the stranglehold and suffocating oppression that was part of their daily life. Young Konrad was not trying to leave Poland; he wanted to stay and work to rebuild the country. He wasn't an easy person to get to know, but he was impressive, as was his father. A brainy bunch indeed, but apart from my irrepressible Gabryś, a group of people whose thoughts were dark and complex.

I spent the next morning deliberately losing myself in my music, practising all morning at the hall. It was lit by flickering fluorescent lights, and I developed an appalling headache. I spent the afternoon reading in my hotel room, counting the minutes before I could get on a plane and leave this proud but tragic country. Tita's cake had run out, so I bought more chocolate at the Pewex to cheer myself up, making sure I had tons of it left to give to Gabryś before my departure.

My guide, Isabella, walked me over to the hall that evening, and I found it half-empty. I had been told that even the cheap tickets were becoming too expensive, and with the Poles being such avid concertgoers, I found this situation inexpressibly sad. I mentioned to Isabella that it was hard for me to see that people were no longer able to attend concerts as they once had. I expected her to reply with an equally regretful remark, but instead she said: "There is no one here tonight because Part II of *The Thorn Birds* is on television with Richard Chamberlain and Christopher Plummer and nobody wants to miss it!"

"But what about you, then?" I asked her.

"Oh, I'm okay, I have my video machine on a timer, and it is being taped for me as we speak!"

I left Poland the next morning for England and felt relieved and guilty all at once; so glad to be out of there but haunted by the depressing scenes I had witnessed and dark visions of the family I had left behind. Never had the red double-decker buses of London seemed more cheerful and welcoming, the shops more colourful and the lights brighter, despite the weather being foggy and cold. Even the London air felt breathable and fresh. For the next few days, I did nothing but eat salads and drink in the atmosphere of a free society.

It was not so long after my visit to Poland that I had a concert with the Pacific Symphony in Orange County, California. A note was sent to me backstage: "Could we come back to see you in your dressing room?" It was signed, Hanna, Lech and Alice. They had finally made it to California. Lech had found a good job teaching at a university. Hanna, as unusual as ever, had become a trained hypnotist and had opened a clinic to help people overcome illnesses and phobias. She drank fresh orange juice every day, and Alice was pink-cheeked and beautiful.

I returned to Poland seven years later, in 1994, for a concert in Katowice with the Radio Orchestra, one of Poland's finest, and as conductor the excellent Kirk Trevor, with whom I have worked happily on many occasions.

Poland had changed dramatically since my last visit and, from a foreigner's standpoint, all for the better. For the Poles, however, this was not entirely the case, and they had many horrific social problems yet to solve as well as the dangers of adopting not only the precepts of democracy, social freedom, and the open market economy of the West, but also all the sinister side effects that sadly often accompany such sought-after advantages. Crime, unemployment, and poverty among pensioners were chronic problems, not to mention traffic jams due to the fact that too many people were now suddenly able to purchase cars and the road system simply wasn't equipped to cope.

The arts were suffering as well, the government no longer automatically subsidising artistic projects and endeavours, orchestras, theatres and musicians. Still, Poland was somehow staying afloat, full of hope and ideals, though sadly lacking in people qualified to take over the governmental and bureaucratic posts once held by corrupt officials of the past regime. Clearly it would take more than a few years before the last vestiges of their communist past would disappear. But Poland does have a great advantage over the other East European countries formerly under Soviet rule in that it receives huge subsidies from North American Poles, who pour money into the Polish economy out of a sense of duty and nostalgia. Over the next few days, I heard plenty of complaints from ordinary Poles, but not a single person regretted the Revolution of 1989, which finally brought about the end of a struggle whose beginnings dated back to 1939, when Hitler invaded their country.

Katowice is not an attractive town. It might improve in appearance if the years of accumulated grime were scraped off the buildings, but not much. An old coal-mining town, it has produced, somewhat paradoxically, some of Poland's finest artists and musicians (Krystian Zimerman springs to mind), and its Radio Orchestra is of very high quality.

I was surprised by the hotel. From the outside, it looked like the same concrete monolith of bygone years, but the interior was perfectly pleasant, with bathrooms that were completely new and actually worked. The television was tuned to CNN. When I thought of how things had been on my last trip to Poland, I found this almost surreal.

I wandered downstairs to have dinner and the surprises continued: instead of the usual pre-1989 clientele (Russians, Bulgarians and other fellow Soviet Bloc citizens, not to mention Arabs from countries not so friendly to the West and a few Africans, Chinese and Southeast Asians), this restaurant was full of Western businessmen – Italians, English, French, German, even some South Africans. The meal was delicious. I had the omnipresent *barszcz*, which I happen to like very much, but I also had perch in a delicate sauce, a glass of French white wine, a lovely big mixed green salad and a fresh fruit salad for dessert. A large Polish family and their friends sat at the table next to mine, celebrating the father's birthday. There was lots of champagne and laughter, and the atmosphere was festive. It really was hard to believe that this was the same country I'd

317

visited seven years previously. Even the shops on my way to the hall were totally transformed. Now privately owned, there was wit, imagination and colour in the window displays, the products similar to what one would find in any western European town.

The Fitelberg Hall in Katowice has one of the nicest dressing rooms. It is almost an apartment, with a full bathroom, a marvellous Steinway to practise on, and a sitting room. In later years, it became almost a second home to me as I rested between recording sessions, practised the Paderewski concerto, read, and ate snacks. On the walls were photos of colleagues who had performed there, going back a very long time. I felt proud that I, too, could be a link in the long magical chain stretching back not just to the Rubinsteins, Arraus, Hofmanns, whose photos decorated the walls, but also to the even earlier, greatest pianists of all, Chopin and Liszt.

The concert went well. I was performing the Liszt E-flat concerto, which is always a big charge to play. Kirk gave a sympathetic accompaniment as usual, and the orchestra, particularly the woodwinds, played marvellously, but unfortunately the quality of the string instruments was very poor. Even the concertmaster had to deal with an inferior violin, which was a shame, as he was a fine performer.

After the reception, Kirk and I went to the station – he was to catch a train to Warsaw, and I was on my way to Salzburg via Vienna to meet Biddy for a short holiday. My train was to pass through the Czech Republic, and although a visa was unnecessary for an American citizen, the Czech government still required visas from Commonwealth countries such as Australia and New Zealand. I had heard this from the Australian violinist Elizabeth Wallfisch, who had also been travelling through the Czech Republic on her way to somewhere and had ended up being cast adrift on a lonely railroad siding by an uncompromising Czech border guard. Worried about this, I had repeatedly asked the girl dealing with travel in David's office to check for me if I, as a Canadian, needed a visa. Absolutely not was her reply, and I believed her. I had also asked for a private sleeping compartment on the train and said I would be happy to pay extra for this luxury. No problem at all, I was told.

The train arrived right on the dot at midnight, and I boarded. Sure enough, there, already undressed down to her bloomers, was a little old lady settling down for the night on the bottom bunk. Suppressing my irritation, since it didn't really matter that much, especially as this was only a two-bunk compartment and therefore less coffin-like, I started to stow away my heavy suitcase and climb up to my perch. My companion turned out to be something of a guardian angel. For starters, she shared my opinion that we should leave the curtain open and the blinds up so we could look out at the passing lights flickering in the dark landscape. She was vivacious and energetic and about 80 years old. She busily showed me where I should stow my suitcase and helped me to do so. We started a friendly conversation, and I told her all about the concert I had just played. Shortly after, we hit the Czech border.

The Polish border guard was puzzled by my Polish visa and kept staring at it, making me extremely nervous. Then my little lady sprang into action, asking what the problem was: with her as translator, he asked me if I had had any trouble entering Poland. I said no, and then, to my surprise, he started to laugh and pointed out to me that the Polish Consulate in New York had stamped my passport 1995 instead of 1994. He didn't seem bothered by this and, after a few jokes over the incompetence of everyone else in the world, he left.

Then a very dour Czech official appeared. When he asked for my visa, I mentally cursed Ingpen & Williams with every fibre of my body and with a sinking heart told him that I had no Czech visa and that I was just passing through on my way to Vienna. A long discussion started up with my little lady (who fortunately also spoke Czech) translating. After a while she began to scold him, but, obdurate and with absolutely no sense of humour, he stood his ground. I was now being totally ignored as my lady escalated her defence, invoking the names of Chopin and Liszt as witnesses to my unimpeachable character. This attracted the attention of the Polish guard who was passing our compartment, having finished his job for the evening. He joined in the discussion with relish, taking my side, and eventually the Czech guard, beaten down by such un-expected, high-spirited opposition, relented and handed me a visa form to fill out. In fact, so brow-beaten was he that he for-got to make me pay the standard visa fee and left looking rath-er stunned. A nasty situation had been averted; I'd had fleeting nightmare visions of wandering in the cold all night, dragging my suitcase behind me, searching for telephones, consulates, visa photographers and some way to get in touch with Biddy, who was waiting for me in Salzburg.

After about an hour, just before the little town of Bohumin, the train, which had been making rather worrying noises, stopped. I was just beginning to feel sleepy but was still fully clothed, lying on my top bunk. Nothing happened – we just sat there for a long time. So my little lady, full of energy, threw on her coat and went off in search of an official who could clari-fy the situation. She was told we were to change carriages and find a seat somewhere else. This was no easy task, as our car had been detached from the rest of the train. Laden with suit-cases, we had to clamber down with no platform on which to land, just a huge gap, gravel and then a steep bank. We could easily have slipped and hurt ourselves seriously. It was all be-coming quite scary, as there was no one to tell us which car-riage we were supposed to use, and the train seemed all but abandoned, with neither passengers nor officials in sight.

My resourceful friend made the decisions for us, and we boarded an empty second-class carriage (the tickets the or-chestra had provided for me had been first class) and settled in for the night, realising very soon that there was no heat, and that the cold December night was finding its way deep into our bones. My little lady was amazing – cheerful, tough and irre-pressible (she was a survivor of the Warsaw uprising, after all) and she remained positive – although we were both exhaust-ed. We tucked ourselves up in our overcoats and told each other stories, laughing a lot. I remembered that I had in my purse some cookies and chocolate that I had brought all the way from Connecticut only three days before, for just such an occasion, and I also had some fruit that I'd kept from the breakfast buffet in the Katowice hotel. We shared my emergency rations and derived considerable comfort from them.

The train began to move, and we started to doze off. At the Czech-Austrian border we were woken up once again by guards, and once again the Czech guard began to make trouble for me. My little lady lost her temper with him, delivering a long and forceful speech on my behalf. He beat a hasty retreat, chastened and humbled by her dramatic rhetoric, and the Austrian guard who followed with his German Shepherd dog gave only a cursory look at our passports. He was a friendly fellow and we chatted amiably while his dog silently ate all the rest of my cookies before we noticed and could stop him.

With all of this hullabaloo and strange nocturnal happenings, it seemed faintly bizarre that we actually arrived in Vienna only 10 minutes late. My little lady was met by her sister and brother-in-law, who lived in Vienna. Not ready to relinquish her role as my guardian angel, she sent her brother-in-law off to find me a carriage for my suitcases and then directed me to the booth where I could change my money. I kissed and hugged her and thanked her and we parted. It is sad that, somehow, I never found out her name. Perhaps guardian angels don't need names.

It was lovely being in Austria, and Salzburg at Christmas time is like a child's most treasured fantasy. Biddy had a long relationship with the city, having been there often with George; she had also, years before, celebrated her 21st birthday there with her parents. As it was exactly a year since George's death, I wanted to cheer her up, and I thought it might be fun for her to have a nice holiday amongst the happy memories. Mozart's hometown was illuminated by a million Christmas lights and adorned with elaborate wreaths, magical Christmas trees, golden angels, and silver bells. We wandered the fairy-tale streets and admired the Christmas Market, sampling the hot *wurst* and warming our hands with mugs of hot cider. And, in the evening, we sat on our balcony sipping champagne and admiring the magical view of the castle and the rushing Salzach River.

We were then to spend a few days in Vienna. My life has been full of surprises, twists and turns, and especially coincidences, but probably the most astonishing occurred on the train from Salzburg to Vienna. Our compartment was already occupied by two people when we boarded in Salzburg, a middle-aged woman, smartly dressed in old-fashioned German travelling clothes, and her elderly male companion. We nodded to each other but did not, *à l'Américaine*, instantly strike up any kind of friendly conversation. Biddy soon fell asleep. She was dressed in her usual, eccentric way, sporting a Tiroler hat with a large feather, which she had bought as a present for Peter, a woollen scarf that she had knitted herself (rather badly), an ancient Dior tweed overcoat that had definitely seen better days (it resembled, at this point, an old beach blanket with a few actual tears in the fabric to add to its decrepitude) little black woollen gloves of the sort the nuns used to wear back in Montreal, a smart, deep-blue Chanel suit that I had bought for her 10 years previously and in which, although it had been dry-cleaned to death, she could still look marvellous – if not for the old tennis shoes she insisted on wearing because they were comfortable.

I was lazily reading *Martin Chuzzlewitt* and looking out of the window, watching the snow-covered Austrian countryside go by when, about twenty minutes before our arrival in Vienna, Biddy woke up and left the compartment for a quick trip to the bathroom. The lady sitting opposite leaned forward and asked me in German if I was accompanying this poor immigrant to Vienna. Trying to figure out a way of breaking the news gently, without embarrassment, I ended up by simply saying that the poor immigrant was actually my mother. To bridge the awkward (but hilarious, I thought) moment, I asked the lady if she lived in Vienna. Noting my uncertain German, she politely answered in perfect English that she was just visiting and in fact, the reason for her visit was to hear a recital of a friend of hers, the pianist Andras Schiff, a colleague of mine with whom I was on friendly terms. We chatted about concerts and pianists and the lady seemed extremely knowledgeable and was obviously a musician herself.

Suddenly, out of the blue, she said: "I was a very great friend of Arthur Rubinstein." I then told her how he had been my mentor and great friend as well, and asked her what her name was. "Gertrud Kottermaier," she responded. The world stopped turning for a second and my heart skipped several beats. It was all too strange to be true. I remembered her name very well as I had read her letters to Arthur after he had become blind, since no one else in the Rubinstein household could read German. Although I refrained from telling Frau Kottermaier the story, I also recalled that it had become a big joke between Annabelle, Arthur and myself when the telephone had rung one day at the Rubinstein home in Paris and Marinha, the sweet Portuguese housekeeper, had run into the sitting room very excitedly, to say that Golda Meir, the former Prime Minister of Israel, was on the phone and wished to speak to the Maestro. Arthur had hurried to the phone, only to find that Marinha had misunderstood and that it was not Golda Meir at the other end of the line but Frau Kottermaier – with whom Arthur was naturally equally delighted to speak.

We then discussed Mrs. Rubinstein and how much we both liked Annabelle, who had recently married Lord Weidenfeld, and how, sadly, neither of us had been able to make it to the wedding.

As the train was pulling into the station, I asked my new friend where she was from in Germany. "Augsburg," she said. I had just been to Augsburg for the first time the month before on a mini-holiday, visiting the conductor Bruno Weil and his wife Mechthild, who lived there, after I had performed with Bruno in Duisburg. Did Frau Kottermaier know Bruno? Of course; she had known him for many years. Frau Kottermaier then gave me her card and said she hoped I would come and perform in Augsburg one day soon and how delighted she would be if I did. I replied that it would be great fun to see her again and also to return to Augsburg, which was an absolute jewel of a place. I then asked her if she also knew Harry Oesterle, who ran Bruno's festival in Irsee. "But of course," she replied, "he is a very nice man, don't you think?"

Five years later, in 1999, I returned to Augsburg at the invitation of my dear friend and frequent collaborator, the American conductor Peter Leonard, who had, by another extraordinary twist of fate, just been appointed Music Director of the City of Augsburg. Up until then my career in Germany had been limited to only sporadic appearances; now it truly felt as though Fate (or God or Destiny) was bringing me to, of all the many towns and orchestras in Germany, this particular one. And so, Frau Kottermaier did see me again and did have the opportunity to hear me perform Mozart's piano concerto K 595. And Harry Oesterle came back into my life.

Although I had only met Harry briefly beforehand, I retained a very fond memory of his kind nature. Being a little nervous of Germany, I felt emboldened to fax him announcing my arrival in his hometown on a date which happened to coincide with my birthday. The New York flight landed at the ungodly hour of 6:10 a.m. in Munich, which I tactfully didn't mention, but I did ask if perhaps he could meet my train when it arrived in Augsburg at eight. Typically, Harry found out the arrival time of the flight coming from New York and was at the airport waiting for me with a birthday cake complete with a burning candle, which caused some consternation amongst the security guards. As my hotel room wasn't ready for me, we drove to his home and ate the cake together and renewed our acquaintance. Over the next few days, we spent most of our free time together as he drove me to rehearsals and took me out for meals and lovely drives in the countryside. The first of the two concerts was thoroughly enjoyable, because it was Mozart and because Peter, the conductor, was an old friend. When Harry drove me back to the hotel that evening, he tentatively asked if I might be interested in seeing where his Festival was held in Irsee, situated in the foothills of the Bavarian Alps. He had to be there the next day for meetings and was going to miss my second performance. Normally I never take trips on the days of concerts, preferring to work quietly in the mornings and rest in the afternoons, but Harry quickly added that they had a relatively new Steinway on which I could practise, and since I was already becoming quite smitten, I agreed he should pick me up the next morning and we would spend the day together ... which was exactly what we did, except that I barely touched the new piano. Harry put me back on the train to Augsburg after saying good-bye, and we both felt inexplicably torn by the thought of perhaps never seeing each other again. During the performance that night I was distracted to the point of ending one of my own *cadenzas*, freshly improvised, in the wrong key.

The next morning, I telephoned Harry from the airport, something I never would normally do as I have a pathological fear of the telephone. When I arrived in Edmonton (where I was to play my next concerts) 20 hours later after a bomb scare at Heathrow airport, there was a fax waiting for me from Harry. I wrote back immediately and from that moment on we started a daily correspondence. After a while – and two huge boxes with reams of faxes – we switched to telephoning each other. I was falling in love and didn't even realise it at first. But it all became crystal clear when we met in Rome, six months later. I had a recital there and Harry took a few days off work to join me. After checking in to our hotel, we decided to go and explore the city. Harry took my hand and we started to walk in that magical place. I knew at that very moment that this was the man with whom I belonged and that I loved him deeply. Amazingly, he felt the same way about me. We knew a transatlantic romance would be difficult, but we saw no other option: it was all so obvious. Naturally, when I returned home there were friends who thought I had taken leave of my senses, but Biddy was immediately supportive, and Harry and I became officially engaged just four months later ... we had still only been together for perhaps a total of eight days.

CHAPTER 15

"Remembrances" ("Efterklang")
by Edvard Grieg

The magic of our days together in Rome had long faded into nostalgic memories as our lives became more and more complicated and I was finally struck down by illness, confirmed by the biopsy I had suffered through in New York where I had been hospitalized overnight.

But dawn ushered in a new world of bright sunshine, blustery winds and tiny puffs of cloud racing high in a deep blue sky. The previous day's winter storm had vanished, leaving behind a sparkling, fresh-faced New York City. It was as if the slate had been wiped clean and a new era was about to begin.

Having only the vaguest recollection of being moved out of the recovery room in the wee hours of the morning, it took me a few moments to grasp where I was. Surprisingly, I felt no ill effects from the ordeal of the day before; in fact, I was raring to go. Lack of food made me a bit light-headed, almost euphoric, as I quickly dressed. I chatted with my roommate – an elderly lady with an awe-inspiring, sunny disposition, who was dealing with bone cancer – while I waited for breakfast, the doctor and Harry's return, not necessarily in that order.

Breakfast was first to arrive and, being ravenous from not having eaten in thirty-six hours, I fell on it with enthusiasm, wolfing down everything on the plate: great chunks of scrambled egg, fatty bacon, and soggy white bread saturated with rancid butter. I gave a fleeting thought to high cholesterol and wondered how a hospital of this high calibre could possibly offer such health hazards as nourishment. Then I carefully scraped the last crumbs off my greasy plate and sat back content.

Doctor Morris arrived, and I greeted her quite cheerfully. Nothing she said – whether it was about radiation, chemotherapy, paralysis or death – could dampen my spirits that morning. I was ready for battle. Now that I was face to face with the most ghastly news anyone could receive – potential loss of life and, equally devastating, the potential loss of life's meaning – what I felt was an absurd sense of relief. The worst had happened, and somehow, I knew that a disaster of this magnitude had been almost inevitable. My body had called a halt to my activities and had decided enough was enough. Now it was up to me to fight back – a great challenge indeed, and perhaps the ultimate adventure.

The next few weeks were a whirlwind of activity, giving Harry and myself barely time to breathe let alone absorb what was happening to us. An operation was tentatively scheduled for the month of May. I cancelled all concerts (including my first Grand Tour of Australia, as well as the initial phase of my Liszt Etudes recital tour) until September. No one could tell me in what state my arm would be following the surgery, so I chose to believe that I would be back on stage by the start of the fall season.

With the knowledge that I was a concert pianist, Doctor Morris had conferred at length with her fellow orthopedic surgeons and oncologists at the hospital, and they had come up with a plan of action to try and save as much of my arm muscle as possible. What the biopsy had revealed was that the mass in my upper left arm was a soft tissue sarcoma. Sarcomas are a rare group of tumours that arise from connective tissues such as muscles. I was extraordinarily lucky to have landed in Memorial Sloan Kettering, as it maintains the largest single-institution database for soft tissue sarcomas in the world.

My own particular tumour subtype was of immense interest to the doctors, as it was very rare, almost unique; at that time only sixteen cases had been identified in the hospital's file of over 5,000 sarcomas. My tumour was large – 12 centimetres in diameter – and was slotted into the Stage 3 or, in layman's terms, "very scary" advanced stage of cancer. To remove the tumour, a lot of muscle would have to be cut out, and a major nerve severed. The doctors would attempt to minimize the muscle damage so that a second, experimental muscle transfer surgery could have a greater chance of success.

My first appointment was with Dr. Kaled Alektiar, a radiation oncologist, who put me on a schedule of external beam therapy, designed to shrink the tumour before the operation. I found Dr. Alektiar to be charming, like everyone at the hospital, kind and very careful to explain the procedures to me in straightforward language. I was to have two sets of radiation therapy: 25 days (or five weeks with only the weekends free) before the surgery, and 10 days after.

In the end, radiation was not difficult for me. The session with the simulator before the treatment began was less than agreeable, and then the breakdown of the skin at the end of the five weeks was painful and repulsive. For the simulator, I had to lie absolutely still for what seemed an eternity in the most uncomfortable positions. During this time, the doctor and his technicians pinpointed where the radiation beam would hit, at various angles around my arm and shoulder. They then made three tiny tattoos as signposts for when they would do the daily setup for the actual radiation process. It was sobering to think what might happen if they were just millimetres off target. This is why one had to lie so incredibly still and hardly breathe during the procedure; it could be quite agonizing.

Determined to appear brave, I tried to imagine I was a victim of the Spanish Inquisition lying on the rack, or maybe even a Polish war hero being interrogated by the KGB. I quickly decided that I wouldn't have lasted very long as a spy and would have volunteered with alacrity, and completely unsolicited, any information desired: restaurant tips, valuable family recipes, how to remove grease stains, inventive fingerings for Chopin etudes, whatever ... These thoughts occupied my mind, and I managed to survive the session without making any kind of exhibition.

328

During the five weeks of radiation, when Harry had to drive me daily into New York City, we had the most wonderful time. I know it sounds odd, but it's quite simply the truth. The hospital tried its best to accommodate out-of-town patients like myself and put our sessions in the middle of the day so we wouldn't have to battle rush-hour traffic. This meant that, when we were lucky, driving into New York, having the therapy and driving back to Connecticut might take only three and a half hours. Fatigue set in by the end of the fourth week, and parts of my arm, particularly the underarm and armpit, became completely raw and burnt. There was a lot of discharge, which was absorbed by a towel that I kept wrapped around the area, and I applied aloe vera and burn ointments constantly.

But for the first few weeks I felt quite fine and was able to practice the piano in the early mornings. The question was what to practice, as I was in a strange sort of limbo with no concerts to prepare and an uncertain future.

Harry shares a birthday with Franz Schubert, his favourite composer, and I had always loved Schubert's piano music, particularly when I heard it performed by my friends Imogen Cooper and Radu Lupu. Arthur himself had urged me to learn the B flat Sonata, sensing that I would have an affinity for the music. But early on in my career, I had decided to abstain from performing Schubert on the premise that for me to communicate the essence of his music convincingly, and also manage the sometimes sprawling and repetitive structures of his works, I would need to have mastered every other composer first and developed great maturity and wisdom.

Harry suggested that work on a Schubert piece might be therapeutic, and I thought his idea was excellent – if ever there was a good time, this was it. Whenever I had a few hours in the early morning, I worked on the four Schubert Impromptus Opus 142. There was no deadline, so I took my time. Every day, it seemed, I uncovered new treasures in these gems of perfection. Deceptively simple, they were nevertheless a marvellous challenge, a kind of music quite different to what I had been accustomed to performing. I often feel that a Schubert piano work is like going on a very pleasant walk across lush meadows filled with wildflowers, perhaps a lovely mountain range in the distance, little lakes and brooks, leaves fluttering in the wind and a nice café with cakes and good company at the end. There are no Victoria Falls, Mount Everests, or Notre Dame Cathedrals along the way, neither are there murders or terrors or violent romantic passions. But the Schubert piano world is beautiful and varied, with plenty of emotion and tension hovering underneath, and its sum total can be more satisfying to the soul and more spiritually uplifting than music riddled with climaxes and extremes. To try and capture and reproduce this extraordinarily complex simplicity required a great deal of commitment and attention. I was happily absorbed and, indeed, extremely grateful to Schubert for this challenge as well as this balm for my soul.

I also practiced some of the Liszt Etudes (Chasse-Neige, Feux Follets, Harmonies du Soir), finding it hard to give them up completely. At the time of the radiation, I would have been right in the middle of the big European tour, performing all twelve of the Liszt Transcendental Etudes. In a way, I was bidding a long farewell to my old friends.

The radiation period provided other interesting and sometimes downright pleasurable side effects. Most importantly, Harry stayed with me. In our entire relationship, this was the first time we had been together for more than just a few days or, at best, a couple of weeks at a time. With the laptop computer and the invaluable help of his assistant and dear friend, Sibylle, back in Irsee, Harry could remain with me in the US and run his festival on the other side of the ocean.

Also, I had never found myself settled in one place for such a length of time since my student years at Juilliard, and Harry and I took full advantage of the situation. Being in New York City practically every day, we became members of the Metropolitan Museum of Art and the Museum of Modern Art. After the radiation session, we visited all the latest exhibitions in those institutions, as well as at the Guggenheim and the Frick museums. The cultural goodies available were thrilling and endless. We were countless times at the opera, Carnegie Hall and Lincoln Centre. And friends! We actually had time for a bit of a social life. We dined on numerous occasions with old chums from Juilliard whom I normally would have seen once in a blue moon, and mostly in backstage situations.

The drives in and out of the city, which lasted anywhere from an hour to three hours each way depending on traffic, could have been a nightmare, but were a joy, for I was with the man I loved. After a while we hit on the novel idea of using this time to improve my German. So, armed with pen and paper and a dictionary, I would carry on halting German conversations with Harry, stopping every so often to look up words when I got really stuck, while he concentrated cheerfully on the perils of New York City traffic which, he said, reminded him of home.

Sometimes we were lucky and the wait at the hospital was only a few minutes. But at other times, when the machines were out of order or line-ups to get into the parking lot stretched around the block, we could be there for hours.

During those five weeks of intense radiation, I formed quite a bond with all the remarkable people with whom I came into contact at the hospital: the other patients, of course, but also the parking lot attendants, the receptionist in the radiation wing, and particularly, the technicians who ran the machines. Sitting in the waiting room day after day, I perceived almost no feelings of sadness, worry, or impatience in the air. Quite the contrary; harmony and calm reigned, perhaps some resignation, but no pessimism and absolutely no despair. These people, whether patients or hospital employees, came in all ages, sizes, colours, beliefs and backgrounds, but somehow this horrible disease clarified one's thinking and cut away any possible remnants of prejudice or envy that might still be lingering in one's ever-so-liberal mind. Sitting in that waiting room also taught me a lot about the sheer resilience and courage of the human spirit, and I felt tremendous waves of affection for all

331

of my fellow sufferers. Upon reflection, what could have been more therapeutic than this kind of spontaneous love?

My sessions were 26 minutes long: nine different angles and a few minutes to set up for each one. The technicians were at first surprised at the complexity of my treatment, until they found out I was a concert pianist. They then offered to play CDs for me over the loudspeaker while I was being zapped. From then on, I would daily experience the curious juxtaposition of, for instance, hearing Mozart concertos played divinely by Murray Perahia while my body was being pierced by supersonic rays.

In the evening when we were home, Harry and I would create wonderful meals. My husband, I was discovering, was an excellent cook, coming by this talent naturally through his mother, who had cooked professionally in her youth. I was happy to chop, slice and clean up afterwards. Harry would then be introduced to the delights of British comedy on PBS, and we sampled a great many videos from my vast collection of old movies.

There were one or two instances when, in the middle of the night, I would wake up in extreme panic with the inconceivable realization that in a few weeks' time my piano playing days could be over for good. But this happened only a couple of times. Most of the time I was defiantly happy.

There was, however, one doctor's appointment that made my blood run cold with fear. Making sure to cover all the bases, Dr. Morris sent me for a consultation with Dr. Robert Maki, an oncologist who specialized in chemotherapies for sarcoma patients. I was nervous about this meeting as, like everyone else, I had mixed feelings about chemotherapy and knew the ravages it could cause. Harry and I had watched *The Sound of Music* the night before the appointment. I felt it was an important part of North American culture that he should know about; besides, I unashamedly admit that I thoroughly enjoy this movie. Anyhow, as we waited in the examining room for the doctor to appear, Harry was trying to remember the words to "My Favorite Things," and we caught an awful and escalating case of the giggles. So much so that when the door finally opened and in came the doctor, he was a little surprised to find us in fits of laughter.

Dr. Maki was a young man with intelligent, boyish good looks. Energetic and voluble, he started bombarding me with statistics and survival probabilities. I soon lost track of the conversation as my mind froze, paralyzed with the enormity of all that he was saying. He was a music lover and had already checked out my website; he was also quite familiar with the case of my brilliant colleague, the Argentinean pianist Martha Argerich, who had suffered from cancer as well and had survived. After much discussion, and since my cancer was so rare and there was so little data on it – and the most recent studies, held in Rome, were inconclusive in their findings as to whether chemotherapy would be of any benefit – Dr. Maki and I decided not to go through with any treatments. I escaped the hospital that day shaking and fearful, but also with a vast sense of relief.

In April, a few weeks before the operation, while my arm healed from the radiation burns, Harry had to fly back to Germany. His presence was at this point necessary at the festival offices in Irsee, plus he had to check up on things at home. After all, when he had flown to America in January, he had expected to be away for only two weeks, not three months. I used the few days that he was away to give the house a spring cleaning and to get my hair cut very short, as I figured it would be difficult to wash after the operation, with my arm in a sling.

Harry's absence and the silent vacuum it created offered an opportunity to mull over what was about to happen to me. Instead, I became an expert at treating my relatively catastrophic situation with a certain degree of equanimity. Perhaps what enabled me to fall so easily into such a sanity-saving course of action was my experience at ignoring the consistently unpleasant situations ubiquitous in a concert career.

To explain a little further:

A performing artist spends his or her entire career living under severe stress, and it is the concert pianist, more than all other performing musicians (who generally travel with accompanists or colleagues and practice only a fraction of the amount a pianist does), who has the most pressure to contend with. There are many reasons, the main one being that in everything we do concerning our work, in everything we face and experience, we are alone. In recital we are alone on stage and ironically, perhaps the loneliest moments of all are during those engagements with conductor and orchestra when we are given between 45 minutes to about two hours of rehearsal time to convince 80 people or so, sometimes all complete strangers, of the validity and effectiveness of our talent. I have, of course, learned a great deal from conductors whom I admire, but so often I have had to deal with a situation where the only solution for a half-way decent and honorable performance is radical compromise or, to put it dramatically, a betrayal of one's ideals. This betrayal contributes to a terrible feeling of isolation.

To be a good performer, one is constantly striving for an ideal – for as perfect a performance as possible. The tension resulting from this constant effort can be, and often is, quite destructive, which is why most of the great pianists who somehow manage to carry on life-long careers develop an extraordinary ability to ignore or simply to forget whole chunks of their lives so that they can continue functioning. For instance, how could one possibly continue working if one spent one's time dwelling on the horror of pre-performance jitters? And what about those seconds of sheer panic when a collaboration with an orchestra seems about to unravel in front of three thousand people? Or those painful rejections and hurtful comments liberally and often daily tossed at us from critics, agents, managers and presenters? Without mentioning those hours of sheer exhaustion on tour, hanging around airports, suffering from colds or the flu and jet lag. Our defense, which we have learned so well, is our ability to forget these trials and tribulations or shove them to the back recesses of our minds soon after they occur. Only by doing so are we able to spend the vast majority of the rest of our time working and preparing in delightful anticipation of another performance, our thoughts leaping over the demon-ridden abyss to those magical moments of fulfillment on stage.

The success of the performance rests totally on the ability of the performer to assert her personality, to cajole, entertain, convince, even lull an audience into believing that she is uniquely qualified for the job. It takes enormous chutzpah and self-confidence. No one can convince an audience if they aren't convinced themselves. Lurking in the performer's psyche is a terrible dichotomy, for along with the chutzpah comes a desperate need to be loved and to please. Such a need brings the inevitable accompaniment of insecurities and anxieties which, coupled with the fact that we live such solitary lives – that we are, by *force majeure,* recluses from very tender ages – leads understandably to the development of many complexes … but also to many rather refined forms of self-preservation.

I survived the demands of my career with equal doses of idealism, naivety, stupidity, courage, hard-earned experience, fear, discipline, and mostly just plain old dogged determination. And now this varied package contributed greatly to the self-defensive barriers I used to shield myself from the current nightmare invading my life. Also, I now had a new and very special secret weapon – my husband Harry, whose support was unwavering but who also never allowed me for an instant to wallow in self-pity. I realized that his was a fundamentally happy nature while I am prone, even at the best of times, to periods of Slavic melancholy. When you love someone, you wish them to be happy: it is as simple as that. And to introduce hours of doom and gloom into our lives just wasn't on. So, I made moderately successful efforts to be cheerful and not to lapse into depression.

The surgery grew ever closer, like some ominous dark cloud blocking my vision with increasing intensity. More x-rays were taken, more suffocating MRIs, more tests. The day before the operation I went to the piano in the afternoon and started to play. I revisited all those old friends to whom I had become so inextricably attached over the years and whose loss I might be facing within hours: Bach's E flat minor Prelude and Fugue, Beethoven's 4th piano concerto and the second movement of Opus 111, endless Mozart but most especially those amazing chromatic passages in the concerto K.491, my beloved Chopin, my new Schubert pieces, Liszt of course, Schumann and Brahms, Ravel, and then back to Chopin. At the end I played through his Barcarolle and the third movement of his B minor Sonata; I feel that nothing more beautiful has ever been written for the piano. I closed the lid and said good-bye. Harry was in tears upstairs. They had told me my muscles would be gone, so I really could harbour no false hopes. But at that moment, exhausted from the lingering effects of the radiation and the afternoon of pure emotion, I prayed for a miracle.

The next morning we were up at 4 a.m. and left for the hospital shortly afterwards. After all the preliminary tests and the insertion of countless needles and tubes, a chaplain came by to chat. I am not particularly religious and am a firm believer that God should not be bothered by me, as He has enough on His plate to deal with. Nevertheless, I listened to her and was quite taken with her imagery of God being like a loyal and loving little dog who stays with us forever. I had brought to the hospital the rosary that had been given to me on the day of my first communion, although I had had to search for it at the back of several cupboards before finding it. Arthur and Elizabeth Pasquinelli had prayers said for me at the Episcopal church in Carmel, and Elaine had given me a holy medal blessed by Mother Teresa. I also had with me a Medicine Buddha from Harry; a Mass was said for me at the Orthodox Church, courtesy of my Greek travel agent, and Lord knows all my Jewish friends, not to mention my Muslim Turkish friends, were praying for me. So, I was well covered spiritually, and this brought me considerable comfort.

The surgery took six hours – far longer than expected. Dr. Morris found a large hole in the bone hidden underneath the sarcoma. There was fear that the cancer had spread to the bones and biopsies had to be taken during the operation. The results were all negative, although I still had to wait an agonizing week for the results of the last and more comprehensive biopsies. Dr. Morris removed the entire tumour, which had shrunk only a tiny bit from the radiation. A large nerve was severed, and large parts of the deltoid and triceps muscles were removed. My arm motion was now, for all intents and purposes, nil, but my finger muscles were saved.

The stay in the hospital wasn't bad, apart from the food (although mercifully my appetite was minimal), and apart from being woken up at all hours of the night for various tests.

I had brought to the hospital a great many CDs and books, but never listened to a single recording or opened a book or even watched television. My brain was just too exhausted and too busy adjusting to the new reality. On my bedside table I kept a photograph taken from a ridge on my favourite walk in the mountainous region of Germany called the Allgäu. I would often stare at this beautiful view of the Bavarian Alps, vowing to return there soon and in perfect health. This was my goal. Harry sat with me every day working on his laptop while I dozed fitfully. Nurses, orderlies and doctors flitted in and out of the room at regular intervals – solicitous, efficient and extremely kind.

Jeff and Melody, and Emanuel and Yoko, arrived together to see me on the third day. It took a lot of courage for them to come, for the spectacle of a colleague in my situation was deeply unsettling. I had been in close contact with Jeff and Melody since Juilliard. We knew each other inside out, and our tolerance for each other's foibles, as well as admiration for each other's qualities, is the kind that exists when only the truest and purest feelings of friendship are present. And one of the silver linings of the whole "arm business" was the revival of my friendship with Emanuel. His wife, Yoko, my erstwhile and very dear roommate from student years, had always stayed in touch, but geography and our busy lives had conspired to keep Emanuel and myself from seeing each other over the last 20 years, except very occasionally. The friendship remained strong, however, and since January nary a day had gone by without some sort of supportive communication from him – either an email from Japan, a phone call from London or messages via Yoko, all of which meant a great deal to me.

The little hospital room reverberated with laughter as Emanuel and Harry tried to out-do each other with a cavalcade of excruciating puns. Melody, with her uniquely contagious laugh, egged them on while Jeff, deadly serious as ever, discussed parallels between my predicament and that of Hans Castorp in Thomas Mann's *Magic Mountain* and presented his views on difficult surgical techniques. Yoko just sat quietly smiling at me, brimming with sympathy, and trying to bring some order to the room. I knew they felt great pity for me, but also a very powerful feeling of "There but for the grace of God go I."

We pianists are semi-prepared for ridiculous everyday accidents – a finger cut while chopping onions, a hand caught in a door, an arm broken after a fall on the ice – but for the most part wounds heal, sprains disappear, and bones eventually knit. We dread these events, but we develop a protective attitude towards our arms and hands, which channel our souls and talents to the outside world, and which are also, more prosaically, our breadwinners. (And incidentally, to insure hands and arms is impossible; the premiums are prohibitive.) But how can one guard against the effects of cancer? To have a muscle removed and from one day to the next have one's whole life's work simply vanish? Visitors to my room saw my arm, strapped and bandaged, completely immobile, without life. I made a joke of it and found myself reassuring them that it was all temporary and that I was optimistic for the future. I love my friends and they love me, but I had the feeling that day they were quite relieved when I became tired and they had the perfect excuse to leave.

Four days later I was released from the hospital. My medical insurance, which had already refused to cover the night in the hospital after my biopsy, now refused to pay for my fourth day of treatments, care, and bed despite the length and severity of my surgery. The bills were astronomical.

Back home in Connecticut my arm healed quickly, although the pain was quite intense for a while. I missed the piano acutely and it didn't take more than forty-eight hours before I went into my music score cupboard and hauled out the Ravel piano concerto for the left hand, a piece I had always wanted to learn but had never before found the time to do so.

The story of the concerto is a remarkable one. It starts with a famous Austrian pianist, Paul Wittgenstein (whose brother was the equally famous philosopher, Ludwig Wittgenstein), who came from a wealthy family and who tragically lost his right arm in combat during the First World War. Not to be stymied by the vagaries of fate, he commissioned the great composers of the time (Ravel, Prokofiev, Britten, Korngold, Hindemith and Strauss) to write for him – concertos for piano and orchestra for his remaining left hand. Now I had only a right arm not the left one, and I was passionately curious to see if it would be possible to perform these one-handed pieces with the "other" hand. It was a staggering relief to find that indeed, with a little shifting of the piano stool to the left, it was not only possible but great fun as well.

Up to that point I had still not cancelled any concerts beyond September 2002, although I had also not actively gone out and attempted to book any new engagements. Now, armed with the knowledge that I could potentially fill the void with this whole array of one-handed concertos written for Paul Wittgenstein, I approached the conductors and presenters where I had been scheduled to perform and offered this alternative. Unfortunately, most of the concerts scheduled for the 2002–2003 season were solo piano recitals, because I would have still been in the middle of the Liszt Transcendental Etudes Extravaganza, which spanned two seasons. Also, many of the orchestras, although sympathetic to my plight, were more or less locked into certain repertoire requirements and were unable to change the pieces for me.

In the end, with the assistance of my kind-hearted friends in the business, twelve concerts were salvaged, so that during the months of my hiatus from two-handed playing, I was still able to be involved with the piano and with performance. Instead of falling into a slump, I now had something to work for and could still cling to the belief that I was a functioning concert pianist. I grabbed onto the Ravel and a month later the Prokofiev 4th piano concerto and held onto them as veritable lifesavers. In particular, the Ravel was an exquisite pleasure. He is a composer to whom I had always been attracted, and I have never understood the reputation thrust upon him of being the ultimate colourist and the archetypical skillful French composer, whose music delights but never moves as it is inherently cold. *Au contraire*, in the delicacy and refinement of his musical penmanship, I have always found deep emotion, including pathos, mirroring what must have been in this sensitive man's soul. Much of this depth of feeling can be found in the "left-hand" concerto.

Harry was exhausted. His back had given out from driving in and out of New York City under such constant tension. We decided that we needed to escape which, on the spur of the moment we did, driving to Cape Cod and taking the ferry to Martha's Vineyard. We stayed in a hotel right on the beach facing a turbulent Atlantic. It was mid-May and still very cold at night, but during the day the sun shone and we even managed to breakfast outdoors. Our best time there was on the last day when we ventured over to Chappaquiddick and strolled on that vast expanse of beach completely alone, the roaring waves still that particular icy blue colour of spring and the seagulls circling noisily overhead. It was magical, the sea air acting as a tonic not only to the physical senses but to our mental state as well.

In the car on the way home we listened to CDs – no piano music, but plenty of Eartha Kitt, Peggy Lee and French songs from the 20s and 30s sung by Charles Trenet, Edith Piaf and Jean Sablon. Somehow a CD of overtures performed by Solti and the Chicago Symphony found its way into the player, and at first we enjoyed listening to an Offenbach Overture. Then Wagner's Prelude to *Meistersinger* began. Suddenly it was all absolutely unbearable. Wagner's music had found the key and the floodgates opened. I had held everything in for so long and now, the effect on me of this extraordinary music with which I had so many deeply moving and happy associations – my student years in New York, Jeff, Solti, Arthur, Bayreuth, and my early discovery of the power of music – was cataclysmic. I completely and utterly fell apart and sobbed.

Hearing this music somehow forced me to face up to what I might be losing. My whole life had been centred around music and the piano – certainly until I had met Harry. Yes, there were plenty of other interests, even passions, in my life, but this relationship to music wasn't a mere passion or interest – this was ME – the piano was ME – music was ME, every molecule, every atom, every strand of DNA in my body screams MUSICIAN. It couldn't just be switched off. I woke up in the morning and automatically wanted to go to the piano – I could visualize myself playing with two hands – I dreamed of it. All my life, nearly every single day I had worked to perfect my art. The thought that it was all over was impossible to bear.

Slowly, I calmed down and Harry, who had remained silent, started to talk to me in German. I had to make an effort to clear my brain and respond in the same language and the terrible moment passed. After a while we put on a CD of Fred Astaire singing Cole Porter.

There followed two more weeks of radiation therapy while New York sweltered in a heat wave. Christopher and Elaine were at the Stratford Festival in Canada, where he was rehearsing *King Lear*. They had encouraged us to use their swimming pool, and as my arm was not breaking down from the radiation this time, nothing could be more delightful than driving out from a steaming New York, where the mercury once hit 108°F on the FDR drive, and throwing ourselves into the deliciously cool water. As a bonus, my "dead arm" operated almost normally underwater.

It was at this point that another astonishing character re-entered my life. The young immigrant from Lithuania, Shmuel Tatz, who had sat in the audience when I'd performed in Jerusalem during the Rubinstein competition back in 1974, was now a world-renowned physiotherapist with offices in the Carnegie Hall building. His wife, Golda, a marvelous pianist, was a pupil of Jeff. It was Jeff who urged me to make contact with Shmuel, which I did shortly after the operation. I desperately needed help keeping the damaged remnants of muscle alive and strong until it came time for the next, crucial, muscle-transfer surgery.

Shmuel has highly original skills, deep insight into the roots of people's suffering, and magical healing powers. He is a genius, something that was obvious right from the first visit. His office has no frills – very functional, old shabby rooms – but he has all the latest equipment. Walking in there was like stepping into some Eastern European country, for the only languages I heard spoken were either Russian or Lithuanian. One wall is devoted to photographs of grateful patients – a Who's Who of the music, ballet, and theatre world – and beyond. There is even a photo, with a heartfelt inscription of thanks, from former Soviet President Mikhail Gorbachev.

And yet, with such renown and so much success, Shmuel is the most un-diva-like person one could ever meet – no designer offices, no designer clothes, no designer home in Westchester, no designer anything. He lives solely for his patients. An intense man with a hint of endearing madness about him, he always gave the impression of caring profoundly about my predicament and that he would do anything in his power to ease the suffering. It was as though he would draw the agonies of pain out of my body by sheer will power and absorb them into his own. And when he felt I was fearful or doubtful, he would abruptly stop treatment, for just a second, and earnestly tell me that all would be well. I trusted him implicitly.

Shmuel worked on my arm regularly for the next few years, until his supernatural talents were no longer required and all I needed was routine therapy. This was fortunate in a way because Shmuel, with no assistance from my insurance, had become unaffordable, other than in a crisis situation. That being said, it is still of enormous comfort to me to know that he is in New York, dashing from patient to patient in a frenzy of concern, always there if and when I need him.

Shmuel has a German counterpart. After the second lot of radiation sessions was over and I passed the final tests with flying colours, Harry and I breathed a sigh of relief and returned to Germany in July 2002. I still needed constant physiotherapy, and this is how I met Matthias Eibeck, an old friend of Harry's. Unlike Shmuel, Matthias' nature isn't frenzied and crackling with nervous energy, but is instead delightfully sane and relaxed. However, he is equally creative, imaginative and knowledgeable and, like Shmuel, has that magical quality of healing power in his hands. He speaks almost no English, so our hour-long sessions became German lessons as well. A strong bond has developed between us over the years and, however physically painful they may be, I always look forward to our sessions. As a lovely bonus, his office is a 25 minute bike ride from our German home and often, in the summer, I happily bicycle along the fields of strawberries and wheat that separate our two villages, feeling carefree and healthy.

I was very careful during this time not to neglect the fingers of my left hand. The arm was incapacitated, but the fingers were fine and needed exercise. So, every day I painstakingly held my left hand up to the keyboard with my right hand, and worked on left-hand passages from pieces like Chopin's Revolutionary Etude, the coda of the fourth Ballade and the finale of the second sonata.

Many solo piano works have been written by various composers for one hand, but I instinctively shied away from learning them. I did learn a beautiful Scriabin Nocturne written for the left hand (which I played with my right hand), as this was a piece that I could use when an encore was needed for the one-handed concerto performances. But as I was convinced of my eventual two-handed return to the stage, and knew that once I was back with both arms operating normally it would never cross my mind to program any of those one-handed works other than the concertos (which are masterpieces in their own right), I tended to avoid them. It was obviously a psychological reaction, which I didn't bother to analyze at the time.

My ever-creative and well-connected husband then decided that surely a custom-designed brace could enable me to lift my left hand up to the keyboard so that I could artificially play two-handed again while waiting for the real thing. The city of Augsburg is home to the Hessing Clinic. Mr. Hessing made a fortune as the first man to design life-like artificial limbs, and the clinic, which he constructed during the second half of the nineteenth century, became famous and very popular under the patronage of the various royal families of Europe. Some of the old buildings remain, originally designed to house, for instance, the Tsarina of Russia and her brood, and there is also a beautiful concert hall on the grounds, reminiscent of Brighton's Crystal Palace, that had been used for the patients' entertainment.

The Hessing Clinic remains an important medical facility. Harry knew one of the leading physicians, Dr. Wolfgang Tressel, who also happens to be an avid amateur violinist, pianist and music lover. Dr. Tressel was very taken with my story and immediately assigned two medical technicians to design a brace. The two were almost silent and rather a Laurel and Hardy pair – one very tall with a slightly crooked face and hair in a brush-cut, and the other short and stocky, with dark hair slicked across his forehead. I went in a few times to be measured and, after two weeks, was presented with a brace constructed out of some sort of plastic material sporting wild psychedelic patterns. When I commented on the dazzling variety of the colors, the taciturn "Laurel" managed a half smile and said, "It is because you are an artist."

The brace was christened Brace Kelly, and she actually did work; I was somehow able to play with both hands. However, after about twenty minutes of use I would develop cramps in my neck, shoulders and upper arms, because the position in which my arm was held was far from optimal. I disliked wearing Brace Kelly and used her sparingly. Paradoxically, she made me feel handicapped and reinforced, in my mind, the fact that my left arm was useless. But she served the purpose of holding up my hand to the keyboard so that I could exercise my fingers, and for this I was extremely grateful to Dr. Tressel and his team.

The summer rolled along; I was able to take many glorious walks in my beloved Allgäu. I am convinced that being outdoors surrounded by such extreme beauty was the best therapy for my health, both mental and physical. Soon, the days started to get shorter and there was a nip in the air; it was time again for Harry's festival. This was not only the festival's tenth anniversary but also Harry's farewell year as Intendant. In what amounted to an inconceivably giant leap of faith, Harry had decided to resign after the current festival so that we would no longer be doomed to endless separations. He also, quite naturally and without any doubts, assumed my next surgery would be a success, and that I would soon be back on the concert circuit, needing his assistance on the road as well as back home booking and organizing the tours.

So, the tenth festival was highly emotional, and it was clear that no one wanted Harry to leave: he was truly loved by one and all. There were farewells, and speeches, and presentations, and tears, and it was lovely to see my husband so greatly appreciated. We were lucky to be staying up the hill, away from all the hustle and bustle of the Kloster, in the B&B of the utterly delightful French lady Marie-José Reichert – where we had spent our honeymoon – who fussed over us like a mother hen and fed us her amazing breakfasts.

What also kept me occupied much of the time was the shocking discovery that the current administrator for the Piano Six
project had been liberally helping herself to Piano Six funds.
The board members were saddled with the brunt of this horrific
problem, but for months on end I, too, would be sitting daily at
the computer sorting through, reading, concentrating, and try-

ing to understand lawyers' briefs and communiqués, account-
ants' summaries and plans of action. It was extremely upset-
ting as the project had been based on the goodwill, generosity
and idealism of all involved. We desperately tried to sort out
the mess without dragging the project itself down into a sew-
er of greed and deceit. Our efforts ultimately paid off, but not
without the astonishing support of the McConnell Foundation,
our first and most loyal supporter, and the Canada Council.
Never in a million years would I have thought that a government agency as large as the Canada Council could display so
much understanding and such a clear vision for the future.

After months of horror, which worried Harry terribly, as
he was afraid the stress was impeding my healing process, we
emerged at the end of the long tunnel into a world bathed in
sunlight. The exhausted Board was finally able to step down
and breath again. A new administrator, the irrepressibly optimistic and experienced Debra Chandler, took over the reins of
operation, a new Board was selected and Piano Six metamor-
phosed into Piano Plus – by adding illustrious Canadian singers, string and wind players to our once all-pianist roster and
expanding to even farther reaches of our country. It was at this
point that I stepped down from my post as artistic administrator; I was worn out from the battles, and my brain had run dry
in the creative ideas department. Angela Cheng kindly agreed
to take over while I, in turn, agreed to do the occasional tour
for the project. Happily, Piano Plus remained strong and vital
for many more years.

October 2002 was full of activity. I was to play my first concert since January (when I had played my last two-handed recital in Irsee), and it was to be in Houston with the great Polish
conductor Stanislaw Skrowaczewski, an old and revered friend
with whom I had worked many times in Minnesota, Toronto,
and at the Proms in London. Originally, I had been scheduled
to play the Chopin E-minor concerto, but Stan had generously
agreed to the Ravel left-hand concerto (a much shorter piece than
the Chopin) and to alter the rest of the program accordingly.

Even without the cancer trauma, this would have been an extremely nerve-racking concert, as the Ravel was a new piece for me, the Houston Symphony was a top orchestra with high standards, and I hadn't performed in public for nine months. At first, Nature seemed to be conspiring against me. To begin with, I had had some CAT scans taken the week before the concert, and the results had not been released by the time I was to leave for Houston. Then, suddenly, a hurricane was announced for the Houston area, and for twenty-four hours it was touch and go whether we could fly down there at all. Luckily, the storm veered off to the south and Houston was spared, but my nerves were frayed. To top it all off, the orchestra members' contracts had just reached their limits, and the players were threatening a strike. Houston itself was like a hot, smelly steam bath and, typically, the air-conditioning in the hotel was positively freezing; Harry caught a cold instantly. Downtown Houston on the weekend is dreadful: too hot to go for a walk, absolutely deserted and with almost every store and restaurant closed.

The morning of the first rehearsal I awoke in the grip of such anxiety that I almost felt ready to call the whole thing off. But then, with miraculous timing, Dr. Morris phoned me less than an hour before the rehearsal was to begin, to tell me that my lungs (to which my brand of cancer was supposed to metastasize, according to Dr. Maki's statistics) were clear and that the cancer was nowhere to be seen. The relief was enormous, and I felt a great wave of positive energy. As I crossed the street from the hotel to the concert hall, I felt I was walking on air.

Immediately upon arriving backstage I bumped into my old friend Stan, who gave me such an exuberant welcome that I breezed through the first rehearsal with absolutely no feelings of apprehension. I also had the wonderful surprise of coming face to face with Uri Pianka, whom I had last seen in Jerusalem, where he had been concertmaster of the Israel Philharmonic Orchestra. Uri and I had performed together at the competition, and he and his wife had kindly taken me under their wing both then and on my subsequent visits to Israel. He was now concertmaster in Houston, and it seemed appropriate and somehow significant that, after playing a major supporting role in the launching of my career in 1974, he should now, 28 years later, be reprising that role at the launching of this new phase of my career.

I now slipped back into the old concert mode and was happy to note the return of that familiar rush of adrenalin. Every aspect of preparing for the concert was welcome: the afternoon spent resting in the hotel room, holding a British mystery in my hand, but dozing off in a fitful, nervous sleep with CNN a distant rumble on the television, then the ritual shower and effort to do something about my hair, my brain working overtime all the while, playing and replaying the Ravel in my head, analyzing every fingering, every phrase, every nuance, every note. At a specific time, I packed up my evening clothes and make-up bag, scores, hairbrush and handkerchiefs and marched across the street (30 seconds of 100 degree weather) to the hall where I was greeted by the stage manager – a solid, tough fellow with great humour and an amazingly gentle streak of calm understanding and empathy which totally belied the rough exterior. I should note here that wherever one plays, the nicest person one can meet, who always provides a smile and the correct words of encouragement, is the last person one sees before going on stage. The backstage crew is more important to us artists than anyone can imagine.

As usual I practiced for half an hour alone on stage, warming up my fingers before the doors opened to the public. This is always a dangerous period because, if something goes wrong during this time, chances are it can become an irreparable mental block before the performance – which is why I take such great pains to make sure such a thing doesn't occur. I find that never playing at full throttle, adopting a little bravado in one's attitude and not taking the occasional or unexpected error too seriously can get me through without too much mental stress. Harry is usually reading in the hall, not listening to my practicing – a non-threatening, silent support.

At this point in Houston, my left leg began to tremble, which rarely happens to me but, let's face it, circumstances were out of the ordinary, and the moment was rather exciting. A quick change, a visit from the conductor full of encouragement, the last minutes of the opening orchestral work, pacing up and down, my hands kept warm in my ancient woollen gloves, a last glance at the score, the futile effort to look ever so casual as I walked across the backstage while the piano was put in place, outwardly smiling, inwardly a mass of quaking jelly, a stern word to myself fiercely repeating that this was a piece I knew inside-out, that I had waited for this moment for months, that the orchestra and conductor were superb, and that I should bloody well go out there and enjoy myself.

And then Stan, the octogenarian with more energy, enthusiasm and curiosity than the entire assembly put together, standing next to me in the wings, said the perfect thing. The orchestra had already tuned, the lights on the stage had brightened and an expectant hush had descended upon the hall. He turned to me and said, "I'm so excited to do this piece with you, and I really think it sounds better with the right hand!"

How could one not be totally charmed by the good humour and positive influence of this wonderful man? And so, with a friendly nod from the stage manager, I strode on in a terrifically good mood, which only intensified as the piece progressed. The applause at the end was thunderous; I got a standing ovation and an excellent review in the following morning's newspaper. By the third and last performance, our interpretation really began to gel into something quite special, and I finally got the glorious build-up, during the last page of the cadenza, sounding almost as monumental and dramatic as I wished it to be.

Pathetically, my left arm, feeling very left out, decided to make its presence felt by aching in the most extreme fashion. I realized that whatever stress I was feeling made a beeline to my body's weakest appendage which, of course, was the left arm. Once I became aware of this phenomenon, after it had occurred during all three concerts, I made a mental note for future concerts to channel some of my powers of concentration into relaxing those few muscles and nerves remaining in my left arm so that the pain wouldn't be so intense.

The weeks following Houston could have been a giant letdown but for the fact that I was once again thrown into a maelstrom of activity: a series of doctors' appointments punctuated by a visit to a fabulous Gauguin exhibition at the Metropolitan Museum, then a quick trip up to Ottawa on Piano Six business, followed by one of the more wonderful experiences of my life: Harry and I flew to Halifax, Nova Scotia, where, in an elaborate ceremony complete with the blare of Scottish bagpipes, I became an Officer of the Order of Canada.

I had been notified of this honour just weeks after my mother died, and it was my great regret that she couldn't be there to witness the event. My decoration was presented to me by

Canada's Governor General, Adrienne Clarkson, who had featured me, years before, on her show *Adrienne Clarkson Presents*. Incidentally, the documentary about me that she had produced had won a prize at the San Francisco Film Festival in the early 90s, much to my utter astonishment at the time.

There was an exceptionally good dinner afterwards for all the new award members and their families. I was lucky enough to sit at Adrienne's table. Harry, too, had a fascinating time at his table of inventors, physicists, and philanthropists. I had never before felt such humility, but also such pride in being Canadian, as I listened to the various citations of my extraordinary fellow inductees.

The next three days Harry and I spent in paradise, or as close to paradise on earth as one can get. Cape Breton Island has always been my favourite Canadian destination, but in October it outdoes even itself. With not a tourist in sight, it was as though we had the entire place to ourselves. It is a wild, unspoiled island of unimaginable beauty, and we made our base at Ingonish, one of its most stunning sites. For the first two days the weather was uncooperative, but still we doggedly hiked along the trails and drove up through Neil's Harbour, Capstick and Meatcove to the northernmost tip at Bay St. Lawrence, where gale-force winds threatened to blow us off the pier.

On the last day the sun finally broke through the clouds. In the late afternoon, Harry and I sat on a large rock with the sea crashing all around us, the deafening roar of the surf pounding in our ears and the wind whipping a fine salt spray off the crest of the waves, forming a soft film of moisture on our faces, the intoxicating smell of the ocean invading our senses. It was a wild scene, with the gulls crying overhead and the red coastline of raw, ragged cliffs stretching for endless miles on either side of us. Jack pines intermingled with the boulders, and then, further inland, the tall dark evergreens lent an air of solemnity and stillness as they stood seemingly unaware of the riot of unbridled fall colours partying all around them – deep reds, scarlets, gold, deep pinks, browns and brilliant yellows.

We were completely alone in the Canadian wilderness after a day chasing rainbows. All afternoon, a fierce battle had been waged between the sun and the massive grey clouds that dashed at breakneck speed across the sky. Rainbows were forming everywhere and we had been chasing them assiduously, determined to find the ultimate, perfect arch. Finally, just as the sun started to fall in the evening sky, there it was – way out at sea – a shining bridge to Valhalla. So entranced were we that we almost missed the large moose who stood munching grass only a few feet away; she seemed incensed that we were paying her no heed and in a giant huff slowly crashed away from us through the dense thicket. Harry and I remained a few more minutes on our rock, breathing in great lungfuls of sea air and watching the sun disappear below the blood-red horizon until a cold, primordial sensation crept into our bodies and, shivering, we returned to the warmth of our hotel.

Back home, I received a call from a very dear friend, the brilliant Austrian conductor, Hans Graf. Although he was now music director of the Houston Symphony (and responsible for my Houston engagement in October) he was still very much involved with his former orchestra, the Calgary Philharmonic, which was at that time in severe financial trouble. Hans knew that I was free and asked if I would like to be his soloist with the Ravel concerto in a large benefit concert to be held in Calgary in a few weeks time. I leapt at the chance. The ushers, the stage crew, the orchestral musicians, and Hans were donating their services, and the Calgary media came up trumps, publicizing the event like mad.

Already at the open rehearsal in the morning, in spite of a raging blizzard outside, 700 people showed up and donated their money generously. This gave us hope that the evening concert would prove to be something special.

By nightfall, the weather had not improved. Would people actually leave their warm, comfortable homes and brave the winter storm to support their symphony? Tickets were sold on a first-come, first-served basis, and Harry and I watched as a queue began to form in the blowing snow, stretching all the way around the block. The hall doors opened at 6:30 and by 7:20 the concert was sold out, with dozens of disappointed supporters sent away. The atmosphere was electric, the excitement and anticipation from this partisan crowd palpable.

Hans has an uncanny ability to bring out the best in me, and this orchestra adored working with him as well. The result was a dramatic, quite exhilarating performance, and when we finished, the applause was deafening. For a moment I asked myself if they were really applauding my interpretation of the Ravel, or if it was simply due to the fact that I was a survivor? Or that they appreciated my doing it for their orchestra? Or were they just cheering to encourage the orchestra?

Then I decided to hell with analysis and reasons – I just wanted to stay on stage and live those moments forever. Euphoria was in the air – I wanted to absorb this gigantic surge of emotion coming to me from the audience. I wanted time to slow down, turning the seconds into hours, as I looked out at the crowd of people who refused to stop cheering. When Hans came back on stage with me and gestured for the orchestra to stand, the audience now made a racket worthy of a hockey game; everyone standing, cheering, whistling and stomping their feet. There was a dreamlike quality to it all, and my heart wanted to explode with joy. I felt whole again. The orchestra joined in and stamped their feet. I glanced over to the double bass section where my old and dearest best friend Marley, from my childhood days at Vincent d'Indy, was leaning on her instrument and smiling over at me – she, too, was a cancer survivor and she, too, was having a great night.

I turned to Hans, to whom I owed this extraordinary experience, and wanted to reach over and take his hand so that we could bow together. He was standing to my left, my arm lay dead at my side, and suddenly, in a cold, starkly poignant moment, the realization that I was unable to lift my hand to clasp his crashed its way into my bubble of enchantment. Hopefully, no one in the audience noticed, but Hans had, and he moved quickly forward to do the reaching himself. The moment passed and I was back, bathed in the warm glow of the spotlight. Yet the reminder cast a pale shadow over the remainder of the evening.

In December 2002 news came that my arm had healed so quickly the doctors had now decided not to wait a year between operations but to do the muscle transfer surgery in January, only weeks away. Funnily enough, I had a hard time adjusting to this change. On the one hand (no pun intended), it would be wonderful to get it all over and get on with my life. But my mind had been programmed for a May operation, and now I was frightened.

My new surgeon, hand-picked by Dr. Morris, was Dr. Edward Athanasian. He was clearly brilliant and exuded knowledge and skill, but he was terribly serious. He asked me exactly how much motion my arm needed to play the piano, and he was surprised at how little is actually required. Perhaps he had seen the elaborate choreography of some of the younger pianists. Dr. Athanasian explained that the operation had been attempted in Switzerland, but never before in the United States; it was in fact ground-breaking.

In medical jargon, it is known as a latissimus transfer – the latissimus being the rather useless muscle that we all have in our backs and that is used primarily by Olympic gymnasts on the ring exercises. Dr. Athanasian was going to reroute this muscle from my back to my upper arm and attach it right under my left shoulder. Just like Dr. Morris before him, he warned me of all the terrible things that could happen during the surgery and his list was impressive: the radiation might have weakened the bone and muscle too much, he might find a recurrence of the cancer, I might hemorrhage, I might need skin grafts, I might need a second surgery taking muscle from the leg instead of the back. My fear level escalated sharply.

Before the operation Harry and I flew to Germany for the Christmas holiday season, and I fell into a period of darkness and depression. It was also unfortunate that over Christmas we spent an inordinate amount of time in hospitals, visiting first

Harry's frail brother Albert and then our friend Sena Jurinac, who had fallen on the ice and broken her arm. The dark and gloomy middle-European December weather did nothing to help.

But then, suddenly, I remembered a day in Paris, in 1977, when I had been out to lunch with friends and Annabelle was in England visiting her parents. I had returned home to the Rubinsteins' house on the Avenue Foch in the late afternoon to find Arthur sitting alone in the darkened sitting-room with tears in his eyes. It was so unusual, almost unheard of, to see him depressed that I was quite shocked. He was almost blind by that time and Mrs. Rubinstein, having been in a particularly frenetic mood, had just left him in the house to sit all day while she raced about Paris on a shopping spree. I sat down beside him and attempted to entertain him with funny stories about the people with whom I had just had lunch.

After a while he interrupted me, took my hand gently and said, "My dear Ninka, you are very sweet, but you don't have to try and cheer me up; I am positively enjoying being miserable." And with an impish grin he added, "To love life unconditionally one must love every aspect of it – and we need these necessary contrasts to be able to appreciate the wonder of it all!" He lived this philosophy every day of his life. He was the happiest man I had ever met.

So, in a funny way, I realized that it had been this way for me during 2002. To look at it objectively, it had been a perfectly dreadful year: I had found out that I had Stage 3 cancer, I had lost the use of my arm, my life-long vocation had been shattered, my future was uncertain at best but, in the end, I had managed to have a rather good time until these last few weeks – and perhaps these last few weeks were just providing me with the "necessary contrasts," as Arthur said!

Things picked up with a visit from our California friends, our wedding witnesses Arthur and Elizabeth Pasquinelli, who marveled at and thoroughly enjoyed the spectacle of Germany at Advent time with the colourful markets, Christmas trees covered with candles, wonderful old crèches in the Baroque churches, *Lebkuchen* and all sorts of cookies and cakes, hot sausages and mulled wine – a true Christmas spirit in the air.

And of course, we celebrated Polish Christmas, a tradition I had brought over with me from America. For our closest friends, I cooked herring salad, *barszcz* (beetroot soup), pierogies, *bigos* (hunter's stew) and a walnut chocolate torte.

In January 2003 I performed the Prokofiev 4th piano concerto for the left hand three times: twice in London, Ontario, with the refreshingly daring music director Timothy Vernon, and for one extra concert when we all travelled up to Barrie, Ontario. It's amazingly fun to play, although quite complicated and, in spots, scary.

All too soon I was back in hospital. This operation lasted only four hours, and Dr. Athanasian almost smiled when he visited me in my room afterwards. All had gone well; I could hear the tentative optimism in his voice. I was back home again in just a few days, thanks to my basic good health and my miserly health insurance, and felt extremely lucky that Harry was there to care for me. I was under the strictest orders not to move my arm at all, not even a millimetre, for six weeks. I had a smart new black brace, aptly named Brace Bumbry. Now came the difficult period when all I could do was wait.

To fill the time, I started to jot down my recent experiences and slowly the outlines of this book began to emerge.

After six weeks, Shmuel Tatz in New York was allowed to start therapy, but it had to be passive therapy: I was still not allowed to attempt moving the arm on my own. I also had another chance to play the Prokofiev; this time in Saskatoon, where the excellent conductor Earl Stafford had the inspired idea of playing, as an encore, a movement from the Malcolm Arnold three-handed concerto! So, after the Prokofiev, a second piano was rolled on and Earl, conducting from the keyboard, played the two-handed part and I the one-handed part.

In early May of 2003, Dr. Athanasian allowed me to cautiously begin aggressive therapy. The new muscle started to be activated, and one morning as I lay on my back on the sitting room floor attempting an exercise that Shmuel had invented for me, I was able to raise my left arm and hold it straight upright. I called to Harry to come and witness what had happened. I then went to the keyboard and found that I could lift my left hand to the keys and hold it there steadily without any problem. My lateral motion was still extremely limited, but I already knew that the music of the Baroque and early Classical composers was now within my reach, and I was ecstatic. I quickly pulled out my Bach, Handel, Rameau, Couperin, J.C. Bach, Haydn and Mozart scores and began an orgy of sight-reading only to realize quite soon that the new muscle tired very easily and that I had to treat it with great respect and caution. Undaunted, I spent my extra spare time devising all sorts of programs that I could perform; there was such immense joy in my heart!

Only a week later, my left arm was able to move slightly more to the left; now I could play some Beethoven, and then, maybe two or three days later, it was clear that Chopin would be back in my life. It wasn't easy to reach those lower notes; my brain had to send all sorts of orders down to the new muscle so that it would respond in the correct manner. At first this process went very slowly, but at least I could reach those bass notes, and every single day the mobility improved. Amazingly, there has never been a single moment of setback. There was plenty of pain and cramping, but the muscle continued to develop steadily and at an astoundingly rapid pace.

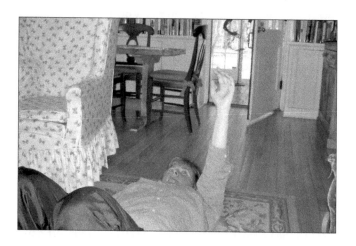

I discovered that all my muscle memory had disappeared, and I was going to have to re-learn from scratch all the arm-muscle movements of pieces, some of which I had worked on for over forty years. This didn't bother me in the slightest. In fact, I found the whole process thrilling. I enjoyed concentrating on the left-hand parts of these pieces and discovering them anew. I found I was injecting a new freshness into my old war-horses, but also there seemed to be a deeper maturity developing in my playing. No longer were there any feelings of urgency in the psychology of my daily work. I took my time and savoured every note and every phrase, playing and re-playing passages for the sheer joy of hearing them and of knowing that this was something I could do once again. I learned to sit at the piano slightly differently and a little to the left of centre.

At first, I could practice only half an hour at a time and never more than an hour a day. But the practice time slowly expanded until I reached a three-hour limit, when the new arm muscle, doing the work of three lost muscles, would start to cramp. I started to think of performing again with two hands and Harry began to book concerts for the following year. My goal and great wish was to return to the stage with a two-handed solo recital on January 13, 2004, in the Festsaal in Irsee. This would be exactly two years since I had played my last solo recital on that very piano in that very hall.

I planned the program: some Grieg lyric pieces to start, all delicacy and charm with no stress or problem for my arm. Then my new Schubert Impromptus, which I had immediately resurrected – the only problem there was in the first Impromptu, when my left hand had to cross over my right hand to reach some chords in the middle upper register of the keyboard. I was still unable to lift my hand that high and that far but, after some experimentation, I found I could reach those notes by going under rather than over my right arm: problem solved. Then, to provide something a little exotic and to perform something of a composer I had championed in the past, the second half started with the two posthumous Mazurkas of Karol Szymanowski. I then wanted to play the B minor Sonata of Chopin, but I truly had no idea if my arm could develop the endurance it would take to get through the last movement, whose left-hand passages were excruciatingly demanding even for "normal" arms. But I was stubborn, and bit by bit the program started to take shape. I was so focused on the planning that I became almost irritated when occasionally I still had to prepare one-handed concerts. However, I did have loads of fun at the actual concerts – the Prokofiev 4th concerto with the Montreal Symphony in September 2003 and again two months later with Hans Graf in Calgary, where Marley prepared for us an extraordinary Sabbath meal that seemed to go on forever and that was absolutely scrumptious. Marley's cancer had returned, but she had boundless energy and was a great fighter. We stayed in close contact and bolstered each other's courage and optimism for the future.

Meanwhile, I was having a lovely time astounding the doctors at Sloan Kettering, who now readily admitted that they had never really expected me to play professionally again. Harry alerted the Canadian presenters, orchestras and media with the news that soon I would be back again, whole. My country responded in the most wonderful, heartwarming fashion, and I received countless messages of support and congratulations. The Canadian concert offers rolled in. Both major television networks planned prime-time news stories the night of my Canadian comeback, which was to be in February of 2004 in Toronto with Beethoven's 4th piano concerto.

But first I had the recital in Irsee, and this recital probably meant more to me than any single performance of my entire life. The week before, I still hadn't played the Chopin Sonata through from beginning to end, so I asked Harry if he would come and listen to my trial run. Somehow it worked, but just barely. I knew that I had to go back to the drawing board to figure out how I could pace myself and my arm a little better throughout the last movement so that exhaustion would not overtake me before the climactic finale. Strangely, this trial run for Harry was the most emotional moment of all for me. I actually wept at the end; tears not of sorrow but of joy, of relief, of gratitude and of exhaustion; the ordeal was finally over.

On January 13th, 2004, I practiced in the Festsaal of the Kloster Irsee just a little in the morning, terrified of straining my arm and totally unsure as to how it was going to react under stressful conditions. We were staying up the hill at Marie-José's and I rested all afternoon. You might think that, having faced death and having been through so much over the past two years, I might have changed my attitude and wouldn't see the point anymore of getting nervous before concerts. But, of course, I was as nervous as ever, although exploding with excitement is perhaps a better way to describe it.

Just about every German person I had ever met in the five years I had been with Harry came from all over the country to hear my concert that night. From Gertrud Kottermaier to Dr.

Tressel from the Hessing Clinic, my mother-in-law and brother-in-law with his girlfriend Inge, Sena Jurinac and her husband, Sibylle and Evelyn (the angels who had enabled Harry to run his festival from America while I was undergoing radiation therapy), Matthias and all his co-workers, the patrons from Harry's ex-festival, such as former Finance Minister (and creator of the Euro) Dr. Theo Waigel and his wife, Olympic champion Dr. Irene Epple, all those dignitaries I had sat next to at the long festival dinners, mayors and district presidents, but also neighbours of ours from our village, old school friends of Harry's, fellow musicians, friends and colleagues – everyone was there. Harry even had two final surprises for me: our friend Lee Rosen from Carmel, California, had managed to arrange his schedule so that he could be there that evening, and an even greater surprise was the presence of Annabelle, who had flown in from London that day; it was almost as if a little bit of Arthur was there as well.

As I stood backstage, I knew that every person in the hall wished me well; just by lifting my hands to the keyboard I would have all their support and enthusiasm. But I wanted more from myself. I was not seeking sympathy. I wanted to be a musician again and to bring something special to the evening – not just a celebration of a small medical miracle. I wanted to honour all those people who had helped me to reach this moment; certainly my friends in the hall, who in so many ways and with such devotion had assisted Harry and me through the ordeal of the past two years, but also Drs. Morris, Alektiar and Athanasian and Shmuel Tatz and all those wonderful nurses, technicians and friends back in North America; and most importantly Harry. I wanted to express my gratitude through my music – not just to get through the concert but to play well, to give something back. I knew the composers would never let me down, but now I must do my part as well.

Matthias ran backstage to give my arm a final massage. I then paused, took a deep breath and walked out onto the stage. I acknowledged the emotional standing ovation with a bow and a smile, then sat down, gathered my wits about me, slowly lifted both hands to the keyboard and began to play the Arietta of Grieg. At first I could barely hear what I was doing: it was as though I was underwater and the notes were all distorted. But bit by bit there was clarity and the old sensations returned; just the feel of the keyboard under my fingers was like a long-lost friend suddenly reappearing. The sounds flowed through my fingers up through my arms, one intact and one damaged but unbeaten, reaching my heart. I was back. I was profoundly happy.

EPILOGUE

After my recital in Irsee I slowly slipped back into my normal schedule and have been playing concerts, giving Master Classes and making CDs ever since.

My new arm muscle, whose development was supposed to plateau after two years, has astounded the medical profession by actually continuing to improve way beyond its original, allotted time limit. Even now I am performing pieces like the 3rd Scherzo of Chopin once again with relative ease, a piece I was unable to manage three years ago due to the weakness of my arm.

The cancer did return – three small metastases to my lungs – small, discreet nodules removed at the Sloan Kettering. And two years ago there was breast cancer, ostensibly caused by the massive radiation I received back in 2003. For this I was treated in Germany. A lot more scars so that my body tends to resemble a map of the London Underground ... but the scars are only skin deep and of little concern, and my health is back to normal.

In 2013, we sold the house in Connecticut and moved permanently to Bavaria to be close to Harry's mother, who was ailing. We built a house right next to hers, and there is a large garden which has become our delight and our hobby.

During the past few years I have been extremely grateful and honoured to receive Canada's highest civilian award; The Governor General's Lifetime Achievement Award, as well as three honorary doctorates. I admit, it is awfully nice to be appreciated in this way.

The world is very different now; lovely, innocent tours in Italy or in England such as I experienced years ago will probably never occur again. But Mozart, Chopin and co. will always be there to enhance the quality of our lives; they are the proof that in these dark, ultra-materialistic and very selfish times, we human beings can still create something of great beauty and incomparable value for the benefit of others.

In recent years young pianists from all over the world are finding their way to my home where they come for a little advice and a lot of encouragement. They delight me with their playing and I do my best for them, to the point of founding a festival where they can perform here in Bavaria.

It is a hard profession. In fact, it is more like a vocation than a profession, and it demands a lifetime of hard work, stamina, courage, humility but above all dedication and love. I believe it is well worth it.

DATES TO REMEMBER

1951   May. Born in Montreal, Quebec, Canada

1955   First piano lessons with my mother

1960   September. Entered École the Vincent d'Indy in Montreal

1962   March. Debut with the Orchestre Symphonique de Montréal in Montreal, Wilfrid Pelletier conducting (Mozart Concerto K.466)

1963   July. Began studies with Yvonne Hubert in Montreal
September. First meeting with Dana.

1966   July. Summer course in St. Germain-en-Laye, France, with Yvonne Lefébure

1967   June. Graduated from "The Study" in Montreal

1968   June. Obtained Baccalauréat and Maitrise from Université de Montréal
–1969 Studies in Paris with Yvonne Lefébure

1969   April. Awarded 1st Prize at Radio-Canada CBC National Talent Festival
August. Began private studies with Sasha Gorodnitzki in New York

1970   October. First meeting with Emanuel Ax and Jeffrey Swann, in Warsaw, Poland
November. Moved to New York and entered the Juilliard School as a pupil of Sasha Gorodnitzki

1974   June. Accepted to the Law School at Université de Montréal
September. Took part in the first Arthur Rubinstein International piano competition in Israel. First meeting with Rubinstein.

1975 January. Met with Arthur Rubinstein in New York; he begins to organise my career

1976 January. Paris debut with l'Orchestre National de France at the Théatre des Champs Elysées.

March. Tour of Spain. First meeting with Annabelle.

April. London debut with the Philharmonia Orchestra, Royal Festival Hall.

First summer at the Rubinsteins' in Marbella, Spain.

October. London Philharmonic Orchestra with Bernard Haitink conducting, Royal Albert Hall

October. Philadelphia Orchestra début, Leonard Slatkin conducting.

1977 January. Cleveland Orchestra début, Lorin Maazel conducting.

Second summer at the Rubinstein's in Marbella.

September. Joint recital with Arthur Rubinstein in Venice, Italy.

1978 March. Beginning of a three-year depression.

August / September. Visited Arthur and Annabelle in Lucerne, Switzerland. First meeting with Sir Georg Solti.

1979 February. New York recital début.

March. Visited Christopher and Elaine Plummer in Connecticut for the first time.

1982 April. Auditioned for Sir Georg Solti in London.

April. Last meeting with Arthur Rubinstein, in Geneva.

April. Left New York and moved to Connecticut.

1985 April. Début with Chicago Symphony and Sir Georg Solti.

1990 May. Returned to Chicago. World Première of the 3rd Liszt piano concerto with the Chicago Symphony, Conductor: Kenneth Jean

May. Took part in Szymanowski Festival held at the South Bank in London as the piano soloist-performing the "Symphonie Concertante" with the Philharmonia and Libor Pesek conducting, as well as 3 solo recitals.

1991	March. Death of Dana.
1992	July. First meeting with Harry in Carmel, California
1993	July. Birth of the idea for Piano Six
	December. Death of my father.
1994	February. Piano Six inaugural galas in Toronto and Québec City
	December. Encounter with Gertrud Kottermaier on the train to Vienna, Austria.
1994– 95	Late spring hiking with Elizabeth and Arthur Pasquinelli in France on the Santiago de Compostela Pilgrimage Trail
1999	May. Performances in Augsburg, Germany, re-united with Gertrud Kottermaier and Harry.
2001	May. Death of my mother.
	June. Marriage to Harry Oesterle in Bavaria.
2002	January 13. Recital in Irsee, Germany of the 12 Transcendental Etudes of Liszt.
	January 31. Biopsy of tumour in left arm at Sloan Kettering Hospital in New York City. Cancer is diagnosed.
	May. The tumour is removed.
	November. Awarded the Order of Canada with the rank of Officer, in Halifax.
	November. Performances in Houston and Calgary of the Ravel left hand concerto (played with my right hand) with Stanislaw Skrowaczewski and Hans Graf conducting.
2003	January. Muscle transfer surgery at Sloan Kettering Hospital in New York
	May. I start practising the piano two-handed again
2004	January 13. Comeback-recital in Irsee, Germany.
	February 26. Performance of Beethoven's 4th piano concerto in Toronto.
2010	Back to normal- 60 concerts around the world to celebrate Chopin's 200th Anniversary year. Honorary Doctorate from Acadian University

2011	Honorary Doctorate from Queen's University
2012	Governor General's award for lifetime achievement in the arts
	BBC music magazine Instrumentalist of the year award.
2013	Awarded an Honorary Doctorate of Letters from Wilfrid Laurier University
	House in Connecticut sold. Residing in Germany.
2018	Juno Award for "CD of the Year" (Classical or Chamber)

LIST OF PHOTOGRAPHS

FÜR AUTOREN A HEART FOR AUTHORS À L'ÉCOUTE DES AUTEURS MIA ΚΑΡΔΙΑ ΓΙΑ ΣΥΓ
TA FOR FÖRFATTARE UN CORAZÓN POR LOS AUTORES YAZARLARIMIZA GÖNÜL VERELIM S
E PER AUTORI ET HJERTE FOR FORFATTERE EEN HART VOOR SCHRIJVERS TEMOS OS AU
INKERT SERCE DLA AUTORÓW EIN HERZ FÜR AUTOREN A HEART FOR AUTHORS À L'ÉC
ÇÃO ВСЕЙ ДУШОЙ К АВТОРАМ ETT HJÄRTA FÖR FÖRFATTARE À LA ESCUCHA DE LOS AUT
MA ΓΙΑ ΣΥΓΓΡΑΦΕΙΣ UN CUORE PER AUTORI ET HJERTE FOR FORFATTERE EE
ZÖINKERT SERCE DLA AUTORÓW EIN HERZ FI
ÇÃO ВСЕЙ ДУШОЙ К АВТОРАМ ETT HJÄRTA F

The author

Janina Fialkowska is a renowned concert pianist
of Polish and Canadian heritage. Having spent
her life traversing the world on tour, she has now
settled in Germany with her husband, Harry, and
enjoys walking, gardening, and reading mystery
novels. She still performs a full schedule of
concerts every year.

The publisher

*He who stops
getting better
stops being good.*

This is the motto of novum publishing, and our focus
is on finding new manuscripts, publishing them and
offering long-term support to the authors.
Our publishing house was founded in 1997, and since
then it has become THE expert for new authors and
has won numerous awards.

**Our editorial team will peruse each manuscript
within a few weeks free of charge and without
obligation.**

You will find more information about
novum publishing and our books on the internet:

w w w . n o v u m - p u b l i s h i n g . c o . u k

CPSIA information can be obtained
at www.ICGtesting.com
Printed in the USA
LVHW080610140222
711067LV00003B/68